THE MISSOURI SESQUICENTENNIAL EDITION

WILLIAM E. PARRISH

GENERAL EDITOR

# A HISTORY

UNIVERSITY OF

# OF MISSOURI

## VOLUME II    1820 TO 1860

### PERRY McCANDLESS

MISSOURI PRESS

# PREFACE

This volume represents an effort to describe and analyze the social, economic, and political conditions in Missouri from the state's admission into the Union in 1821 to the brink of the Civil War in 1860. I have tried to adhere to the purpose for which this series was conceived by writing the history of these years in a manner of value to the layman as well as to the historian. If I have failed to strike that elusive balance, it is because of my concern for making a sound synthesis of the Missouri story easily available to the interested general reader.

In addition to the credits contained in the Essay on Sources, I am especially indebted to several individuals and institutions. Portions of this book started with the research done on my doctoral dissertation at the University of Missouri. To Lewis Atherton, my graduate adviser, I owe a very special thanks for his continuing advice and encouragement in all phases of my career. My friend and colleague William E. Foley acted as a constant consultant on many knotty problems, and his freely shared skill greatly enhanced the style of the narrative. William E. Parrish, the knowledgeable general editor of this series, saved me from possible errors and made positive suggestions that served to improve the final product. Much good advice from R. Leslie Anders, my office partner for many years, is reflected throughout this book. I am indebted to Mrs. Judy Scheer, my graduate research assistant, for doing basic research on several topics and for carrying out a host of chores related to the preparation of the manuscript.

I wish to acknowledge the University of Missouri for financial assistance enabling me to spend two full summers working on this project, and Central Missouri State College for granting me a summer study leave in the early stages of my research. This book could not have been written without the excellent collection of source materials at the State Historical Society of Missouri in Columbia. Its able staff members served me well on this project, as they have done on many previous occasions. Likewise I have enjoyed the use of the materials and services of the staff of the Missouri Historical Society in St. Louis.

Finally, for the patience, understanding, encouragement, and sacrifices of my wife and two teen-agers Anne and Richard, along with their more tangible aid in putting the manuscript into final form, I am most deeply grateful.

The author alone is responsible for any errors of fact or interpretation.


P.M.
Warrensburg, Missouri
January, 1972

# CONTENTS

# INTRODUCTION

At the time of its admission to the Union in 1821 Missouri stood at the far reaches of the American frontier. Beyond lay "the Great American Desert" and the Rocky Mountains, where few could contemplate any settlement of consequence aside from the Indians already there or those who might be sent to join them. Yet, within the next 40 years—by the eve of the Civil War—settlers had begun exploring those regions and beyond. America jumped the Rockies and reached the Pacific shore, leaving Missouri as the center of a flourishing nation. In that interim she had played a major role in western development because of her pivotal geographic position and the restless energy of her people. Her leaders, especially in Congress, had been in the forefront of the struggles to secure for the West the benefits and opportunities needed by a rapidly expanding area.

Missouri also found itself central to the North-South sectional crisis. Settled originally by a population largely French and Southern with a heritage of slavery, the state began to receive a large influx of immigrants both from the North and from Ireland and Germany by the late 1840's. These immigrants brought new ideas, tending to weaken the old sectional ties, although they found "the establishment" well entrenched both politically and economically. The tumultuous decade of the 1850's involved Missouri in a sea of emotional issues along both East-West and North-South axes. When Civil War erupted, its choice for allegiance was not an easy one.

Professor McCandless, in this second volume of the Missouri Sesquicentennial History Series, follows the story of the state and its people through these formative years after statehood.

Designed to detail the state's development and the role it has played both regionally and nationally, this series was undertaken by the University of Missouri Press to mark Missouri's 150 years of statehood. The University of Missouri generously agreed to underwrite leaves and research assistance for the various authors to complete their work. Each author is a specialist in his field, and the volumes are based on extensive research in both primary and secondary sources. Because the format calls for a general survey of each era, rather than a highly detailed study, footnotes have been limited to explanatory matters. The reader will find a more detailed bibliographic essay accompanying each volume to point him to materials used and to offer suggestions for further study. Subsequent volumes will trace Missouri's story through the Civil War and Reconstruction periods, during the age of the Populists and the Progressives, and from World War I to the present.

William E. Parrish
Fulton, Missouri
January, 1972

# CHAPTER I

# THE NEW STATE IS LAUNCHED

THE western orientation of energies in the United States in the years following the close of the War of 1812 had a profound effect upon the Missouri Territory. The rapid population growth, the opening of new areas for settlement, and the increasing tempo of economic development brought the disadvantages of territorial government to the attention of more and more Missourians. Following the failure of the first session of the Fifteenth Congress to act on a privately sponsored petition for statehood, the territorial legislature adopted a memorial requesting admission into the Union in November, 1818, and submitted it to Congress the following month.

The memorial set forth three major points to demonstrate the need for statehood: a population "little short of 100,000"[1] with an anticipated rapid increase; a land area too extensive for effective administration; and a territorial system that denied its residents their full rights. "There are many grievances," the memorial read, "of which your memorialists might complain, and complain heavily too, and many that are much more easily felt than described, yet most of them, it must be confessed, are inseparable from the form of government under which they live." The memorialists chose not to complain of old grievances, but there were "rights, privileges, and immunities, belonging to citizens of the United States, which your memorialists would proudly claim, to which they aspire, and with which they pray to be invested."

Missourians quite naturally desired personal political equality with citizens of the already existing states and the greater degree of home rule that would come with statehood. As territorial

1. The population was probably nearer 50,000, but since no official figure was available, Missourians understandably may have augmented the figure somewhat.

residents they were subject to congressional decisions that were without basic constitutional limitation and in which they had no vote. With statehood Missourians would greatly increase their power over internal affairs and consequently limit congressional control over the state, and they would gain a voice in shaping national policy.

Missouri had reached a point where national action was highly important to the area and its people. Thomas H. Benton, editor of the *St. Louis Enquirer*, set forth perhaps as clearly as possible the needs of Missouri in an editorial on June 16, 1819. Undoubtedly filled with aspirations for a high political office such as the United States Senate, Benton editorialized on the subject, "Objects of Public Interest with the People of Missouri; the Accomplishment of which requires the aid of the National Government." He saw the territory's most pressing needs as statehood, adjustment of the Spanish land claims, protection of the frontier, promotion of the fur trade, more efficient operation of the salt springs, the sale of all lead mines to private enterprise, and a series of internal improvements connecting the area with the East, the Gulf of Mexico, and the Great Lakes.

Despite the continuing desire and apparent readiness for statehood, some twenty months passed between the presentation of the statehood memorial from the territorial legislature and Missouri's admission into the Union. A bitter debate over slavery erupted in Congress and across the nation that prevented an otherwise routine action on Missouri's request. The controversy did not arise from any differences within the territory— Missourians wanted the institution unrestricted in their state. Instead, the slavery question divided sections of the country, and the fight over the admission of Missouri to the Union became a national issue.

When Missouri's request for statehood came before the second session of the Fifteenth Congress, the nation stood balanced with eleven slave states and eleven free states. Slave state representatives would continue to be outnumbered in the House of Representatives, however, because population trends clearly favored the free states. In the House, the antislavery forces were making efforts to restrict slavery in new areas. Congressman

Arthur Livermore of New York had, for example, proposed in April of 1818 a constitutional amendment to prohibit slavery in any new states, and later that year Rep. James Tallmadge, Jr., of New York opposed the admission of Illinois because he was not satisfied that its constitution adequately prohibited slavery. Congress voted down Tallmadge's opposition, and Illinois was easily admitted, but the above actions were indicative of a sentiment for restriction. The admission of any new state was of vital importance to the South, and it was imperative that Southerners look to the Senate to protect their interests if the South was not to become a minority section.

In February of 1819, a House committee reported out a traditional statehood enabling bill for Missouri, but when the bill passed, an amendment proposed by Representative Tallmadge had been added. This amendment had two distinct provisions: one was to restrict the further introduction of slaves, and the second was to provide for gradual emancipation of future slave children. Neither of these restrictions actually interfered with the rights of existing property in Missouri, but eventually the institution of slavery would have come to an end in the state. Voting separately on the two clauses the House passed the first by a vote of 87 to 76 and the second 82 to 78.

As might have been expected, the Senate rejected the Tallmadge amendment on February 27, 1819. All senators from slaveholding states voted against both parts of the amendment, as did Illinois Senators Ninian Edwards and Jesse B. Thomas, both of whom held indentured servants, who were slaves for all intents and purposes. Perhaps Tallmadge's earlier reservations about the Illinois Constitution had not been unfounded. The Senate vote, however, must have reflected some concern, even in the North, about the amendment's constitutionality with regard to property rights: the senators defeated the clause to free the future children of slaves 31 to 7, and the clause to prohibit the further introduction of slaves 22 to 16. Congress adjourned without reaching an agreement, and Missouri remained a territory.

Missouri's request for statehood precipitated the formation of the territory of Arkansas, and the antislavery forces in the House led by John W. Taylor of New York moved to prohibit the extension of slavery into that new territory. Congress defeated

3

the Taylor proposal and organized Arkansas as a territory without restriction on slavery in March, 1819.

From a constitutional standpoint there was a difference in the two cases. There was precedent in the Northwest Ordinance of 1787 for congressional restrictions on slavery in the territories; many Southerners agreed that Congress had such power, but they opposed its exercise in southern latitudes. On the other hand, Missouri was seeking statehood, and there was a greater question on the right of Congress to limit a state's control of its domestic institutions.

Outside of Congress, antislavery forces enlarged and sharpened the tensions created by the Missouri question as they prepared for the next round. Late in the summer of 1819 antislavery reformers organized an "Anti-Missourian Crusade" to swing public opinion against Missouri's admission as a slave state. This movement involved important national figures including William Tudor, editor of the *North American Review*. Northeastern fears of southern congressional power, bulwarked by the voting strength in Congress provided by the slave count for representation, aided the Missouri opposition. In private quarters and in Congress, Missouri's admission involved a basic struggle for sectional political power that transcended slavery as an issue. But the Tallmadge amendment, and all similar proposals, also ran counter to a strong current of white supremacy that had fixed slavery firmly in the South. The gate of Missouri's admission into the Union did, indeed, swing on complex hinges.

Early in the Sixteenth Congress, a House committee reported a Missouri statehood bill without restriction. In January, 1820, while the bill was before the Committee of the Whole, John Taylor proposed an amendment excluding slavery or involuntary servitude from the new state. The bill with Taylor's amendment, which was more restrictive than the earlier Tallmadge amendment, finally passed on March 1, 1820.

While the House debated the Missouri question, the Senate was also at work. Seeking to speed action on Missouri, the Senate tied her admission to Maine's request for statehood. Massachusetts had consented to a division that permitted the Maine area to seek admission to the Union, provided it could be gained by March 4, 1820. Pressure was on the free states to compromise on

4

Missouri in order to get Maine admitted before the deadline. It was also difficult for the free forces to support Maine's admission without any restrictions while insisting on the limitation of Missouri's right to control her own institutions. In considering a House bill passed on January 3 admitting Maine without restriction, the Senate added two amendments before it approved the measure. One amendment enabled Missouri to form a constitution without slavery restriction; the second was Jesse B. Thomas's well-known amendment limiting the area of expansion of slavery with the prohibition of slavery elsewhere in the Louisiana Purchase north of 36° 30′. In this form the Maine bill went back to the House, where it was rejected twice in February as that body moved ahead with consideration of its own bill and Taylor's restrictive amendment. The Senate refused to accept the House bill, but a solution based on the Thomas amendment was in the cards, and with Speaker Henry Clay dealing in the House, events moved quickly. A conference committee appointed to seek agreement recommended that the Senate withdraw its amendments to the Maine bill, that both the House and the Senate strike out the Taylor restrictive amendment to the House bill on Missouri, and that the Thomas amendment be added to the House Missouri bill. These recommendations were followed, and the Missouri Compromise was completed on March 3, 1820. In substance, the compromise admitted Missouri as a slave state, Maine as a free state, and prohibited slavery in the Louisiana Purchase north of 36° 30′, except in Missouri. On March 6, 1820, Congress formally authorized the people of Missouri to frame a state constitution and organize a government, with only the stipulation that the constitution be republican in nature and that it contain no provisions repugnant to the Constitution of the United States.

The lack of a voting representative in Congress had not silenced Missourians during the debate over their future. John Scott, their territorial delegate to Congress, vigorously advocated Missouri's right to statehood without restrictions. During the Tallmadge amendment debate Scott announced that the spirit of freedom was such among Missourians that "if admitted into the national family, they would be equal, or not come at all." While Congress struggled in the slavery controversy, the uproar coming out of Missouri intensified. By petitions, memorials, editorials, speeches, mass meetings, and toasts, Missourians denounced Congress for delaying statehood and for attempting to dictate the status of slavery. Any limitation upon the new state, Missouri spokesmen argued, grossly violated the constitutional guarantee of equality among the states. Missourians also charged that Congress had failed to adhere to the provisions of the Louisiana Treaty of Cession, which had pledged to the people of the territory both statehood and protection of property.

A toast delivered in 1819 at a Fourth of July celebration in Marthasville typified local sentiments: "Messrs. Tallmadge and Taylor—Politically insane.—May the next Congress appoint them a dark room, a straight waistcoat and a thin water gruel diet." A protest meeting in St. Louis attended by many of the leading territorial residents adopted Thomas H. Benton's forceful resolution declaring the right of the people of the Missouri Territory, "to form a constitution and state government, whenever they deem it expedient to do so, and that a second determination on the part of Congress to refuse them admission, upon equal footing with the original states will make it expedient to exercise that right." Central Missouri politician Duff Green's toast in support of Missouri's admission without restriction— "The Union—It is dear to us, but liberty is dearer"—reflected an American inconsistency, since restriction would have reduced human bondage in the state. Missourians appear to have convinced themselves that the abolition of slavery in the state was against the welfare of the slaves. The slaves had no spokesmen, and no one had an honest talk with them.

Whether or not the Tallmadge amendment was a violation of the letter of the Louisiana Purchase treaty is debatable. Decades later, court decisions would hold that political restrictions as a requisite for admission could not be held binding after statehood. Aside from any legal basis, Missourians simply believed that they had a right to equal statehood, and that Congress was attempting to deny that right.

Underneath all of the "legalisms" and "rights," Missourians wanted to maintain the status of slavery. Although slaveholding was limited, Missourians generally considered the attack on slavery as a threat to property rights. More importantly, a sub-

6

stantial majority of the residents had come from slaveholding areas, and many of them viewed slavery as an institution essential to white supremacy. No significant antislavery sentiment existed in the territory.

When the enabling act was finally passed, the *St. Louis Enquirer* announced the "happy intelligence" in an extra on March 25, 1820. In its next regular issue, using headlines perhaps for the first time in Missouri, the paper proclaimed:

> Gratifying news from Washing-
> ton.—King and Clinton defeated.—
> The Senate triumphant.—Final pas-
> sage of the Missouri State Bill with-
> out restriction.

But with self-righteous anger, editor Benton announced in the same issue that, had the bill been longer delayed:

> The people of the United States would have witnessed a specimen of Missouri feeling in the indignant contempt with which they would have trampled the odious restrictions under their feet and proceeded to the formation of a republican constitution in the fullness of the people's power.

Benton reflected much popular sentiment, even if his language was somewhat dramatic and anticlimactic.

Missourians generally viewed Tallmadge and Taylor not only as their foes but also as representative of an evil and oppressive power; since compromise appeared to have been essential, Clay and Thomas were considered as Missouri's true friends. Missourians, however, may well have been wrong. The institution of slavery was not as important to the state as Missourians appeared to believe at the time, but in a more general sense, because of the fundamental unfairness of slavery, the Tallmadge amendment, rather than the Thomas amendment, would undoubtedly have better served the interests of the state, as well as the nation.

The many and widespread celebrations did not deter Missourians from proceeding with the framing of a constitution. The enabling legislation authorized all free, white, male citizens of the United States who had reached the age of twenty-one and who had resided in the Missouri Territory for three months prior to the election to vote for members of the constitutional convention. Delegates were apportioned among the fifteen existing counties. As prescribed by the enabling act, Missourians went to the polls during the first week of May, 1820. The election of delegates and the discussion over the nature of the future constitution occasioned only limited controversy, and the absence of national or local competing political parties contributed to the lack of organized debate. Limited proposals for mild restrictions on slavery were made, but a part of the press played up restrictionist sentiment far beyond its real significance. While the *Missouri Gazette*, edited by Joseph Charless, carried some suggestions that the question of further admission of slaves might be submitted to the voters after a few years, the *St. Louis Enquirer* attacked such proposals as abolitionist and editorialized as if the opponents of slavery were on the verge of securing supremacy in the state. Editor Benton attacked a straw man, but the image of a giant killer would prove helpful to his political career. He boasted after the election that not a single confessed restrictionist had been elected to the convention. In fact, there had been no real contest between advocates of restriction and nonrestriction. Of an estimated 7,000 to 11,000 voters participating in the election, probably less than 1,000 favored any form of restriction. With candidates in only five of the fifteen counties, the restrictionists had their greatest strength in St. Louis County, where they polled about 400 votes. The remainder were scattered throughout Jefferson, Lincoln, Washington, and Cape Girardeau counties.

Although the enabling act permitted all adult, white males to vote for delegates, the so-called "common man" or "frontiersman" was not elected to the convention that launched Missouri on the road to statehood. Rather, it was composed of the wealthy, generally conservative men who had dominated territorial affairs. This forty-one-member body contained land owners, doctors, and educators, but it appears to have been dominated by a combination of businessmen and lawyers. All but four of the delegates were of financial means, and fourteen of them were among the most wealthy men in the territory. That Missouri was not fully a rough frontier was evidenced by the educational level of the delegates. At least twenty-six had attended college or studied under outstanding men, while others had gained competence through self-education. The urban influence, especially from St. Louis, was important in shaping the convention's work. A great majority of the delegates had been residents of a slaveholding state. David Barton, Edward Bates, John Cook, Jonathan S. Findlay, John Rice Jones, and John Scott—all representing the older, more established areas of the state—took particularly active roles in preparing the constitution, but no one man can be given credit for writing the document. Of these six convention leaders all but Findlay, who was primarily interested in land sales, were lawyers who went on to play important roles in the political life of the state. Barton and Bates were from St. Louis, Jones from Washington County, Cook and Scott from Ste. Genevieve, and Findlay from Howard County.

The Jacksonian movement was just over the horizon in 1820, but the forces of popular democracy exercised little influence in either the election of delegates to the convention or in the writing of the constitution. The convention produced a constitution typical of many already in effect, combining provisions drawn from at least fifteen different state constitutions, with those of Alabama, Illinois, and Kentucky supplying the greatest portions of Missouri's first supreme law.

Separation of power existed through the three traditional branches of government, and there was a bicameral legislature. The county served as the basis of representation in the lower house, with each assured of one representative in that body. A system of apportionment allotted additional representatives for the more heavily populated counties.

The executive branch included a popularly elected governor and lieutenant governor. Both were to serve a four-year term, longer than those in many other states, but the governor was not allowed to succeed himself. If the office of governor became vacant, the lieutenant governor was to be only an acting governor; if more than eighteen months of the term still remained, a special election had to be held to fill the vacancy. Other officers with executive and administrative functions were an adjutant general appointed by the governor for an indefinite term; an auditor, an attorney general, and a secretary of state—all appointed by the governor for four-year terms; and a treasurer selected biannually by the General Assembly. The governor was to give the General Assembly information relative to the state of government, along with recommendations for such measures as he thought necessary and expedient. This established a constitutional mandate through which the governor might exercise some legislative initiative and leadership. The chief executive had the power to veto legislation, but his veto could be overridden by an absolute majority of each house, after having considered the reasons for the veto. This, contrary to providing an avenue for aggressive leadership, limited executive authority and created a balance of power favorable to the General Assembly.

The constitution provided for a judicial branch with a state supreme court, circuit courts, and a court of chancery with jurisdiction in matters of equity and probate affairs; the General Assembly was authorized to establish additional inferior courts. An unusual detail in the constitution set the minimum salary of the governor and judges at $2,000 a year—a substantial amount for that time. Debate in the convention concerning the judicial system revealed an important division of opinion that was to carry over into early state politics. Edward Bates, a member of the committee on the judiciary, drafted the provisions for a strong, independent judiciary. He represented those individuals, including David Barton, who wanted an independent judiciary to check the popularly based legislature; Alexander McNair and a smaller group sought to make the judges subject to popular election and to limit judicial review of legislative actions. The Barton-Bates position prevailed in the convention, but the court question carried forward as one of the specific issues in the first election, as the constitution's judicial article aroused popular criticism.

In setting forth the powers and functions of the state government, the constitution was very brief. It assigned all lawmaking to the General Assembly, with few mandates or limitations upon the exercise of that power. The constitution did charge the legislature to encourage education and internal improvements, but it went no further on those subjects, and the legislature was authorized to charter one, but only one, bank. The document also contained the usual Bill of Rights, which restricted the government in the areas of personal and property rights. The most specific limitations upon the power of the legislature were those related to the protection of slavery. No law could be passed for the emancipation of slaves without the consent of the owner, or to prevent bona fide settlers from bringing slaves into the state, but trial by jury was provided for the slaves. Reflecting the fear of problems that might stem from having free Negroes, the constitution required the General Assembly to pass the necessary laws to prevent free Negroes and mulattoes from coming to, and settling in, the state.

This latter provision soon caused new trouble with Congress and delayed Missouri's final admission into the Union. In outlining the structure of local government the constitution granted the General Assembly almost blanket power in defining the authority exercised by local units and their officials. Following the pattern of the time, the first Missouri Constitution with its very limited restrictions upon legislative power was not a code of law, but an instrument framed to establish the organization and procedure for governing. This reflected the convention's faith in the legislative branch of government. In the future, Missourians would have second thoughts about such unrestricted power.

The constitution did continue the national trend toward the liberalization of the suffrage by granting the right to vote to every free, white male citizen of the United States who was at least twenty-one years of age and who had resided in the state one year before the election and in the county or district for three months preceding the election. Not so democratic, however, was the restriction of elective officials to members of the General Assembly, the governor, and the lieutenant governor. Likewise the voters could not act directly on constitutional amendments, which were to be proposed by a two-thirds vote of each house and ratified by the same majority at the first session of the next legislature.

The enabling act contained five important grants to the state, subject to action by the convention, that would exempt all public lands of the United States sold after January 1, 1821, from taxes for five years from date of sale and all bounty lands granted for military service during the War of 1812 for three years if held by the patentee or his heirs. The convention passed the necessary ordinance, and Missouri received grants of the sixteenth section or its equivalent in each township for the use of public schools; all salt springs, not exceeding twelve in number, with six sections of land adjoining each; four sections of land for a seat of government; thirty-six sections of land for a seminary of learning; and 5 per cent of the net proceeds of the sale of public lands in Missouri for making roads and canals. Of the latter sum, three-fifths was to be spent under the direction of the state legislature within Missouri, and two-fifths was to be spent by Congress on highways leading to Missouri.

Although the Missouri territorial legislature previously had complained that the territory was too extensive to administer, it had asked for a state of considerable size. Congress reduced the proposed area between 25 and 30 per cent, but at the time of admission Missouri ranked second in size among the states, and the convention made the boundaries set by Congress a part of the state constitution.[2]

The convention completed its work in five weeks and formally adopted the constitution on July 19, 1820. Contrary to a growing trend, the framers did not submit the document to the people for approval, but no serious objections were raised to this course of action.[3]

2. Congress had cut from the area requested by the memorial a strip of land 60 miles wide and 200 miles long from the western border, a strip equal to three tiers of counties from the north, and some 5,000 square miles from a southeast projection below 36° 30'. The original request had placed the boundary on the Mississippi River at the thirty-sixth parallel, running southwesterly to the White River and then along that river to 36° 30' and thence due west. There seems to be no clear explanation for the inclusion of the southeast Bootheel in the new state of Missouri. According to tradition, John Hardeman Walker, a significant landowner in the area, led the effort to get the Panhandle into the proposed state of Missouri and successfully enlisted John Scott and other political figures from the Jackson area to support its inclusion. The few people living just south of 36° 30' west of the Bootheel apparently made no effort to be included in the future state of Missouri.

3. Of the state constitutions in effect in 1820, 6 of the 24 had been submitted to a vote of the people. From 1820 to 1830, the Missouri Constitution was the only one out of 6 adopted that was not approved by the voters.

Missourians now turned their attention to the first state elections scheduled for August 28. They would choose a governor, lieutenant governor, representative to Congress, and the full membership of both houses of the General Assembly. The General Assembly would then select two United States senators, and the governor would appoint the judges and necessary administrative officials.

Opposing political parties did not exist in Missouri in 1820. Common to the national pattern during the "Era of Good Feelings," all Missourians who labeled themselves at all politically were Republicans. Nevertheless, politically active combinations sought to win public office in order to secure policies favorable to their interests. The most powerful faction was a relatively small, conservative combination of businessmen, speculators, and lawyers centered in St. Louis. This group, which editor Joseph Charless of the *Missouri Gazette* termed the "little junto," was composed of old French leaders and their American allies, with common interests principally in the fur trade and in a liberal policy for the confirmation of the vast Spanish land grants. Businessmen such as Auguste Chouteau, Charles Gratiot, and Bernard Pratte; Edward Hempstead, perhaps the leading lawyer in the territory; and William Clark, territorial governor, were prominent members of the St. Louis establishment. Associated with the junto were a few men of similar interests outside of St. Louis, including John Scott, lawyer and territorial delegate to Congress from Ste. Genevieve, and Duff Green, political leader and speculator from Howard County in central Missouri. Benton, although he denied it, was also close to this faction.

The little junto was not without opposition. An antijunto faction composed largely of the more recently arrived American land speculators and their allies had emerged near the end of the territorial period. The two groups divided primarily over land policy, with the control of the vast unsettled land of Missouri as the prize. The newly arrived Americans—including Rufus Easton and William Russell—opposed confirmation of the Spanish grants. The two major voices of opposition to the little junto were editor Charless and John B. C. Lucas. Lucas, a former Missouri territorial judge and member of the Board of Land Commissioners, had never associated with the older territorial leadership; he also nursed a growing hatred for Benton, who had killed his son Charles in a duel in 1817. Well educated, strong-willed, and lacking in sociability, he was the most important opponent of confirmation of the Spanish land claims held by speculators.

Lines between the little junto and the antijunto were not, however, always clear. Neither group had any real organization, and alliances sometimes shifted. David Barton, a lawyer and popular territorial official, was probably closest to the antijunto group, but, since he did not openly oppose the other faction, he managed to secure support from both groups for public office. Both groups by choice represented the upper-class, conservative individuals in the state; neither made any effort to appeal to the interests of the majority of Missourians. Their common interests brought them together in the fight for statehood, but differences over potential political jobs and policy soon marred that newfound unity.

Joseph Charless announced with assurance that the little junto caucus had determined the allocation of new offices. The governorship was to go to William Clark; Benton and John Rice Jones were to be the two United States senators; the superior judges would be David Barton, William Harper, and John B. Cook. Charless gave the little junto more credit for discipline and power than it really had. Internal conflicts and the unexpected results in the popular elections would upset plans of the caucus, and the men named by Charless would not get their designated jobs.

As election day approached, there was evidence of a growing, although unorganized, opposition in the rural areas against domination by a "St. Louis Clique"—a term that applied to all St. Louis politicians. Reflecting this sentiment, an "Old Supporter" writing in the Jackson *Missouri Herald* stated that although he supported James Evans for delegate to the constitutional convention, he would vote against him for the General Assembly because he had joined the St. Louis politicians.

Alexander McNair swamped William Clark, territorial governor and candidate of the St. Louis establishment, in the contest for governor. McNair had been associated with the established territorial political leadership, but his administration of the land office in St. Louis from 1818 to 1820 had turned the big speculators against him while, at the same time, he gained the support of many of the newly arrived settlers. As a member of the constitutional convention McNair opposed some of the undemocratic features of the constitution, and before the convention adjourned he announced his intent to run for governor. He conducted a vigorous campaign throughout the state in an effort to win rural support, and his opponents accused him of doing too much campaigning in tippling shops and in back streets among "the dirtiest blackguards." Clark, who was out of the state because of the illness of his wife in Virginia, was unable to campaign. His earlier policies on Indian affairs had not been restrictive enough on the Indians to satisfy many Missourians, and this may have cost Clark some votes.

William H. Ashley, a wealthy landowner who had also conducted a successful gunpowder manufacturing operation at Potosi, became the first lieutenant governor of the state. Although he had not yet entered the fur trade in which he later would gain both fame and fortune, he did have an attractive military record. Ashley defeated Nathaniel Cook, a prominent southeast Missouri political figure and member of the constitutional convention, and a favorite of the St. Louis caucus. The voters returned John Scott to Congress as their first full-fledged representative.

The elections for the General Assembly also reflected a reaction against the constitutional convention and the St. Louis clique. The new legislators did not come from the older territorial leadership. Like the Old Supporter, many Missourians apparently had turned against the St. Louis politicians. To his friend Scott, Benton wrote that all of their calculations had failed; his own election to the Senate, Benton believed, would be much more difficult than had been anticipated. The election results thus shocked the old guard into intense action to line up votes for the Senate positions and to gain support for the appointive posts. There were also increased internal strains; the junto lacked true unity, and some members saw better opportunities in a noncontrolled General Assembly. Still, no new candidates of the people appeared to challenge seriously the original aspirants to office, and the political posts were finally filled from the territorial power elite.

The General Assembly met in joint session on October 2, 1820, to elect the state's two United States senators. On the first ballot, with each legislator voting for two candidates, David Barton received 34 votes, Thomas H. Benton, 27, John B. C. Lucas, 16, Henry Elliott, 11, Nathaniel Cook, 8, and John Rice Jones, 8. Barton and Benton—each with the required majority—were duly elected. In naming Edward Bates as the first attorney general and John D. Cook, John Rice Jones, and Mathias McGirk as the three judges of the state supreme court, Governor McNair did not draw from outside the old order.

The selection of the two senators reveals much about the forces at work in early Missouri politics. Barton's election was virtually assured: he had St. Louis support without being too strongly attached to either faction, and his long-established personal popularity in out-state areas could override the growing opposition to the city clique. He did not, however, possess the tremendous political power often credited to him. He was not elected by an overwhelming vote, and eighteen of the fifty-two legislators cast neither of their two votes for him.[4]

4. There have been several errors recorded in various accounts of the election of Benton and Barton to the United States Senate in 1820. The more dramatic explanations of Benton's election have been corrected in recent publications, but some old accounts state that Barton was elected by a unanimous vote for the first Senate seat and that, after additional balloting with no one receiving a majority, he was given the privilege of naming his colleague and chose Benton. Another part of old accounts is that even with Barton's aid Benton's election was most difficult. Benton's supporters, according to accounts, realized they were one vote short and worked in a long night session with Marie Philippe Leduc, a holder of large areas under Spanish land grants, until he was convinced that his interests would fair better with Benton in the Senate than with Lucas. Another crisis supposedly was reached when it appeared that Daniel Ralls, pledged to Benton, was too ill to attend the session of the General Assembly. He was carried into the hall on his bed and his vote—that of a dying man—reportedly gave Benton the one vote necessary for a majority and victory.

Part one of the above accounts is an error of fact. The *Journal of the General Assembly* shows that only one ballot was cast, with each member voting for two separate candidates. Barton and Benton both were elected on this one ballot, and Barton did not have a unanimous vote. There is no evidence to disprove the Leduc story, but he certainly did not need

The selection of Benton was not so sure, although he, too, had the support of an established territorial class. Since his arrival in St. Louis in 1815, he had been personally associated with the little junto; as an attorney for the fur-trade interests and the Spanish land claimants, his favorable position on their political concerns was well known. Lucas charged that the Spanish land claimants secured Benton's election. Although there was no organized party, Scott revealed the existence of an informal working association that was undergoing an internal struggle for office in a series of letters he wrote to select individuals pleading for unity and for Benton. Duff Green was tied with the old territorial leadership, and, although he was not personally in favor of Benton, gave him his support for the sake of group unity.

These special interest and factional forces alone were not sufficient to secure Benton's election, evidenced by the fact that he received only three of the seven votes from St. Louis while Barton got them all. The base of political power in Missouri, as elsewhere, was shifting from the conservative, established upper class to the masses; if Benton did not recognize the shift in the election period of 1820, he was, nevertheless, the beneficiary of that new power. Had there been available a man of the people, Benton might well have been defeated. As it was, however, he won, not because of his association with the St. Louis clique, but because of the state-wide support that must have come from his well-known political program. A successful candidate needed a state-wide reputation acceptable to a substantial portion of the people and there was a lack of such men available for the Senate. Of the announced candidates, Cook, Elliott, and Jones were little known throughout the state. Lucas—not a popular personality—had incurred powerful enemies and had not attracted any offsetting support. Men well known as business leaders sought influence, but not office; they would probably not have been acceptable to the masses.

---

to be convinced that Benton was more favorable to Spanish land grants confirmation than Lucas, who was the most vocal and bitter enemy of such confirmation. Benton's supporters may well have been interested in getting the Ralls vote recorded, but Benton did not need it. To be elected, a candidate needed a majority of the votes cast. If Ralls had not voted there would have been fifty-one votes cast, twenty-six of which were for Benton. The point is that Benton had strength in his own right.

Barton, with his already developed state-wide popularity, was a logical choice, as was Benton, who had developed a state-wide reputation as a political spokesman through his editorship of the *St. Louis Enquirer.* More than the other aspirants, Benton had developed and made public a political program for Missouri; he had pointed out the need for support by the national government and had vigorously supported the popular majority in the fight against restriction. Since he had not been a member of the constitutional convention, he was not directly associated with the unpopular features of the constitution. His close personal association with the special interests of the St. Louis clique was probably not universally known throughout the state, and he very carefully stated his political program so that measures beneficial to special economic interests had significant elements of popular appeal. For example, Benton voiced his support for liberal confirmation of the Spanish land grants in such a way as to woo the many holders of smaller claims, while at the same time he stressed the benefit of the fur trade for all of Missouri.

The elections of 1820 must have made a significant impression upon Benton. He could not discount the support of special economic groups and the old political power elite in furthering his election to the Senate, yet they had not dictated his selection. Was the election evidence that he had been wrong in associating his political ambition with the few? Could it be that the real source of political strength lay with the masses, even for a senator elected through the refining processes of an intermediate body? Benton's future actions indicated that his answer to these questions was a strong yes, and his future success indicated that he was right.

With the adoption of a constitution and the formation of a government to their advantage, Missourians awaited the presumed routine acceptance of their work by Congress and subsequent formal admission into the Union. When the Missouri Constitution was placed before Congress in the middle of November, 1820, however, a strong effort to block Missouri's entry into the Union as a slave state produced a second debate that raged, bitter and intense, for several months. Centered in the northern-dominated House, the opposition zeroed in on the clause in the state's constitution requiring the General Assembly to enact legislation to prevent free Negroes and mulattoes from settling in Missouri. Pointing out that Negroes were granted citizenship rights in some northern states, opponents argued that the right to enter and to settle in any state was one of the guarantees of the national constitution, which prescribed that: "The Citizens of each State shall be entitled to all Privileges and Immunities of Citizens in the several States." In addition, they charged that the provision in Missouri's constitution was an insulting reflection upon every state where Negroes were citizens.

Opposition in Congress to Missouri's constitution should not have been a surprise, for the dedicated restrictionists had not accepted the original Missouri compromise as final. In less than a month after passage of the compromise, antislavery forces in the Pennsylvania legislature introduced a resolution that condemned the Missouri Compromise and requested the state's congressional delegation to vote for the admission of Missouri only if that state's constitution provided for the gradual abolition of slavery. Similar resolutions were introduced in Indiana, New York, and Vermont. Although only Vermont passed the resolutions the actions themselves indicated there was still opposition to the admission of Missouri as a slave state. In the weeks following passage of the Missouri Compromise, antislavery newspapers and spokesmen continued to voice opposition to any slave status for Missouri. The editor of the *Western Herald* in Steubenville, Ohio, informed his readers in May, 1820, that the friends of freedom still had a chance to keep Missouri free because Congress had not yet approved a constitution for the state. In February of 1821, a member of the House of Representatives introduced a resolution requiring Missouri to provide for the gradual abolition of slavery before being admitted. The measure was defeated, but the sixty-one votes cast for the proposition constituted a repudiation of the Missouri Compromise by a substantial majority of the representatives from the North.

Some congressmen were undoubtedly sincere in their continued objections based on constitutional interpretation. Others may have wanted to avoid any action that might imply congressional approval of the type of state legislation required by the Missouri Constitution. Most Missourians believed, with good reason, that northern congressmen were trying to force Missouri to become a free-soil state or block her admission to the Union. There were, on the other hand, northern congressmen who supported Missouri's admission for a variety of reasons, without restrictions. Some were sympathetic to the southern position, while others like the two Democratic senators from Maine distrusted what they considered the federalism of many of their northeastern colleagues. Missourians did have cause to think the state was being singled out for unfair treatment, because other states had similar laws against the migration of Negroes. Senator-designate Barton informed Missourians from Washington that the constitutional objection was a pretext for the antislavery forces to delay admission. As Barton read the opposition, it erroneously believed that enough restrictionist sentiment existed in Missouri to alter the state's position on slavery.

Henry Clay, influential in shaping the first Missouri Compromise, again worked out a course of action that was adopted by Congress in late February, 1821. The bill, which passed the House (87 to 81) and the Senate (28 to 14), provided for Missouri's admission into the Union on an equal footing with the original states, upon the fundamental condition that the objectionable clause in the state's constitution should never be used to support the passage of any laws by which any citizen of any of the states of the Union should be deprived of his privileges and immunities to which he was entitled under the national constitution, and that the General Assembly of Missouri should pass a solemn act assenting to that condition. Upon receipt of such action, the President was to proclaim Missouri a state of the Union.

Missourians were unhappy with the congressional measure, but they appear to have viewed the action as political, and they complied accordingly. Without controversy the General Assembly passed the required act, but so phrased it as to defend the rights of the state to the point of near defiance of congressional power. The act declared that Missouri had already assented to abide by all provisions of the national constitution and that the General Assembly had no power to change the state's constitution other than by the procedure prescribed therein; but as Congress desired the General Assembly to declare its assent to the stipulated conditions it would do so, for "such declaration will neither restrain, or enlarge, limit or extend the operations of the constitution of the United States, or of this state, but the said constitutions will remain in all respects as if the said resolution had never passed."

The solemn act, approved on June 26, 1821, was forwarded to Washington, and, on August 10, 1821, President James Monroe proclaimed the admission of Missouri into the Union as the twenty-fourth state of the Union—the second west of the Mississippi. The Missouri General Assembly later violated the compromise by enacting legislation in 1825 and in 1847 that excluded free Negroes and mulattoes from coming into the state, but the national government never challenged the legislation.

Although the formal admission of Missouri into the Union was delayed for over a year, the state government began to function almost immediately after the August elections in 1820. The First General Assembly convened in the Missouri Hotel in St. Louis on September 18, and Alexander McNair took the oath of office as governor the following day. The transition from territorial status to statehood required Missourians to assume the responsibility for establishing state governmental machinery and to determine basic policies for the state. The convention had produced the constitution, but its implementation and the actual assumption of political functions still had to be accomplished. The new state would also have to develop its role in national affairs. There were controversies over certain undemocratic features of the constitution, personal rivalries, and normal political quarrels over policies, but the disputes did not interrupt basic order and stability; Missouri's internal transition from territory to state was made in a relatively smooth manner.

The selection of a capital site was one of the first matters taken up by the General Assembly. After considering several towns, the General Assembly agreed to locate the state government in St. Charles, where a building had been offered, until October 1, 1826, when it could then be moved to a permanent site as prescribed by the constitution. In accordance with the constitutional mandate, the legislature appointed five commissioners representing various parts of the state to select a capital site on the Missouri River within forty miles of the mouth of the Osage River. The commissioners selected an area equal to four sections of public land, although it was located in parts of seven different sections—where Jefferson City stands today—but their report endorsed Cote Sans Dessein, the largest settlement in the prescribed area, as the first choice for the capital site. Since the enabling act had specified only four sections, there was some concern that the area selected might not be granted to the state. Cote Sans Dessein was lacking in public land, and controversies over land titles were common. Many Missourians favored the Cote Sans Dessein location, with Angus Lewis Langham, a townsite speculator, being its most active promoter. In late 1821, the commissioners reported that Langham had apparently secured the necessary land titles and would give the state almost four hundred acres of land if the seat of government was located at Cote Sans Dessein. The deliberations of the General Assembly were not fully recorded, and consequently it has never been clear why front-running Cote Sans Dessein lost the capital to the Jefferson City site. Word from the General Land Office that the lands selected would qualify for the grant from the national government, evidence that the Cote Sans Dessein site remained embroiled in title problems, and fear of possible reactions against the activities of promoters like Langham probably influenced the General Assembly's final decision. In early 1822, the state legislature directed the commissioners to lay out a town that it already had named the City of Jefferson, which through common usage would soon be called Jefferson City.

The First General Assembly enacted legislation necessary to make the constitution operative by adopting statutes that defined the duties and functions of administrative officers and organized a state militia. As local governmental units were not established by the constitution, the General Assembly created counties and other political subdivisions by statutes that prescribed their organizational structure and powers. The most important unit of local government was the county court, with three judges, established to handle probate business and to administer county affairs. These courts, although the officers were called judges, did not have regular judicial functions, and the judges were to be appointed by the governor.

To meet the financial needs of the state, the First General Assembly adopted a traditional set of revenue laws. A general land, lot, and improved real estate tax was imposed at the rate of 25¢ per $100 evaluation; slaves and livestock were taxed at the same rate; and the rate for furniture was 50¢ per $100 evaluation. The signs of affluence were also targets, as pleasure carriages were taxed at 1 per cent of their value and watches at $2 per $100 evaluation. Although not a requirement for voting, a poll tax of $1 was levied upon every white male over twenty-one years of age. Legislation also was enacted requiring payment of a license fee to operate various types of business establishments and to practice certain occupations. Among the highest were the license cost of $20 to sell wine and liquor for six months and the $100 charge for a six-month license for auctioneers.

Before the new state could move forward effectively, it had to ride out its phase of a national depression. Although the effects of the Panic of 1819 did not reach Missouri until the latter part of 1820, the state was in a severe financial crisis by the spring of 1821. Problems related to the depression overshadowed all other concerns of Missourians. Extensive land speculation, supported by the liberal credit and unsound paper issues of many banks throughout the country, contributed greatly to the depression. As the economic boom collapsed, banks sought to protect themselves by calling in loans and curtailing credit; bank-issued notes circulating as currency depreciated greatly and many banks failed. All these conditions further depressed the economy, and heavy speculation throughout Missouri helped to draw the state into the national maelstrom.

Migration into Missouri Territory was somewhat unique and proved advantageous to Missouri's economy. In the years just before the panic, men from eastern areas who had sold their improved farms at good prices moved westward, with many settling in Missouri. With their capital they purchased frontier land, but still had sufficient money left to increase capital and commodity demand in Missouri. This inflow of money had provided one means to pay for eastern goods being shipped into the state. As the depression hit the East, this kind of migration slowed, and the capital that previously had been brought in was soon expended. Since much land speculation in Missouri had been based upon expectation of sales to newcomers, land values fell.

The depression affected every class and most individuals in the state and caught debtors, small farmers, merchants, and speculators with obligations they could not meet. Merchants and other creditors could not collect money due them for merchandise or services, paper currency depreciated, and banks could not collect their loans. Commodity prices dropped drastically, if, indeed, a cash purchaser could be found. Many debt and tax obligations had to be defaulted. Property that had been worth up to $10,000 could not be sold for over $500. Corn sold by farmers at their door to newcomers at three to five dollars per barrel dropped to a market price of ten cents a bushel. The newspapers were full of long lists of property sold for taxes. There were frequent executor sales to settle private debts, and individuals were sometimes placed in jail for failure to pay obligations. The two banks chartered during the territorial period both failed—the Bank of St. Louis in 1819 and the Bank of Missouri in 1821. Although poor management of both banks undoubtedly contributed to the state's depression, Missouri was left without needed currency and banking services.

The impact upon the individual was direct and disastrous. The honest, hard-working person was unable to meet even his most modest obligations. A farmer who worked harder would only produce an unmarketable surplus. The merchant who had advanced credit in good faith lost his investment and could not pay his creditors. Those holding depreciated or worthless bank notes understandably came to dislike paper currency and the institutions that had issued it. The absence of capital, credit, or markets weakened the incentive for economic expansion or development. The land speculator was hard pressed with his now overpriced land and big debts in a contracting economy.

To many there appeared to be very little the individual could do to help himself. The depression produced demands for state action to provide relief and to bolster the economy. Just how the state government should respond to these economic problems produced one of Missouri's earliest political contro-

versies. Debate was not between those favoring state intervention and those favoring a policy of *laissez faire*. Most Missourians
considered some state action necessary, but they disagreed concerning the extent and nature of the state's role. Some, who
thought the General Assembly needed only to create a state
bank, argued that a properly chartered bank could make capital
and credit available and issue a new, sound currency that would
serve as a medium of exchange to open the channels of trade
and also serve as an instrument to pay debts and taxes. Others
thought the role of the state should be even more extensive and
include provisions for more direct relief to individuals caught
in the depression squeeze.

When the special session of the General Assembly convened
in the summer of 1821 to pass the solemn act required by Congress for Missouri's final admission to the Union, the growing
demands for relief required legislative attention. In his address
to the General Assembly Governor McNair called attention to
the great public and private distress resultant from the depression, but without any course of action to recommend he could
only suggest that, "If there be any feasible plan of relief, the
public exigencies seem imperiously to require its adoption; if
it can be done without trenching out the fundamental principles
of the Constitution."

The General Assembly, determined to act with or without
specific recommendations from the Governor, rejected the demand for a state bank favored generally by the more conservative, older leadership, and instead passed a series of laws for the
relief of debtors, and authorized a form of state-issued currency
to stimulate economic recovery without the "evil" banking institutions. The special session enacted a very moderate stay law
under which land sold for debt could be redeemed by its owner
within thirty months by paying the buyer the purchase price
plus 10 per cent. If, however, the creditor made the purchase,
the property could not be redeemed with less payment than the
debt. Actually, the law gave little debt relief, and it held up clear
title to any buyer of property involved. Other laws abolished
imprisonment for debts on contract and exempted some essential personal property including pieces of furniture, one cow,
and one spinning wheel from sale for execution of debt.

The most ambitious and controversial legislation of the special session established a state loan office, authorized to issue certificates in denominations ranging from fifty cents to ten dollars, which were to be loaned to individuals on land and personal property security. Loans could be made up to $1000 with interest at 6 per cent. To give these certificates value as a common circulating medium of exchange, the law made them receivable in payment of taxes or debts due the state and payable for the salaries of state officers. As the loans were repaid, the certificates could be retired or reloaned according to need, but 10 per cent of those issued were to be withdrawn annually. Missourians were actually not very original in devising the loan office operation, since similar practices had been employed in most of the American colonies.

In the 1821–1822 regular session, the General Assembly completed its relief legislation with a rather complicated although far from radical stay law. This law provided that if a creditor sought to foreclose on a loan he had to agree to settle for no more than two-thirds of the value of the property sold or agree to a stay of execution for two and one-half years, provided the debtor could show warrant for leniency and could secure bond for full payment. The operations of the loan office were also extended with the provision that all state payments could be made with the loan office certificates. In a limited way, through special legislation, the certificates could be loaned to individuals to establish a business in the state.

Strong opposition developed against the loan office on the grounds that its certificates lacked adequate financial backing. The refusal of many merchants and creditors to accept the loan office issues further undermined their value, and they began to depreciate as early as January, 1822.

The debate over the relief laws and the loan office was heated and intense. Missouri newspapers gave extensive coverage to the issues, with prorelief arguments directed toward the farmer, debtor, and poor man generally, while antirelief articles emphasized respectability, knowledge, and a general property-holding conservative approach. The prorelief arguments sought to justify payment of obligations measured by labor and produce equal to the value of the debt at the time it was incurred. The opposi-

tion cried out about dishonesty and emphasized sanctity of contract and the tyranny of majority rule. Farmers, landholders,
and speculators generally supported the legislation, while most
lawyers, merchants, and creditors opposed the programs. Edward Bates, for example, resigned as attorney general, at least
in part to protest relief legislation. During his successful campaign for the General Assembly in 1822, Bates declared the
legislation an outrageous and unconstitutional violation of individual and property rights. Like other conservatives, he appealed to the judiciary as the true shield of the people and
called upon the courts to declare the action of the General
Assembly unconstitutional and void.

Although class positions and class arguments were involved
in the relief issue, there was no absolute alignment along any
fixed class lines. The fact that a man was a debtor or creditor,
buyer or seller, farmer or merchant, or landholder or nonland-
holder entered into his decision, but the situation was not the
same for all men within a single major class, and the interests
of some crossed any arbitrary class definition. Many of the
businessmen of St. Louis wanted an increase in the amount of
currency in circulation, for the supply was inadequate to do
business, but their concern was not the same as that of a debtor's.
A debtor supporting relief measures might have been a small
farmer or a businessman trying to meet varied financial obligations; he may have been a poor man by all standards, or a man
generally classified as a large property holder, but in debt for
his holdings; he was frequently a land speculator. The voting
in the General Assembly did not indicate any major sectional
divisions. In fact, the vote from every county with more than
one representative was divided.

In operation, the relief laws do not seem to have won great
popular support, and even friends of relief saw limited value in
the final legislation. Many charged that the program served the
large landholder and the big speculator rather than bona fide
farmers, and certainly the speculators had been a major force
behind the adoption of relief legislation.

A series of unfavorable court decisions soon invalidated the
stay laws. A lower court in Cooper County declared the stay
legislation unconstitutional in March of 1822; the state circuit

court in St. Louis held the legislation void the following July on the grounds that it violated the constitutional guarantee against the impairment of contracts; and the state supreme court confirmed these decisions. In November, 1822, the General Assembly repealed the measures.

The loan office suffered a similar fate. The St. Louis state circuit court in February, 1822, ruled that the act violated the United States Constitution because it provided for the issuance of bills of credit by the state and attempted to make something other than gold or silver legal tender. The state administration then moved to dismantle the loan office operations. No new loans were to be made, and debtors were called upon to pay 10 per cent of their loan every six months with an opportunity to retire their full debt with an 80 per cent payment. Officials ordered the destruction of all certificates received by the state.

With the loan office certificates declared unconstitutional some borrowers sought to avoid repayment of their loans. The state supreme court continued to hold that the loans had to be repaid, but in 1830, in *Craig* v. *Missouri*, the Supreme Court of the United States declared the Loan Office Act unconstitutional and ruled that the notes under it were not collectable. As a result the state lost approximately $43,000, along with uncollected interest. The counterfeiting of certificates proved a further cost to the state, when a final accounting disclosed that approximately $180,000 in certificates had been issued while over $188,000 had been redeemed.

Not all agreed that the loan office principle was a failure. Some believed the operation could have been successful if the certificates had been made legal tender and more of them had been placed into circulation. Some opponents had not even debated against a regular currency issue, and the broader questions of currency and note issues remained unsettled. Missouri, with the rest of the nation, recovered from the Panic of 1819, but not before many men had suffered financial losses.

The relief program undoubtedly had some impact in shaping the nature and personnel of the party system that subsequently developed in the state, but the division in 1821–1822 was far from clear. Because the relief legislation was related in some ways to the needs of the masses, many prorelievers were found later in the popular-based party of Andrew Jackson; any absolute correlation is by necessity impossible. Proreliefer Duff Green, later a leader in the Jacksonian movement, was a land speculator in the early 1820's. Benton, seriously considering his political future, stood aloof. Even Andrew Jackson condemned similar legislation in Tennessee in no uncertain terms. John Miller, Missouri's first Jacksonian governor, in his biennial message to the General Assembly in 1826, termed the loan office as impolitic and unconstitutional. The fact is that the mainstream of Jacksonianism in Missouri supported hard money. The entire package of relief legislation undoubtedly caused the traditionally conservative, property-holding, creditor class to form a more united front. Although to some members of this class such legislation might offer needed relief, they feared this kind of power in the hands of a majority.

No clear-cut distinction or political division between the acceptance of the philosophy of *laissez faire* and that of a very positive role of government in social and economic affairs emerged in the very early years; nor was there any particular consistency on such basic alternatives by individuals or interest groups. The state's first chief executive certainly did not use his office to launch Missouri under any precise, predetermined economic-political philosophy, but Governor McNair did recognize that the state government could be a positive force in economic planning and direction. They had a "destiny," he told the legislators in November, 1821, to awaken the slumbering energies of their countrymen and to "be the instruments of ameliorating the conditions of your country, by well-planned systems of encouragement to the development & application of its internal resources." Other than a recommendation for the construction of a tobacco warehouse to aid in the marketing of Missouri tobacco, he did not, however, suggest specific programs. When the General Assembly convened in November of 1822, he had no positive suggestions to deal with the depression-created problems, and he could only urge the strictest political economy and emphasize that the most effective source of relief was in the private industry and economy of the citizens.

In 1822, McNair did propose the establishment of agriculture societies to promote improved agriculture methods and the enactment of laws for the inspection of flour, beef, and pork to enhance the marketing of those Missouri products. He also urged the General Assembly to utilize the land grants for the establishment of public schools and begin the construction of internal improvements such as state roads and river improvement, but he offered no specific programs. In another area, McNair urged consideration of legislation for aid to the aged and the infirm and the establishment of a state hospital along the Missouri River to serve the many boatmen and passengers who had to be left by the boats due to illness and were dependent upon charity for medical service and other accommodations.

It is perhaps unfair to expect a new state government to involve itself in such operations, especially during a depression. Although the General Assembly did provide for the establishment of an inspection system for tobacco going on the market, little else concrete came out of the Governor's suggestions.

Although the Missouri economy was still in the pioneer stage and the entire nation might be hurting from the Panic of 1819, the state's future seemed nonetheless bright. Energetic and able leaders with experience rooted in the territorial years moved quickly to promote the settlement and development of the new state.

# CHAPTER II

# THE PEOPLE AND THE LAND

Missouri's natural endowments made the state easily accessible and highly attractive to settlers. As the westernmost outpost of American settlement, Missouri was strategically located within the nation's great central river system. The Ohio River, a major route of western travel and commerce, flowed into the Mississippi River on the state's lower eastern border. With the Mississippi as its eastern boundary, much of Missouri was attached to the central nerve of the mid-American water system. The Missouri River, flowing through the heart of the state, served as the major highway for the far western trade. St. Louis, a well-established city of some 5,000 persons in 1820 at the confluence of the Missouri and the Mississippi, was located in the key of an extensive river system that reached into and far beyond the state.

Smaller rivers served as routes into the more remote parts of the state. The Chariton and the Grand rivers flowed from the north into the Missouri, while the Osage and the Gasconade joined the Missouri from the south. Only small and relatively unimportant tributaries flowed into the Mississippi north of the Missouri River, but to the south the Meramec, the St. Francis, the Current, the Black, and the White rivers drained Missouri's lands into the lower Mississippi. Missouri waterways flowed through approximately 8,000,000 acres of highly fertile bottom land—almost one-fifth of the entire acreage of the state. Complementing the rich lands, the new state offered the added attractions of a moderate climate, long growing seasons, ample rainfall, and abundant timber. To an agrarian-oriented people the river routes to good land offered an attractive opportunity.

Mineral resources that might attract mining operations and aid in the state's economic development were abundant. Lead had been important from the earliest days, and although their extent and value were unknown, other minerals found in Missouri included coal, flint, gypsum, iron ore, kaolin (clay), marble, saltpeter, silex, and zinc.

Missouri contained several distinct geographical regions, and the patterns of settlement and economic development of each region reflected its special characteristics. The area north of the Missouri River was termed the Northern Plains. With some internal physical variations, the Northern Plains have a generally rolling surface; rounded hills with broad, shallow valleys have different qualities of soil, but the region as a whole is productive of cereals and grasses. The soils of the loess hills in the northwestern part of the state and along the Missouri River possess outstanding productive value. The area lacked extensive timber, but enough areas provided ample woods to meet the needs of the settlers.

The Ozark Highlands area covers a major part of the state south of the Missouri River. Although there are some relatively

GEOGRAPHY OF MISSOURI

Each of Missouri's geographic regions—the Northern Plains, the Ozark Highlands, the Western Plains, and the Bootheel—offered a variety of attractions to settlers, and her abundant waterways supported a thriving agricultural productivity and interstate trading activities.

smooth plateaus, most of the area is too rough and hilly for general agriculture, and the soil is generally of poor quality. This region offered the least to the average early settler, but the abundant timber and mineral possibilities added much to the over-all opportunities in the state.

The Western Plains form something of a rough triangle based on the north by the Missouri River from just west of the mouth of the Osage River and on the western border down to the Ozarks. This area was easily adaptable to general farming with its relatively smooth surface or gentle slopes, slow streams, and fertile soil. Coal was also available in the region by simple strip mining.

A limited area in deep southeast Missouri was composed of flat lowland. Although this has been drained and is today one of the most productive and valuable land areas of the state, the region was not attractive to early settlers because too much of it was swampland. Each major region contained rich bottom lands, with those adjacent to the Mississippi and Missouri rivers being most important because of their easy accessibility.

At the time of statehood, the greatest portion of Missouri's nearly 66,000 inhabitants resided along the Mississippi River from the Arkansas border northward to Pike County and along the Missouri River as far west as Ray and Lafayette counties. A small number of persons coming north from Arkansas along the White River had settled in southern Missouri, and there was also a small settlement in what is now the Springfield area.

In 1820, approximately 85 per cent of the Missourians reported agriculture as their major economic activity. The small, general, highly self-sufficient farm was common. Farmers, especially in the off season, engaged in a variety of other economic pursuits. Although there were some large landholders, these were usually speculators; large plantations had not yet developed in the state. Important nonagriculture activities included fur trading, lead mining—which was centered in the region just south and west of St. Louis—frontier merchandising, common skilled and semi-skilled craft work, and the processing of lead, tobacco, grain, and other extractive products. Land speculation also occupied the energies of important men. The older French and first American arrivals retained their Spanish claims, while the post–Louisiana

Purchase Americans sought land for future resale. In spite of confusion over the still unconfirmed Spanish land claims and the holdings of other speculators, newcomers could easily acquire land.

Missouri entered the Union with a surprisingly large professional class dominated by lawyers. Generally attracted to frontiers that promised growth, many attorneys were especially drawn to the Missouri Territory because of the great amount of litigation involved in confirmation of Spanish land claims. As a group, the lawyers had been very active in territorial affairs; the new state was well endowed with capable men of the bar who would play important roles in shaping its future.

Urban development predated statehood. The establishment of the early towns usually preceded extensive agricultural settlement. The towns then contributed to the development of the region's agriculture and were in turn influenced by that growth. Although Ste. Genevieve was the earliest permanent settlement in Missouri, by 1820 St. Louis was by far the most important city of the new state. The city, with its advantageous river location, was the seat of government—a fact that attracted many lawyers—and it served as headquarters for the western fur trade, probably the biggest single business of the valley. Still somewhat steeped in French influence and led by the old French families, the city was by 1820 beginning to show a predominant American tone. A new, aggressive American leadership, aiding in the establishment of urban institutions, helped prepare St. Louis to receive and direct the flow of immigrants and goods into the whole trans-Mississippi region. Ste. Genevieve, with a population of between 1,500 and 2,000, was second in size and an important center of economic and political influence in the area south of St. Louis. The most important western town, third in population, was Franklin. Founded on the Missouri River in 1817, it quickly became the gateway to a vast and fertile region and the economic center for the growing Boonslick country. By 1820, Franklin had a population of nearly 1,000. Four other towns could boast a population of over 500: Cape Girardeau, Jackson, Potosi, and St. Charles. Leadership in the areas of culture, economics, and politics centered in all these major towns, especially St. Louis.

34

The majority of people in the new state could be classified as self-sufficient, pioneer farmers, but there were many variations from any possible norm. In all the settled areas there were men who had accumulated considerable wealth. In central Missouri this class had accumulated wealth chiefly through farm enterprises and land speculation. In the southeast the wealthy were usually Americans who had either come to the area before the Louisiana Purchase and had secured large landholdings from the Spanish or had prospered in the lead mining operations. Men from Kentucky and Tennessee who—after having sold their land there at a high price—had come to frontier Missouri, represented the state's newer wealth. In addition, there were French landowners and merchants especially in St. Louis, and the American land speculators, businessmen and professionals who represented an upper class based on wealth and status.

Social institutions and cultural activities in 1820 were generally in the frontier stage throughout the new state. Most Missourians possessed rather rough and often crude social characteristics. Outbursts of lawlessness occasionally erupted, and members of the "better classes" criticized the abundance of overindulgence in drinking, fighting, gambling, and general moral laxity. If a minority took undue advantage of the freedom from restraints usually imposed by traditional legal or social institutions found in more established areas, the majority were basically good people seeking to establish for themselves a workable system in which to live. Actually, there were important islands of culture in this western outpost of settlement where the cultural and social life of a few rivaled that of Easterners. A scarcity of books, music, art, or drama was the rule for most Missourians in plain homes with meager furnishings, but for the elite few these luxuries were a very real part of their lives.

Missouri soon attracted thousands of settlers. Her population increased during the first four decades following statehood seven times that of the nation as a whole. The state moved from a rank of twenty-third among the twenty-four states in 1820 to a rank of eighth among thirty-three states in 1860. In absolute figures, the census reported Missouri's total population as 66,557 in 1820; 140,455 in 1830; 383,702 in 1840; 682,044 in 1850; and 1,182,012 in 1860. The census omitted Indians from the count, although there may have been as many as 6,000 living or hunting regularly within the state in 1820.

During the first decade of statehood, newcomers tended to locate in the "T" areas formed by the Mississippi and Missouri river boundaries. The Mississippi line was pushed north to Marion County, formed in 1826, and the some fifty-mile-wide corridor along the Missouri was extended to the western border, effecting the organization of Jackson County in 1826. Some settlers moved into the area north of the Missouri and west of the Mississippi with the resultant creation of Randolph (1829) and Monroe (1831) counties.

In the 1830's a heavy surge of migration opened new areas of the state and pushed settlement away from the original river corridors. The present counties adjacent to the Missouri River on the north and the Mississippi on the west had all been established by 1837. Due principally to the attractiveness of the Chariton Valley, present-day counties in the northeast had also been organized in a triangle framed by a line running along the Mississippi from St. Louis to the northern border, then diagonally to a point in the center of the state. Much of the Western Plains area also had been settled by 1837, and counties had been formed along the Osage River from the southwest to its point of contact with the Missouri; with the exception of Moniteau and Bates, all present counties had been organized in the region between the Osage and Missouri rivers. Some settlers also entered the Ozarks, but this movement resulted in only three counties covering all of the southwest corner of the state. The other region greatly influenced by a population movement in the 1830's was the Platte country. The addition of the Platte Purchase to Missouri in 1837 extended the state's northwestern boundary from the original line running due north from the mouth of the Kansas River westward to the Missouri River. This area filled in so rapidly that four counties had been organized in the region by 1841.

During the 1840's settlement north of the Missouri River increased so heavily that by 1851, with only two exceptions, every county had its present boundaries; south of the river only eight present-day counties were lacking, and all of these were in the

Ozark region, which offered the fewest economic resources. By 1860, with the exception of Worth County, the state's present 114 counties had been established.[1] The settlement of new areas away from the river corridors, especially after 1840, reflected new elements of livelihood in the backgrounds of the immigrants coming to the state.

The 1850 census, which tabulated nativity for the first time, confirmed that the migration into Missouri since the Louisiana Purchase had been primarily from the south. Almost two-thirds of Missouri's residents born in the United States but outside of the state reported Kentucky, Tennessee, or Virginia as their birthplace; the number of persons born in slaveholding states exceeded the total from free areas 187,518 to 76,592. By conservative estimate more than two-thirds of the people living in Missouri in 1850 traced their origins back to Kentucky, North Carolina, Tennessee, or Virginia. As a slaveholding territory and state, Missouri became the final destination of many western-moving southerners who had bypassed the area of the Old Northwest where slavery was not allowed. Many of Missouri's more than 87,000 slaves in 1850 had been a part of this southern migration. Even this strong southern orientation did not make Missouri fit the traditional southern stereotype. Kentucky and Tennessee were border states, and the settlers from Virginia and North Carolina were from the back-country farm class rather than the plantation areas. The states of the deep South actually supplied fewer people to settle Missouri than did the free states.

Despite its predominantly southern population, Missouri always contained an important segment of residents whose attitudes, experiences, and interests had been shaped by their free-state backgrounds. After 1840 these residents became an increasing force in the state, and, with little money and much courage, they extended settlement throughout the state. Most of those settling north of the Missouri River were from northern states and were not slaveholders. Economic possibilities in

1. Under the authorization contained in the state constitution of 1875, the voters of St. Louis County approved a plan in 1876 for separation of the city of St. Louis from the county. The city retained certain functions of county government.

areas other than agriculture attracted a growing number of Northerners, whose numbers increased at a more rapid rate during the 1850's than did the ranks of their southern counterparts. The last area occupied—the plateau and hill regions of the central Ozarks—was peopled by a class seeking to continue a frontier style of life. Many of those came from the poor class of the Tennessee and Kentucky hill country and found in the Missouri Ozarks a familiar environment with improved soil and water resources, but without the pressure or competition of their former more energetic and efficient neighbors. These people were not slaveholders, and they hardly fit the southern "image."

Foreign immigrants also contributed significantly to the diversity in Missouri's economic and cultural development. With an increased migration each decade, the number of foreign-born Missourians in 1860 exceeded 160,000 and made up 13.6 per cent of the state's population. Germans constituted by far the largest national group in Missouri, accounting for slightly over 55 per cent of the foreign-born and 7.5 per cent of the total population. Since many of the Germans had left their homeland in search of greater liberties, they created an active force in opposition to slavery.

Gottfried Duden holds an important place in the story of the German migration to Missouri. Concerned about the status and the future of the common people of Germany, this rather well-to-do lawyer and public official of Mulheim on the Ruhr came to the United States to investigate the possibilities for German migration to a new land. Traveling by land after his debarkation at Baltimore, Duden arrived in St. Louis in the fall of 1824. Impressed with what he saw of the Missouri region, Duden purchased a farm in what is now Warren County. While he operated his farm only for a short time, he did make extensive observations of the area's resources, with an eye toward suitability for a possible German immigration. Returning to Germany in 1827, Duden wrote a report in which he enumerated the opportunities in Missouri, encouraged migration, and offered detailed instructions for those who desired to go.[2] The book,

2. *Report of a Journey to the Western States of North America, and a Residence of Several Years on the Missouri (during the years 1824, '25,*

published in 1829, was widely read, and subsequently thousands of Germans "followed" Duden to Missouri. Although he was overly romantic and optimistic in his report, Duden did point out that careful planning for the trip was a necessity, that some capital was essential, and that agriculture offered the best vocational opportunity. Disappointed immigrants later criticized Duden for his subjective evaluation of the area, but generally those who had the greatest difficulties were those who had ignored his advice. The over-all successes of the Germans in Missouri, however, were indications of the general soundness of Duden's recommendations.

The German settlers who came to Missouri differed both in social background and in motives for leaving their homeland. They came in organized groups or as individuals, but in nearly all instances they settled in closely knit communities where they could retain more easily the language and customs of their Old-World homes. Well-educated Germans with status in the old society who either had to flee or chose to leave after the unsuccessful revolutions against the undemocratic government of the 1830's and late 1840's comprised an important part of the migration into the state between 1830 and 1850. Organized religious groups of different persuasions also came to secure greater freedom of worship. The largest number of German immigrants—representing farmers, merchants, craftsmen, and professional men—came simply to improve their lot in life.

Disappointed by the failure of the revolutionary movement in 1832–1833 and influenced by Duden's book, Frederick Muench and Paul Follenius organized the Giessen Emigrant Society. The group, plagued with sickness and other misfortunes, arrived in St. Louis after having exhausted their funds for a communal land purchase. The society disbanded, but the people settled in St. Louis, St. Charles, Franklin, and Warren counties. Another organized group of some 600 Saxons moved into Perry County in 1839, after leaving their native state because of limitations on their freedom of worship. These conservative and strict followers of Luther joined in organizing the Missouri Synod of the Lutheran Church. By 1840 German Catholics had also come

'26, and 1827), dealing with the Question of Emigration and Excess Population.

to Missouri; Westphalia, established on the Maries River in 1835, became the center of the numerous German Catholic settlements in Cole, Maries, and Miller counties.

Germans from the eastern part of the United States also contributed to the growing population of Missouri. Organized in 1836, the highly structured German Settlement Society of Philadelphia hoped to establish a settlement in the more isolated West, where a traditional German culture could be more easily perpetuated. In part because of Duden's book, the Philadelphia Society selected the Gasconade River valley as a site and sent out an advance agent, who purchased about 300 acres of land from individuals and some 11,000 acres from the government; they then established the town of Hermann as a focal point for the settlers of the society. There were, of course, many other organized group movements, not to mention the thousands of individuals who moved on their own. A heavy migration in the decade of the 1850's doubled the German-born population. A large number of these immigrants settled in St. Louis, but other areas of special concentration included Franklin, Gasconade, Osage, Cole, Chariton, Buchanan, and Andrew counties.

As a whole, the German immigrants were a stable, hardworking people. For those with an agrarian background, Missouri's cheap and productive land offered a real opportunity, and they took advantage of it. The Germans tended to stay put; they involved themselves in limited land speculation, and as land passed from father to son a family stability arose within the German communities. They were also good farmers. Most of the land selected by the German farmers was outside of the river corridors. They wanted cheaper land, but their choice also reflected a desire for greater isolation, a dislike for slavery, a fear of lowland sickness, and an attachment to river bluffs and hilly regions similar to those of their homeland. In lesser numbers, German merchants, craftsmen, and professionals—classes that were to provide valuable contributions to Missouri life—concentrated most heavily in St. Louis.

The second largest group of foreign settlers came from Ireland. After the Irish migration of the late 1840's and 1850's, the 1860 census reported over 43,000 Irish in Missouri. Conditions in Ireland different from those in Germany brought the Irish to

Missouri. Ireland's potato famine of the 1840's triggered an exodus to America as thousands came in search of better economic opportunities. The bulk of the Irish, most of them farmers, entered Missouri with only meager resources and generally settled in urban areas where they hired out as day laborers because they lacked the money to buy land. They consequently proved an important source of labor, especially for water transportation and for the construction of Missouri railroads. The Irish were most heavily concentrated in St. Louis, Buchanan, and Jackson counties.

In contrast with the influx of German and Irish settlers, the number of immigrants from other foreign areas remained small. The English scattered throughout the state; those locating on farms settled primarily north of the Missouri River, where slavery was not prevalent, while others chose an urban area, particularly St. Louis. The few French immigrants, preferring to live in St. Louis, contributed to the cosmopolitan character of that county, whose 1860 population was over 50 per cent foreign born. French cultural influences from the pre-American period—the Catholic church, a now-corrupt form of the French language, steep-roofed cottages, and narrow streets—remain in evidence in the Ste. Genevieve and St. Louis areas still today.

Settlement patterns in Missouri reflected the diversity of the people and their origins. Several of the traditional western-moving groups made their appearance on the Missouri scene. A relatively small number of the most primitive type of settlers, to whom land ownership was not imperative, limited their farming to a small garden plot, which they worked under very crude methods, to supplement a diet of wild game, fish, berries, and fruits. Most of these primitive farmers avoided the major river areas and squatted on public land in the more isolated areas where they could maintain the characteristics of a back-country society. If a more organized civilization encroached upon their privacy, they would move on to a new area.

Other settlers were interested in land ownership, but inclined to view possession of the land as a fluid investment. These men commonly acquired more acreage from the government than they could cultivate, with the hope of selling all or part of it at a profit. They might even clear timber, break sod, or fence in some of the land to increase its resale value. They were prepared to sell improved land, but they were not the real speculators on western lands. The hardships of starting over again on virgin soil did not deter this class; they were content, perhaps willing, to be the vanguard of a new frontier.

Stability marked a third group. Individuals in this class purchased land in an area of their choice and made improvements aimed at permanent tenure. In so far as their capital allowed, these men frequently purchased more land than they could cultivate while it was available at low prices and took great pride in the ownership of their land.

As on any land frontier, professional speculators in Missouri sought to buy choice lands cheaply and then to sell them dearly as supply lessened and demand increased. The land speculators were often unpopular, but they performed vital functions in the opening and developing of new areas.

There was no clear-cut time progression in Missouri from the entry of the primitive pioneer to the development of a final ordered and stabilized society; some of the earliest immigrants brought fine horses, slaves, and capital with them and purchased fertile land easily accessible by river—enabling them to effect a smooth transition to a new way of life.

Land acquisition occurred in various ways. At the time of Missouri's entry into the Union, national government lands were being auctioned at a minimum price of $1.25 per acre in plots as small as eighty acres. Although no credit was allowed, a farm site could be purchased in Missouri for a relatively small outlay of capital. With some obvious exceptions most land went at or only slightly above the $1.25 minimum price. By prior agreement or sometimes as a result of personal pressures, men at auctions frequently held the bids down. Some of the land never came up for auction because men had already settled on a selected spot and were allowed in most areas by special legislation to purchase it for the minimum price before it was put up for auction by the land office. The right of general pre-emption was granted by Congress in 1841.

Most land auctions sold off only superior lands, leaving abundant good farm land available through direct purchase from the government at $1.25 per acre. After a long struggle that had been launched almost immediately after statehood by Missouri's Thomas H. Benton, Congress approved a law in 1854 graduating downward the price of public land once offered at auction but still unsold. This action, although quite late, opened almost 14,-000,000 acres of public land for sale at reduced prices.

Just how much of the public land was sold directly to the bona fide farmer or picked up by the speculator cannot be traced. While speculators clearly purchased substantial amounts, it is questionable whether they made great profits, and much of the speculation was done on a small scale by individual farmers.

The actual price paid for Missouri land obviously varied by time, location, and quality; any meaningful generalization is impossible. Records indicate that many Missouri farmers did get their land directly from the government at the $1.25 minimum price. Duden reported good land was available at the minimum price from the government or at a slightly higher price from individuals. In the prime Boonslick country at a public land sale in 1827 the average price for over 20,000 acres was approximately $1.50 per acre. The best land sold at auction increased in price as it passed from one individual to another, with some acreage in the more desirable locations being reported in the 1820's at $4 to $12 per acre; in the mid-1830's land in central Missouri brought between $10 and $20 per acre; farther west, a resident reported land could be had around Liberty for $5 to $6 per acre. The price of individually owned land frequently included improvements and therefore varied according to the location and the extent and nature of improvements. This difference in price is illustrated by the experience of the agent for the German Settlement Society of Philadelphia who purchased approximately 11,000 acres of public land for $1.25 per acre and 300 acres of private land at about $5.00, all in the Gasconade River valley in the mid-thirties. The depression of 1837 reduced land sales, and the public entries continued to be slow during the decade of the 1840's. The graduation act of 1854 increased public land sales, and with land offered for as low as 12½¢ per acre vast areas passed from the public domain into private hands.

By the end of 1820 approximately 550,000 acres of public land had been sold; by the close of 1830 the total had reached nearly

1,700,000 acres; sales in the decade of the 1830's put the total to just short of 7,000,000. The census of 1850 reported almost 10,-000,000 acres in farm land, and this figure doubled by 1860. This meant that approximately one-half of the area of the state was in private hands and classified as land in farms.

After securing land the new arrivals settled down to the tasks of production and development. Those with capital might purchase an improved farm, while those with lesser financial means selected an unimproved homestead requiring steps to provide immediate shelter. Frequently a tent had to suffice until a log cabin could be constructed, often with the help of neighbors. Most cabins were crude and their furnishings plain and scanty. New settlers sometimes brought a few items with them, mainly those with sentimental value, but for the most part they had to get along with the barest essentials. With his family, and possibly slaves or hired hands, the farmer next turned his attention to the task of clearing his land for cultivation. He girdled the larger trees and felled smaller ones to cut for wood supply. To supplement the limited supplies, the farmers planted cereal grains, vegetables, and even fruit trees as soon as an area was cleared. Poultry, hogs, and cattle supplied a major part of the family's basic food needs, with wild game, fish, berries, and fruit adding variety to the diet. Hides, cotton, and flax provided basic materials for making clothing. Even in the earliest years the most isolated farms had access to a town or trading post offering basic necessities along with a selection of nonessentials and even a few luxuries. Because of currency shortages on the frontier, supply and service exchanges were often conducted by barter. Nevertheless, most early farmers by necessity remained highly self-sufficient, devoting only limited attention to production for commercial purposes.

Frontier life placed demands on every member of the family. With leisure time limited, social life was closely tied to economic activities. Cabin raising, wood chopping, sap collecting, and cornhusking provided opportunities for social gatherings. On these occasions men tested themselves in such strengths and skills prized on the frontier as wrestling, jumping, running, and shooting, with a dance often climaxing the day's activities. The loneliness and isolation of the pioneer settlers kept them always eager to persuade relatives and old friends to settle nearby. They wrote to friends and relatives in their old home communities extolling the virtues of their new-found home and praising Missouri's fertile soil, healthful climate, and abundant resources.

Crude agricultural techniques prevailed in Missouri throughout the pre–Civil War period, but farm operations in the state soon progressed beyond the simple, self-sufficient pioneer stage. During the 1830's the transition was particularly noticeable. As owners prospered they replaced the simple log cabins with brick or frame houses. The quantities of cleared and fenced land increased while commercial production grew in importance. As some men became more successful than others, a form of class structure also began to appear. The transition did not proceed everywhere at the same rate, and different stages of farming existed in the same regions. Moreover, a significant number of arrivals, even in the early 1820's, brought sufficient capital, livestock, supplies, and slaves to avoid existence in a basic pioneer stage altogether.

Early town development contributed substantially to the agricultural refinement. The town offered the farmer such services as corn grinding, wheat milling, and blacksmithing, while general stores supplied a variety of goods. Local manufacturers provided a market for the farmer as did the merchant or commission man who gathered area produce for export. In offering opportunity to exchange farming information and local gossip, to enjoy social and recreational activities, and to participate in public affairs, the towns—especially the county seats—became social as well as economic exchange centers for rural Missourians.

Agricultural production and specialization increased in Missouri, but farming techniques remained largely unchanged. Missouri farmers showed little interest in fertilization, conservation, or other improved methods. As long as land remained productive, plentiful, and cheap, most saw no reason for immediate concern, preferring instead to continue the old but familiar ways. Rank-and-file farmers generally preferred inefficient cultivation of a large area to the more effective concentration of labor on a smaller field. Instead of cultivating, they were "scratching" the soil. In contrast with their American counterparts, most German farmers, coming from a country where land was scarce, made more effective use of the soil. They looked upon Missourians with great disdain as crude farmers indifferent toward their farms.

Missouri farmers were slow in adopting the farm implements and machinery that became available in the years before 1860. Reluctance to change, the distance from implement manufacturers, and the lack of specialization in small grains most easily adaptable to machinery contributed to the lack of mechanization on Missouri farms. Steel plows, common and improved harrows, cultivators, and various types of seed sowers were among the most popular machines in use in 1860. Hay rakes, threshing machines, and reapers were less common because of their cost and because they were not considered as essential.

At least a few farm leaders and nonfarmers who were interested in the general development of the state sought to improve farming practices. To meet the apparent lack of agriculture knowledge and to promote better farming methods, Missouri newspapers published numerous articles encouraging fertilization and improved techniques. Most newspapers carried information relative to the most suitable crops for given areas and advice on the potential market of various farm products, along with suggestions for the planting of fruit trees, gardens, and even vineyards. Question and answer columns handling specific problems of area residents were common newspaper features. In the late 1840's a popular magazine, the *Valley Farmer*, represented a more specialized approach in the effort to improve Missouri farming.

Between 1841 and 1861 growing interest resulted in the establishment of forty-nine agricultural societies dedicated to the promotion of improved livestock breeding and crop production. These societies sponsored local fairs and exhibits where information could be exchanged and quality seed and livestock purchased. In 1853 the General Assembly chartered the Missouri State Agricultural Society and provided it with an annual appropriation of $1,000 to purchase premiums and awards to be given at fairs. The act authorized the society to send agents into the counties to encourage and to aid in improving farming techniques. Two years later the legislature provided $100 yearly

46

to any county agricultural society organized to advance agriculture so long as it would meet certain state requirements. In the same year, a private group founded the St. Louis Agricultural and Mechanical Society and invested $65,000 in land and buildings for a fairgrounds providing excellent facilities for the exhibition of livestock and produce. The agriculture fairs undoubtedly did contribute to the improvement of farm methods because farmers could see demonstrations of better practices in the fair exhibits and apply this first-hand knowledge to their own farming.

A limited number of individuals engaged in their own agricultural experimentation. At his garden near Franklin, John Hardeman conducted experiments and made extensive observations on the production of wheat, corn, trees, and grapes until the Missouri River washed his property away in 1826. In a similar endeavor German immigrant George Engelmann studied Missouri vegetation and collected plant specimens, which he later donated to the Missouri Botanical Gardens in St. Louis, first opened to the public in 1860.

Missourians demonstrating real imagination included the Fort Osage farmer who wrote early in 1823 that he had grafted apples on sycamore and cotton trees and that some of his neighbors had tried peaches on black walnut stock. Other Missourians experimented unsuccessfully with crossing buffalo and domestic cattle. Procreation was possible, but the offspring of the buffalo female proved difficult to domesticate; the domestic cow and buffalo bull were difficult to mate; and the delivery of the offspring proved a physical problem for the cows. Efforts to establish a silk culture in the 1820's—with an imported silkworm expected to thrive on Missouri's black mulberry trees—failed. In the late 1830's interest in silk production was revived by the introduction of the *Morus multicaulis* species of the mulberry tree. The cultivation for sale of the species, however, contributed to a speculative craze that advanced the price of trees from four dollars per hundred in 1836 to thirty dollars per hundred in 1839. But Missouri was not a suitable area and the craze died, resulting in losses to those who had been tempted by the worm.

If most Missourians were reluctant to strive for improvement of farming techniques, there was no reluctance of native born and newcomer to open new acres for farming. The United States census reported 2,938,425 acres of improved and 6,794,245 acres of unimproved farm land in 1850; in 1860 the amount had jumped to 6,246,871 acres of improved and 13,737,939 acres of unimproved farm land. The total cash value of Missouri farm land rose rose from $63,225,543 at mid-century to $230,-632,543 in 1860. Land values are indicative of an area's wealth and economic development. Seventeen of Missouri's 113 counties had land in farms with a value of over $4,000,000 in 1860, all of which were located on the Mississippi River north from St. Louis or along the Missouri running westward to Buchanan. In general, the farther removed from the two river base lines the lower the county's land value. The Ozarks stood out as the least developed part of the state as measured by the value of farm land.

Because of the increased acreage being brought under cultivation, rather than because of the increased production per acre, the quantity of farm output in Missouri increased rapidly in the decades just prior to the Civil War. An important aspect of Missouri agricultural production was its diversity. Large quantities of most major crops common to the United States including corn, wheat, oats, rye, barley, and buckwheat were being produced in the state, with the exception of cotton. Missouri ranked second in the nation in hemp production from 1840 to 1860 and was seventh for tobacco in both 1850 and 1860. Further diversity existed with the widespread production of a variety of fruits and vegetables and a specialization in grape production in some German communities.

Missourians produced a large quantity of livestock, and the state has a rich pre-Civil War history in improved livestock breeding. Although most stock animals in the early years were a rather mixed, scrubby lot, as early as the 1830's Missouri leaders took steps to improve the quality of their livestock. Many Kentuckians who had migrated to Missouri brought with them their interest in fine animals, along with some superior stock from their native state. At first primary interest centered on fine saddle and race horses. Quality horses were a sign of status, and men took particular pride especially in their carriage and riding horses. The love and appreciation of fine mounts made horse racing a favorite sport, and in nearly every community the race track was a central point of attraction.

An active concern for the improvement of other types of livestock reflected more practical economic interest, but pride remained a factor. Men most active in improved stock breeding were usually community leaders, often business or professional men, who owned land and had enough money to experiment and to buy improved or even pedigreed animals. Theodore Jenkins and Anthony Rollins, along with the Rollins sons James S. and John W., were among the prominent leaders in Boone County; other county leaders were George Tompkins in Cole County, Nathaniel Leonard and Sterret Barr in Cooper County, Henry Larimore and Thomas C. Anderson in Callaway County, and James H. Adams of Clay County. Barr's specialty was Arabian horses, and Adams was a major mule producer; the others were primarily cattlemen.

Like cattlemen elsewhere, the Missouri cattle producers favored the Durham or Shorthorn breed. The Shorthorns were valued for their size, early maturity, smoothness of flesh, high percentage of choice cuts, and, perhaps most importantly for Missouri, their tremendous prepotency. A calf produced by a common native cow mated to a Shorthorn bull was usually of good quality, with the offspring receiving more characteristics from the Shorthorn bull than from the cow. Improved cattle were brought into the state rather early, and before 1840 the number of blooded cattle must have been sizable. The first approved pedigreed Durham bull in Missouri was probably Comet Star, purchased in Ohio in the late 1830's by Nathaniel Leonard and James S. Hutchison for a reported $600. After 1852 rivalry grew among breeders for prize stock and the effort to build purebred herds increased.

Production of an improved line of sheep centered in Clay and Andrews counties, but the effort throughout the state ranked Missouri ninth in sheep raising in 1860. Missouri's sizable corn crop contributed to a large-scale hog production. Pork, the most easily preserved meat of the time, served as a basic staple and as an easily marketable product. Within the first year of statehood, William Lamme and R. S. Barr and Company of Franklin offered through the local *Missouri Intelligencer* to advance money to farmers, at legal interest, for the purchase of barrels, salt, and other needed articles to put pork into a marketable condition; the firm also proposed to market the pork for a 5 per cent commission. Between 1830 and 1860 the increase in hog production led to the establishment of packing houses in nearly every river town, which increased hog production even more. In the number of hogs produced, Missouri advanced from fourteenth in 1840 to fourth among the states in 1860.

As late as 1841 contemporary sources made little reference to breeds of hogs, but after that date the need for animals with a larger weight and earlier maturity increasingly became a subject for discussion in the newspapers. Most Missouri hogs probably were raised with minimum care, but there was important improvement with the introduction of the Berkshire, which was being grown in many of the states. The production of an improved hog may have been more widespread than was true of other livestock, but the men who worked for an improved breed of hogs and who raised good hogs received less attention or prestige than those who related to cattle, horses, and mules.

Missouri also became well known as a center for the production of mules. These sure-footed, strong, and tough work animals could draw or carry and withstand exposure to harsh weather conditions; comparatively immune from disease and easy to feed, the mule played an important role in the premechanized age. Missourians were introduced to the merits of this animal through the Santa Fe trade. They enhanced the line by improved breeding, and the famed Missouri mule became a major state export. Thousands of Mexican mules, jackasses, and jennets entered the state from the Santa Fe trade. Missourians bred the jacks with their mares and developed a propagation of considerable proportion. Additional efforts to produce an improved mule were under way by the mid-1830's. Anthony W. Rollins was one of the first to import jacks from Kentucky, and, some time around 1835, jacks and jennets began to be imported from Europe. These imports greatly improved the quality of the jacks used to sire the famous Missouri mule. When the mules of John H. Adams won first prize at a big St. Louis fair in 1857, after he had offered to wager $1,000 that he would win against all comers, the Missouri newspapers laid claim to Missouri mules as the best in the world. A favorite work animal in the South, mules produced or handled by Missourians soon had a major market in the southern states. By 1860, Missouri ranked sixth nationally in mule production.

According to the 1860 census, the total value of Missouri livestock exceeded $53,000,000, with only six states having livestock of greater value. With the 1850 value less than $20,000,000, there had been a significant increase in livestock production during the decade.

Missouri's geographic position created a major business opportunity for the sale of cattle to Oregon, California, and Colorado. Although there had been some earlier export of cattle, the major trade developed in the 1840's. In 1846, 38,000 head of cattle moved out of St. Joseph headed for Oregon. During the gold rush and mining excavation periods, a cow purchased in Missouri for $10 often brought $100 to $150 in the West. Men in Missouri saw a chance to possess western gold without going west to mine it. St. Joseph and Kansas City both became major centers from which great numbers of cattle were started on the long drive west. An estimated 110,000 cattle started for California from the banks of the Missouri River in 1856. The sale of cattle and mules to the wagon trains and of beef to the many military posts west of Missouri became an important business of growing towns. To meet the sudden demand Missourians began to import additional cattle from Texas. Fear of transmitting the Spanish fever caused some resistance to Texas cattle entering Missouri, but enterprising cattlemen conducted major drives to Kansas City and other points on the Missouri River prior to the Civil War. Probably as many as two-thirds of the cattle that arrived in Kansas City in 1858 were from Texas. Smaller numbers of Texas cattle also crossed the state to St. Louis to help supply eastern markets.

As the white settlers took possession of and developed the land they dislodged the Indians from their Missouri homes. By 1820 the Indian population was so sparse and so generally passive toward the newcomers that they created no significant barrier to settlement in the new state. Duden reported that probably no Indians had been seen in his neighborhood for ten years, except those going to St. Louis to trade.

The Osage, largest of the Indian tribes, occupied areas south of the Missouri River along the branches of the Osage River. A major portion of the Shawnee and Delaware tribes was concentrated in the Cape Girardeau area, and another segment of this tribal grouping lived on the James Fork of the White River in the southwestern portion of the state. The remaining two tribes, the Sacs and the Foxes, generally roamed north of the Missouri River, but they maintained villages in the northeast near the Mississippi River. In addition to these five principal tribes, a band of Kickapoos had been moved to the Pomme de Terre region in 1819 after ceding their land in Illinois and Indiana. Three of the largest migratory groups who hunted in the area, but generally maintained villages outside the state, were the Missouris, Iowas, and Kansas. Within fifteen years after statehood even this small remainder of the native peoples would be pushed from the state.

Observations of these Indians by missionaries, settlers, and travelers indicate that they were generally friendly, congenial neighbors. The founders of Harmony Mission in present-day Bates County recorded that their reception by the Osage in 1821 was pleasant and that the Indians were amiable and hospitable. The missionaries recorded that they observed no traits of great fierceness and cruelty normally associated with a barbarian people. Such comments undoubtedly reflected the attitude of many Americans who, without evidence, considered all Indians as savages.

Even though most Missourians came to acknowledge the Indians' congeniality, they continually disapproved of their life style and code of behavior. In measuring the Indians by their own standards, they naturally made a negative assessment of Indian culture. Missionaries who endeavored without success to teach agricultural techniques to the Osage reported them as living in a state of poverty and degradation. Missourians who evaluated a man by his work performance scoffed at the Indians' cultural heritage of hunting during the spring and fall. Since the male Indians deemed manual labor a disgrace, suitable only for the newly arrived settlers and for Indian women, white people generally viewed them as indolent.

The Indians also failed to meet the settlers' code of personal conduct. Missionaries noted the apparent unfamiliarity with the qualities of neatness and cleanliness and criticized the Indians' moral code for its disregard of chastity and modesty. The Indians' rejection of the white man's culture and their continued adherence to traditional life styles caused George Sibley, Indian Agent at Fort Osage, to report in 1820 that like all people in a state of ignorance, they "are bigoted, and obstinately adhere to their old customs and habits." Popular democracy and equality were favorite themes of both speakers and listeners during these years, but applicable only to a white man's society. In the rhetoric of the time, the Indians were savages with most references to them unfavorably connected with ambush, scalping, bloodshed, and savage yells. There was a somewhat different point of view, however. The degeneration and misery of the Indians in Missouri and other western areas were regarded by some as the result of their relations with the white man. The childlike Indians, the "noble savages," originally trusted white men and consequently often were taken advantage of by unscrupulous traders and settlers. It was painful to these observers to witness the loss of power and independence by a once proud people, particularly when they saw it to be the result of white oppression and cruelty.

Some missionaries suggested the establishment of trading centers closer to the Indian villages because while visiting distant settlements the Indians often encountered irresistible temptations such as strong drink. Coupled with the Indian's uninhibited curiosity was the open evasion by whites of protective laws that forbade selling liquor to Indians. As whites moved into an area, it became impossible to isolate the Indians.

However they viewed the Indians white settlers tried to justify policies designed to remove the Indians from their tribal lands so as to open those areas for white occupancy. Missourians attempted repeatedly to influence national Indian policy. Sen. Thomas H. Benton strongly advocated Indian removal. He believed that removal could open the way for the expansion of white settlements, bring great natural resources under more efficient development, and save the Indians and their culture from becoming more degenerated and depraved through contact with the white men. The national government, he stated, deserved praise for its policies that were designed "to cherish and protect the Indians, to improve their condition, and turn them to the habits of civilized life." In less flowery rhetoric, Benton bluntly pointed out that the white men were relieved of a "useless and dangerous population" within their boundaries. In similar manner, Timothy Flint, a frontier minister and author, extolled the "steady dignity, moderation, benevolence, untiring forbearance" of the government's Indian policy in warding off evil and providing all practical good to "this unhappy and declining race of beings" as the admirable goal of the government's policy. With a smug sense of the superiority of their own civilization, the settlers simply could not understand the point made by a knowledgeable Osage who suggested to George Sibley that he, "Talk to my sons, perhaps they may be persuaded to adopt your fashions, or at least recommend them to their sons; but for myself, I was born free, was raised free, and wish to die free." Although he admired much about white society, the Osage thought it held its own people and everything it touched in chains.

The national government promoted Indian constriction through treaties in which an Indian group ceded one area in exchange for another unsettled area usually farther to the west. Indians frequently negotiated treaties under duress; they misunderstood the white man's concept of exclusive property rights and often encountered misrepresentation by government officials. The national law did prevent individuals from dealing with the Indians for the land, but the Indians still received only token payments.

During the territorial period, the federal government had negotiated several treaties to restrict Indian land holdings in Missouri, but immediately after achieving statehood Missourians sought a more effective solution to the Indian "problem." On March 3, 1821, the Missouri General Assembly requested the national government to extinguish all Indian land claims within Missouri, to stop Indian immigration into the state, and to remove those eastern tribes that had been moved earlier into the territory by the federal government. Under continuing pressure from Missourians the national government negotiated a series of removal treaties with the Indians between 1823 and 1832. Treaties with the Iowas in 1823 and with the Sacs and Foxes in

1824 secured the area north of the Missouri River. The Osage gave up title to their extensive ownings in the western part of the state in 1825. In the southeast the Shawnee surrendered their claims in 1825 and 1832; the Kansas ceded their lands in the Jackson and Clay county area in 1825; and the Delaware turned over their claims to land in the southwest and White River region in 1829 and 1832. A treaty agreed upon in 1832 with the Kickapoos in the Pomme de Terre area extinguished the last Indian claims in the state.

In return for their cessions, most of the Indians received land in a designated Indian Territory in Kansas that was generally regarded as unsuitable for white settlement, in addition to a limited amount of cash, some provisions, and a pledge of assistance to aid them in the agricultural development of their new homelands. Even as they moved, the depleted ranks of the early inhabitants of the land suffered from food shortages, inclement weather, sickness, and harassment by whites who stole their horses.

The completion of a treaty of removal was not always followed by the immediate movement of an entire Indian tribe. Some tribal members refused to acknowledge the validity of a treaty, and others occasionally returned to hunt in the state. Missourians supported the national Indian Removal Act of 1830 passed to enforce treaty agreements; in early 1833 the state government authorized the sheriffs of five northwestern counties to recruit posses and prevent Indian bands from hunting within their jurisdictions.

Despite the attitudes toward the Indian that prevailed in Missouri, racial encounters were not characterized by indiscriminate animosity between the two peoples. Atrocities were few; violence was limited; where provocations did produce destructive reactions the punishment was usually mild and executed with regard for the laws. From statehood until the Indians were removed from the state, there was no full-scale outbreak of warfare between the two races. Only a few incidents in outlying areas caused any difficulties.

One such armed encounter, known as the "Big Neck War," occurred in 1829 between the Iowas and a small group of settlers near present-day Kirksville in Adair County. The area in question had been ceded to the United States, but the Iowas insisted that the treaty allowed them to stay in the area until 1834. While on a hunting trip a band of Iowas confiscated the meat from hogs killed by their dogs, but they refused to pay the damages or leave the area. Authorities summoned a local force of twenty-seven men under Capt. William Trammell to handle the situation. A parley between the settlers and Indians was arranged, but during the meeting a member of Trammell's group opened fire, killing the brother of Big Neck, the Indian chief. The ensuing battle left three Indians and two white men dead and several wounded. Fearing retaliatory Indian attacks, residents of the area appealed to Gov. John Miller for help. The Governor responded with a request for federal assistance, which authorities honored by dispatching troops to confront the Indians. The Iowas, fearful of retribution, left the area and moved northward to the Des Moines River, but those involved in the incident later voluntarily submitted to authorities, who tried and acquitted them.

A similar episode occurred in northwestern Missouri in 1836 as a result of the Heatherly incident near Grand River. The Heatherly gang, an infamous family living on the outskirts of settlement, attempted to sell whiskey to Potawatomies emigrating to new homes west of the Missouri River. When the Indians refused to buy, the gang stole some of their horses. The Indians, believing them to be members of a rival tribe, pursued the thieves. The Potawatomies came upon the Heatherly encampment, were fired upon, and in their return fire killed two of the Heatherly group. To cover their guilt the Heatherlys spread tales of thousands of Indians on the warpath, causing some settlers to leave the frontier for refuge in more populated areas. Gov. Daniel Dunklin sent 200 militiamen to the area with orders to expel all of the Indians from the state. National authorities sent Capt. Matthew Duncan from Fort Leavenworth to investigate the incident in the interest of the policy and responsibility of the national government. When the investigation was completed, it was obvious that a few unscrupulous white men had provoked a friendly Indian tribe, and that there was no cause for the fear that had reached panic proportions.

A final armed confrontation, known as the Osage War, occurred in 1837 when militia units drove hunting parties of the Osage, Shawnee, and Delaware into Kansas and Arkansas. This effort ended the Indians' sojourns and hunting expeditions into Missouri. Nicholas Hesse, a German visitor to Missouri in 1835–1837, concluded that the Indians had learned their lesson by experience, and the powerful state militia deterred any further hostility.

As Missourians were pressing for the removal of all Indians from the state, the number of black slaves was increasing from 9,797 black slaves in 1820, to 25,091 in 1830, to 114,931 by 1860. Although the total number of slaves increased over the years, the percentage of slaves in the total population dropped from a high of 17.8 per cent in 1830 to 9.8 per cent in 1860. Slavery in Missouri was black slavery. Few Indian slaves from earlier times in Missouri remained into the American period, and the state supreme court declared Indian slavery illegal in 1834.

Rather strangely, black slavery in the state was not a creation of the law, since no territorial or state statute ever specifically authorized it. The treaty made for the purchase of Louisiana guaranteed the property to the inhabitants, and, although not specifically stated, the property was assumed to include slaves. The territorial code did fix the legal definition of a Negro as any person whose grandfather or grandmother was a Negro or who had one-fourth or more Negro blood, and all blacks were assumed to be slaves. The law also permanently fixed the status of a slave as the personal property of his master. In 1857, the state supreme court ruled that slavery had existed under Spanish and French authority, that it had continued in the territory under the United States, and that no legislation was necessary to support the institution.

Having won the fight against the right of Congress to restrict slavery in the state, Missourians did provide constitutional and statutory protection for the institution, but they never attempted to formulate a legal definition of slavery or to designate any class of people as slaves. The Constitution of 1820 provided that no slave could be emancipated without the consent of the owner or without payment when such consent was given. The General Assembly enacted the slave code necessary to sustain the system so that slaves could be sold or traded as their owners desired. A slave could not, without his master's consent, buy or sell anything; he could not hold property; nor was he allowed to testify in any trial of a white person. Assemblies of slaves were generally forbidden. Their marriages were not recognized by law, and in 1847 it became illegal for any person to teach a slave to read or write. Legislation to guard against the escape of slaves further restricted their already limited privacy by authorizing county courts to establish patrols with power to enter slave quarters and arrest or lash any black found out at night without a pass. In addition many towns and counties had special rules to regulate the activities of the local slave population. The criminal law that governed slaves imposed especially severe penalties for conspiracy to rebellion, insurrection, murder, criminal assault on women, and resistance to an owner or overseer.

Special restrictive laws also regulated the governing of free blacks. In part to guard against the possible creation of unrest among the slaves and in part because of white racial attitudes, the General Assembly passed legislation restricting the migration of free blacks into the state, despite the solemn act to the contrary approved in conjunction with the second Missouri Compromise. An 1825 law excluded Negroes from the state unless an individual could show by naturalization papers that he was a citizen of another state—a virtual impossibility—and an 1847 statute flatly denied free Negroes entry into the state. Although never fully enforced, the laws did help restrict the number of free blacks; with 376 in 1820, the number grew to 1,478 in 1840, to 2,618 in 1850, and to 3,572 in 1860. No free Negro could live anywhere in Missouri without a license from the county court of his residence, and the posting of bond for good behavior was a frequent requirement. Black assemblies could be held only if a white official was present; likewise, free blacks could not testify in the trial of a white man.

Missouri law did provide some protection for slaves and free blacks, but these so-called "rights" always remained within the framework of a system of black bondage. The constitution gave the General Assembly a mandate upon which laws were written for some legal protection of the slaves against inhumane treatment by their owners. A slave had the right to trial by jury, and he could bring a suit for freedom to the court if he could show cause that he might be illegally held. The law permitted manumission subject to numerous restrictions, but such action was more tolerated than approved. To be manumitted by his owner a slave had to be of sound mind and within designated age limits, and the master was legally subject to payment of costs should the freedman become a public charge. Slaves could be freed in several ways: by will; by masters for moral or ethical reasons; or for financial considerations, where a slave was sold to his own friends or relatives who in turn freed him. Incomplete records have hindered attempts to estimate the number of slaves emancipated by their masters, but the number was apparently small. Scattered statistics indicate that in such large slaveholding counties as Boone, Howard, and Greene there were few manumissions, with probably only a few hundred emancipated throughout the state before 1861.

Under Missouri law the act of enslaving a free person was a serious offense, but the black man—with the disadvantages of his color, the burden of proof, and the cost—had only limited legal redress. Ownership of property appears to have been the best evidence of free status.

Slavery existed throughout Missouri, but river counties contained the heaviest concentration. The largest slaveholding county at mid-century was St. Louis with a reported 6,000 slaves; Howard County came next with almost 5,000; ten other river counties each held over 2,500 slaves. In the decade before the Civil War slavery grew most rapidly in the area from Callaway and Cole counties up the Missouri River to the Kansas border and along the western boundary of the state. These counties, which held some of the newer and more productive lands in the state, produced large amounts of hemp—the single most important Missouri crop raised with slave labor. Every county had some slaves; those with limited numbers were represented by Mercer, Oregon, Ozark, Putnam, and Shannon counties, with less than twenty-five slaves in each.

There was no class of large slaveholders in the state, and only a small percentage of Missourians owned any slaves. It is estimated that about 24,000 masters owned all of Missouri's 115,000 slaves in 1860, and the number of slaves held by individual owners varied greatly. A study of St. Louis revealed that 497 owners possessed a total of 1,383 slaves. The largest holding in Ste. Genevieve County was 78, the second was 32, and in one township the 32 slaves were owned by 10 masters. In Callaway County, of 636 slaveholders, 173 had 1 slave each, and 102 had 2 each for an average of 4.67 per master.

From statehood to 1860, most Missourians vigorously defended slavery even though a small percentage of them actually owned slaves. The reasons for such total proslavery commitment are unclear, although economic self-interest was undoubtedly involved. Scholars have suggested that within the slaveholding group was the best natural talent for leadership in the state. Slave proponents were an aggressive group, and the general conservative reluctance to any change played into the hands of the advocates of the *status quo*. Many Missourians, including nonslaveholders, reflected the prevailing racist attitude of the nineteenth century and viewed slavery as a social system by which to keep an "inferior race" in "its place."

Although the plantation labor system of the deep South never developed in Missouri, slavery nonetheless constituted an important part of the labor force. Missouri hemp producers used slave labor extensively for the arduous work of breaking hemp and removing the pith. General practice required a slave to break at least 100 pounds a day, and for every pound above that the slave received one cent. The task system appears to have been limited to hemp processing, although tobacco production relied upon slave labor to a lesser degree. In the rural areas most male slaves worked as general farm hands, while in St. Louis and other urban areas they frequently worked as domestic servants. The female slave most commonly performed household duties. Slaves also worked in Missouri mines and iron works, on river boats—although freight handling was reserved for white workers—in factories, as blacksmiths, and as carpenters.

The hiring out of slaves was common in the state. Widows seeking a source of income and a release from the responsibility of the care and supervision of slaves, or masters with slaves they had inherited or no longer needed frequently followed this practice. Some masters may have considered the ownership of a slave for hire as a good investment and perhaps even a mark of prestige, but there was no specific practice of purchasing slaves for this purpose. The contract usually required that the renter supply quarters, food, clothing, and medical care for the slave along with an annual payment to the owner amounting to approximately 14 per cent of a male slave's value; rates for female rental were slightly lower.

A German immigrant to Missouri commented that slavery was morally wrong, and that the first commandment of the North American apparently was to make money. Whether or not slavery actually helped to fulfill that commandment will probably always be open to debate. Nevertheless, despite some contention that slavery was a conspicuous waste rather than an economic advantage, the best evidence indicates that most Missourians considered slavery profitable and acted accordingly. Nor was slavery in 1860 a "dying" institution in Missouri.

Slave values continued to rise throughout the pre–Civil War years. A strong male slave increased in price from approximately $500 in 1830 to almost $1500 by 1860, and Missourians throughout the state brought in new slaves during the decade of the 1850's. The total monetary value of the slaves in Missouri at any given time defies precise measurement, but certainly it reached a peak in 1860.

Politicians who spoke on the slavery subject in the critical 1850's believed it was profitable; even those who argued against slavery in the interest of free labor implied quite clearly it was a cheap labor source, and some admitted that hemp and tobacco could be produced only with slaves. Still no clear relation seems to have existed between slaveholding and wealth. There were men of wealth who did not hold slaves, as well as some slaveholders who were certainly not considered well-to-do.

The extent of personal antislavery sentiment in Missouri cannot be accurately measured. Because of the strong popular support of the institution in the state, few men dared to speak out against it. A brief flurry of emancipationist activity in the mid-1830's proved to be short-lived and ineffective. In 1835 the General Assembly submitted to the people the question of calling a convention to consider possible revision of the constitution; some antislavery spokesmen demanded that abolition of slavery be a first order of business for the convention, but the call was defeated by a margin of almost 2 to 1. Advocates of emancipation favored some form of colonization for Missouri Negroes. The Missouri State Colonization Society, organized in 1839, actively supported this concept, but it colonized very few slaves. Abolition of slavery without removing the blacks from Missouri was not even a topic for discussion.

Vigilante groups often dealt with suspected abolitionists. When the Reverend Elijah P. Lovejoy, proprietor of the *Observer* in St. Louis and already under suspicion for his antislavery views, dared criticize both the mob burning in April, 1836, of mulatto Francis McIntosh—charged with stabbing a law officer —and the judge who upheld it, the minister's office was attacked, his printing equipment tossed in the river, and he was forced to leave the city. The president of the newly established Marion College near Palmyra in northeast Missouri, who spoke out too strongly against slavery for that section, lost his job and had to leave the state in 1835. At the same time proponents of slavery forced two other men to leave Marion County for receiving American Colonization Society literature.

The state legislature had given little attention to the abolition movement until the petitions presented to Congress in the mid-1830's produced a heated national debate. On February 1, 1837, without a dissenting vote in the House, the General Assembly passed a stringent law prohibiting the spread of abolitionist doctrines or any action to disrupt the institution of slavery. Under this statute a third offense was punishable by life imprisonment.

The capture of three men accused of attempting to entice some slaves out of the state produced considerable excitement in Marion County in 1841. When the trio appeared at the pre-arranged place to meet the slaves whom they were allegedly to guide to freedom, they were met instead by armed men who guided them off to jail. The three were tried and given twelve-year sentences. Missouri law did not allow a black to testify against a white, and the only witnesses were the slaves who had been approached by the accused. Authorities got around this technicality by allowing the slaves to testify to the master who then testified in court. The event spurred the formation of vigilante committees in each township of the county to examine strangers; if good reason could not be given for their presence, they were expelled and threatened with fifty lashes if they returned. In other counties similar vigilante groups were organized to offset the limited but greatly feared work of the underground railroad. George Thompson, one of the men imprisoned as a result of the Marion County episode who later became known as the "prison bard," stated that while he was in jail at Palmyra his counsel told him that reading the Declaration of Independence or the Bible to a slave violated Missouri laws. By 1846, Gov. John C. Edwards had pardoned all three men convicted in the Marion County affair.

The subject of abolition got short notice in the constitutional convention of 1845. An abolitionist petition from a solitary individual was presented by a delegate who personally opposed it, on the grounds that he nonetheless had an obligation to submit it. The convention voted 64 to 0 not to receive the petition. The proposed constitution, subsequently rejected by the voters, would have made no change in the status of slavery. Had it been accepted it would have further restricted free Negroes by requiring all newly freed blacks to leave the state. The politics of slavery in the fifteen years preceding the Civil War are best discussed within the context of those times.

Any truly accurate general description of the nature of slave life and of the relations between master and slave in Missouri is probably impossible to secure. Writing as a free man after the Civil War about his life as a slave in Missouri, Henry Clay Bruce described both good and bad personal relations between masters and slaves. Undoubtedly there were elements of what was often labeled the "patriarchal" attitude and operation within the Missouri slave system, and on the surface at least relations appear to have been generally good and orderly. The property value of slaves must have deterred damaging physical abuse by a master even if he was so inclined, but passions, blindness, or an assumed need to discipline often resulted in physical punishment, most usually by whipping. Under the law a slave could not be put in jail for a minor offense unless his master requested it, but when the slave was found guilty of an offense, the master was frequently the one who administered the flogging. Public opinion appears to have been hostile to harsh treatment of a slave, unless it was as just punishment for an action or alleged action that was a threat to the community or the system.

Most masters exercised some concern for the physical well-being of their slaves. They provided plain but comfortable housing facilities and allowed some social activity in the slave quarters. They often permitted slaves to work perhaps one afternoon a week to earn money for their own use and, where the slaves were known, their owners allowed them some freedom of movement within the immediate community. Slaves sometimes attended the masters' churches, and the ban on their own slave religious services was not always enforced. If a black minister preached that it was the will of God that blacks were slaves, and that they should accept this fact, he was probably free to hold religious services. At times slaves could learn to read, and although never legally recognized nor registered, they entered the bond of marriage. Many masters did have a certain affection for their slaves, and the segregation of the races was not as complete as in the decades after Reconstruction. A master frequently tried—if only for self-interest—to shield his slave from the law. Discovery, however, led inevitably to swift and often cruel punishment. But one factor appears to have been almost universal: the black people were considered an inferior race; they had no real rights, only privileges granted by masters or the white law. A more open assertion of racist sentiment in Missouri increased as the nation moved toward crisis after mid-century.

How the slave viewed the institution and his lot is another question. Unfortunately for history the slaves were unable to leave much source material about slave life and attitudes. Slaves, too, differed in respect to relationships with their owners. Some had an apparent regard, perhaps affection, for their masters, while others showed their dislike by outright resistance or physical violence. The slave code and legal and vigilante action against blacks or whites who threatened any existing order indicate that the community feared slave rebellion and that some such reactions did occur, although there is no record of any slave insurrection of consequence in the state. An attempted uprising in Lewis County, where slave-master relations appeared to be generally stable, never got beyond the collection of weapons, and those involved were sold farther south.

One of the worst features of slavery was trading. Lewis County may not have been typical of the entire state, but in that county most slaves were sold or traded at least once during their lifetime. Slave sales and slave traders were common in Missouri, as was slave mobility within as well as in and out of the state. Missourians took pride in the belief that their form of slavery was milder and better for the blacks than the various forms in the deep South, and slaveholders vigorously denied charges that they were breeding for the southern slave market. Missouri slaves were sold to Southerners, but always with the insistence that such sales were made only when necessary because of financial reverses, an excess of laborers, or to be rid of chronic troublemakers.

The generally unsatisfactory nature of the lives of Missouri's free blacks can be assumed, but their more positive role in Missouri society needs further research. The number of free blacks in Missouri increased from 376 in 1820 to 3,572 in 1860, but percentage-wise they remained small in relation to the total white or black population. The increased number of free blacks came from procreation, from individual acts of emancipation, from the purchase and subsequent freeing of friends or relatives from slavery by free blacks, and from illegal immigration.

Some of the free blacks entered more highly specialized vocations than their indentured brothers, but as a general rule the forces of white society restricted them to employment in areas with the common characteristic of hard physical labor. When the free blacks of the state were required to secure new licenses by an act of the General Assembly in 1847, the records for the city of St. Louis show their occupational listings included blacksmiths, bricklayers, carpenters, coopers, engineers, firemen, miners, nurses, plasterers, tinners, tobacconists, and vegetable dealers; the most common skilled vocation open to the free blacks was that of barbering. The free blacks of the city were a sober and industrious group of people.

Limited evidence indicates that the free blacks, like the white society, seem to have had their own class structure. There was something of a free black aristocracy in St. Louis that stood out by the wealth, property, education, general way of life, and influence of its members. Collectively, this class was worth millions of dollars, with the richest single free black worth perhaps a half-million dollars. The blacks secured their wealth in a variety of ways. Some of them profited in real estate operations or cattle buying; some were butchers and vegetable dealers, while others owned their own business, such as a coffee house; some had inherited property from their masters, and a few were successful gamblers. A number of free blacks had prospered as proprietors of their own barber shops, but they were not among the richest of their class. The more wealthy blacks, although segregated from their white counterparts, lived in similar upper-class homes, dressed in the latest fashion, sent their children to Europe to be educated, held elaborate parties, and tried to secure a "right" marriage for their children.

As old and new settlers took up Missouri land and moved the state's economy from a pioneer stage to a more developed and complex form, Missourians also produced a more sophisticated political system and shaped the nature and role of government for the state. In the political processes of this young, western state, the forces of Jacksonian Democracy would play a major role in shaping the state's political structure and procedures.

# CHAPTER III

# THE EMERGENCE OF
# JACKSONIAN DEMOCRACY

Demands for constitutional change loomed large in Missouri politics during the years of the McNair administration. Reflecting the popular dissatisfaction with the old political leadership and the undemocratic features of the state's new constitution, the First General Assembly proposed ten amendments to that document. Certain of these amendments would abolish the minimum $2,000 salary for judges and make that item a matter of ordinary legislation, transfer the power to appoint judges from the governor to the General Assembly, abolish the office of chancellor and turn cases of equity and probate over to the regular courts, and vacate the offices of judges of the supreme and circuit courts at the end of the First General Assembly or as soon thereafter as their successors had been duly appointed and qualified. The remainder of the proposed amendments sought to abolish the minimum $2,000 salary for the governor and make that a matter of legislation and to reassign the appointive power for an auditor, attorney general, and secretary of state from the governor to the General Assembly.

Supporters of the amendments sought to alter the existing constitutional balance by reducing the power of the courts and of the executive while increasing the General Assembly's role in state affairs on the grounds that the legislature was closer to the people. Opponents charged that legislative fears that the current court judges would throw out the recently enacted relief legislation had motivated the proposed revision in the judiciary.

Since the amendments had to be ratified by the succeeding legislature, they were an issue in the election of 1822. The first burst of public indignation had subsided, and the older leaders with increased energies re-established their positions of power and prominence in the contest. Only six of the original fifty representatives and four of the original eighteen senators were in the Second General Assembly. More conservative in its make-up, the new assembly ratified only those amendments that abolished the office of chancellor, repealed the required salaries, and vacated the judicial offices. The rejection of all the various proposals to transfer appointive powers from the governor to the General Assembly meant that no change was made in court personnel. Since the most important changes relating to increased popular government had failed, a current of popular dissatisfaction awaited harnessing by men like Thomas Benton, who was soon to take the reins of the Jacksonian bandwagon in Missouri.

While Benton emerged as the leader of one political faction, David Barton became the spokesman for a more conservative group. A correspondent for the *New York Commercial Advertiser* wrote of Benton and Barton in 1828: "On every political subject, they are antipodes; and, they seem to have for each other no great personal friendship. They never converse or associate either in public or in private. In debate, they are uniformly opposed on every subject." Although the extreme differences referred to in 1828 had developed gradually, these two men represented the political divisions and philosophies of government that were forming in Missouri immediately after statehood. The competition was intense, but within a decade Jacksonianism emerged victorious in Missouri, making Benton king of the hill.

Benton's personality and political technique contributed much to his ultimate success in politics. His aggressive, dynamic personality and impressive physical appearance helped him establish his political image by playing the role of solon and Roman senator. An aristocrat in tastes and action, Benton continued to emulate the customs and habits of the upper-class elite, even after he had come to depend upon the masses for political support. He remained cool and aloof in personal associations and never stooped to the handshaking political role. In the West, even in the midst of the Jacksonian movement, men voted for aggressive, fighting leaders who expressed and symbolized western interests, values, and popular aspirations. Frontier politics did not require a political leader who lived in a log cabin or rose from the ranks of the masses; on the contrary the Jacksonian "common man" most generally looked to successful men from an upper stratum to lead the cause. Image was nevertheless important, and Benton, combining opportunism with a sense of honest regard for the people, developed and successfully projected his image as a leader in whom the western agrarian common people could put their faith and take pride.

Barton stood at the pinnacle of popularity and power when Missouri entered the Union. As a forceful speaker, his hard-hitting sarcasm, sometimes bitter and vindictive, enabled him to hold his own in the turbulence of Missouri's frontier and personal politics. In his early years Barton may not have been as intemperate as his enemies charged, but his bouts with the bottle caused talk, and the unfortunate habit became a major factor in his later life. How much this hurt him politically on a rough, hard-drinking frontier is questionable. Barton's downfall in Missouri politics probably came because he failed to convince the majority of Missourians that his program for strong national government and a compliance with an older federalism were in the best interests of all Missourians, rather than a special few.

Members of the dominant territorial power elite had united to form a common front in 1820 in an effort to maintain their favored position, but personal rivalries for office and influence continued to create differences among individuals. Benton and Barton were never close personal friends, and their final break in 1824 stemmed in part from their earlier differences. Both personal animosities and political differences contributed to the 1823 duel in which Thomas Rector killed lawyer Joshua Barton. Barton had charged William C. Rector, the surveyor general and brother of Thomas, with favoring his family in the letting of contracts and then falsifying the records to cover his action. Thomas admitted that the charges were partially true, but nonetheless he issued the challenge that resulted in Barton's death. Immediately after the duel, Barton's law partner, Edward Bates, repeated the charges and succeeded in securing an official investigation, which led to William Rector's dismissal in 1824.

The duel may not have altered existing political alignments in the state's shaky political structure, but it intensified them and brought them more into the open. William Rector was associated with the McNair administration and was also a personal friend of Benton's. This Benton-McNair-Rector faction was vigorously denounced by David Barton, Joshua's brother, and Bates, who had resigned as attorney general; the former group responded with accusations of their own. As the two factions hurled charges and countercharges at one another, the truth appeared to have been of limited importance. The two groups did not evolve into political parties, but the Barton-Bates alignment had begun to take form while Benton was moving from the elite side of the stage to direct the drama of the early Jacksonian farmers. Likewise, debate concerning important national issues helped solidify further the emerging political alignments within Missouri that would in time relate to the national Democratic and Whig parties.

Benton was in a quandary as he started his senatorial career. He could not ignore the special interest groups that had contributed to his election, and neither could he overlook the rising tide of popular power opposed to the same long-dominant economic and political groups. Consequently, he sought a middle course. He served the Spanish land claimants well during his first term by aggressively supporting liberal, general legislation for confirmation of still-unsettled claims, but to offset his connection with the large claimants he stressed the benefits the legislation would provide to the many farmers with small unconfirmed claims. Benton was instrumental in securing legislation to abolish the factory system so hated by the fur traders, and he also pressed for securing legislation to promote the fur trade through Indian treaties, military protection, and tariffs. The fur trade and the opening of the West, he emphasized, would benefit the entire state economically not only with the fur itself, but also from handling the necessary trading goods and provisions. An energetic, first-term senator, Benton supported measures extending the national road to Missouri, providing funds for river improvement within the state, and placing tariffs on Missouri-produced lead, hemp, salt, and fur; he withheld, however, his full endorsement of the principle of a national system of internal improvements or the principle of protective tariff.

In the first session of the Eighteenth Congress (1823–1824), Benton introduced an amendment to abolish the electoral college system, which he termed undemocratic because it intervened between the people and the object of their choice. His amendment provided that each state would divide itself into districts equal in number to its delegation in Congress, with the voters of each district to vote directly for candidates for the offices of President and Vice-President. The candidate who received a majority vote in a district would be credited with one vote; the candidate with the majority of the district votes would be elected. Congress failed to approve the amendment, but Benton, with some modifications, kept it constantly before the people. With introduction of the amendment in 1824 Benton placed himself ahead of the field in support of the growing popular democracy that would soon take shape around the personality of Andrew Jackson. Barton voted to postpone indefinitely the proposed amendment.

In seeking to transfer his base of political support, Benton also introduced a bill proposing to graduate downward the price of public land. In essence he wanted the price of public land to be reduced by 25¢ per acre each year it was offered for sale but passed over, with any piece of land unsold after it was offered at a price of 50¢ (he later lowered this figure to 25¢) subject to free donations. By making land increasingly available to all, regardless of their financial resources, Benton fashioned a specific program to provide for a greater equality of opportunity—a major aspect of the Jacksonian movement. The graduation idea was not new, but Benton renewed it and gave it greater energy and direction. His introduction of the proposal late in the 1823–1824 session of Congress necessarily precluded any debate on the subject.

Barton charged that Benton had introduced a proposition that on the surface had great appeal for campaign purposes, but that was, in fact, a very complicated issue presented late to avoid serious discussion of its terms. Barton may have been right, but in the light of the great interest in cheap land and the opportunity it offered, many Missourians found even the suggestion of a graduated price appealing.

In spite of the growing political factionalism, the state elections of 1824—apparently lacking any excitement—failed to bring any specific issues to the people or to produce any open opposition. The state issues of relief and constitutional amendments were dormant, and Benton's land and electoral college proposals had not yet created enough attention to influence the voters. Frederick Bates, an affluent St. Louis attorney and former secretary of the Missouri Territory, won the governorship with the support of important St. Louis businessmen and land speculators. His opponent, William Ashley, had organized the highly successful Rocky Mountain Fur Company two years earlier and had also played a key role in organizing the state militia, in which he held the rank of general. Despite his defeat, Ashley had a base of considerable popular support that would benefit him in future elections. The voters returned John Scott to the House of Representatives by a wide margin.

When Missouri's first two senators were seated, Barton, who had drawn by lot the shorter four-year term, sought re-election in 1824, and Benton came out openly against him. This clear-cut public split was no major surprise, and it came more from personal rivalries than from a party formation. The men had never been close personal friends, and their positions on opposite factions were intensified by the Barton-Rector duel. Moreover, Benton's shift to a more democratic political base and his programs to support that shift probably widened their differences. When a series of letters written by Scott in 1820 fell into Barton's hands, convincing him that Scott had tried to secure Benton's election to the Senate at his expense, hostility deepened. Scott also had written that Barton should be satisfied with a position on the state supreme court.

The senatorial contest in the General Assembly was not based on any serious political questions. Opponents of Barton concentrated their campaigns on his alleged immorality, especially his drunkenness. Barton did not have the same cross-factional support as in 1820; in fact, charges were made that a St. Louis group of politicians was more concerned with the defeat of Barton than with who might be elected. The opposition's William Clark failed to defeat Missouri's political favorite, and he won re-election by a margin of 50 to 15.

The presidential election in November, 1824, accelerated the breakdown of a common Republicanism and the emergence of two political parties both nationally and within the state. During James Monroe's second term, national growth, economic change, and old and new sectional differences were all creating conditions and diverse needs that hindered any unification of the body politic. Sections, states, local groups, and the people in general were pushing for a greater role in national affairs. The continued dominance of the Presidency by Virginia specifically and by the eastern aristocracy generally also produced a wide and growing dissatisfaction. Many Westerners blamed the congressional caucus, with its exercise of a candidate selection power, for the continuity of the Virginia dynasty. In 1820, James Monroe had been elected President without opposition, but by the spring of 1822 there were at least sixteen presidential candidates representing all parts of the nation. The arduous campaign soon reduced the field to five serious contenders: William Crawford, John C. Calhoun, John Quincy Adams, Andrew Jackson, and Henry Clay.

William Crawford of Georgia had no following in Missouri even before illness forced him, for all practical purposes, from the race. Duff Green, editor of the *St. Louis Enquirer*, backed John C. Calhoun until he withdrew in favor of accepting the vice-presidency. John Quincy Adams, able and dedicated, had few supporters in Missouri. His close identification with the Northeast and with federalism made him unacceptable to most Missourians. Benton and other Missourians also blamed Adams for the loss of western territory through the Adams-Onis Treaty with Spain in which the United States gave up any claim to Texas. In contrast, Andrew Jackson, a popular national hero and a Westerner, was well received by Missourians. Even as somewhat of a political novice and with only a vague program, Jackson nonetheless appealed to the spirit of voter unrest. His position in Missouri also was aided by Duff Green's decision to support him after Calhoun's withdrawal from the race.

Henry Clay, a Kentucky resident, was truly a great favorite with Missourians, and he carried the state by a substantial popular margin.[1] Both Clay's nativity and his image brought him state-wide support, as did his opposition to the hated national caucus. Clay's western heritage helped him carry outstate

1. Clay, 2,042; Jackson, 1,168; Adams, 186; Crawford, 37; scattered, 5.

agrarian regions, while his espousal of the American System won him urban support. Jackson, who finished second in Missouri, received his strongest support in outstate regions, whereas Adams's limited number of votes had come out of the most highly developed urban centers where, quite surprisingly, he received almost one-fourth of the votes cast in St. Louis and slightly over 15 per cent in the district surrounding that city.

All three of Missouri's members of Congress supported Clay in the campaign, although Benton was the most active participant. Benton's campaign for Clay did not include unqualified support for Clay's program of protective tariffs, national internal improvements, and the national bank; in fact, Clay had not been his first choice. In May of 1824, Benton had been party to a plan to bring out a Crawford-Clay ticket, but Clay had rejected the second spot. Practical political considerations, coupled with opportunism, probably accounted for Benton's enthusiasm for Clay. With the political appeal of Jackson still untested, Clay appeared to be an almost sure winner in Missouri. Barton, although not as active a campaigner as Benton, gave his support to Clay, probably based on political considerations similar to those of Benton, but he was also in greater agreement with Clay's nationalism.

Despite his commitment to Clay, Scott tried to cool the quarrels being generated over the presidential contest in Missouri. Calling all of the candidates able and distinguished Republicans, he condemned attempts to label any of them as Federalist—an obvious reference to criticisms being made against Adams. Scott must have recognized the likely possibility of a close vote that would throw the eventual selection into the House of Representatives. If that should occur, he said in July, 1824, "I vote not as a citizen of Missouri, but as the Representative of Missouri; the vote belongs to the people, and not to me, and the voice of the people will in such case as far as practicable be the voice of the Representative." He asked Missouri Republicans to close ranks behind the candidate who emerged victorious.

When the votes were in, no candidate had a majority nationally, and the election went to the House of Representatives for a final decision. Clay had finished fourth, thus eliminating

Missouri's favorite, and illness had removed Crawford, who ran third, as a serious contender. For the House, then, the choice was between John Quincy Adams and Andrew Jackson.

As Missouri's lone member of the House of Representatives, John Scott had the final responsibility for casting the state's vote. He had committed himself to vote in accordance with the wishes of the people, but their wishes were difficult for him to gauge. Since Clay, the first choice of Missourians, had announced for Adams, Scott debated whether or not to follow the Kentuckian's wishes, because Missourians had demonstrated a preference for Jackson over Adams. Caught in a whirlpool of politics, Scott asked for instructions from the General Assembly, but that body could not agree on how to instruct him.[2] When he asked both Missouri senators for advice, he received conflicting replies. Barton recognized the accountability of a legislator to the people and the principle of the right of instruction, but in the case of a presidential election in the House, Barton contended that a representative was not bound by the preference of the voters of the state. If all representatives were so bound, Barton argued, the election could never be resolved, and the constitutional provision that sent the election to the House would be nugatory. To him, this particular vote was cast under the au-

2. Several instruction resolutions were proposed in the General Assembly, but none were passed. In December a resolution was submitted in the Senate to instruct Scott to vote for Jackson if Clay should not qualify —a fact generally known but not official. The resolution lost 9 to 7. After official word that Clay had not qualified, a resolution to instruct for Crawford was defeated 14 to 0.

In the House a resolution was introduced to instruct Scott to vote for Jackson because he was Missouri's choice of the candidates, but Robert Wells's amendment to postpone any instruction carried 30 to 22. Wells, who was to be elected later to Congress as a Jackson man, made repeated unsuccessful efforts to secure passage of a resolution that ruled it improper to instruct on this subject. A final resolution to instruct Scott to cast Missouri's vote for Adams lost by a vote of 43 to 2, in favor of indefinite postponement.

Just what the voting in the General Assembly indicated about the strength of the candidates is difficult to say. Clearly, Adams and Crawford were unacceptable. It is possible that Jackson supporters were reluctant to risk a vote on instructions in favor of Jackson fearing that a defeat, or even a narrow victory, might be worse than no action based on the lack of power for the General Assembly to instruct a representative in such cases.

thority of the Union, not the state, and it was the representative's duty to vote in the interest of the whole for whomever he believed to be the best man. If Barton's reasoning did have some validity in principle, his choice of Adams did not win popular support throughout Missouri.

Benton's advice was straightforward: the vote Scott was to cast belonged to the people of Missouri, and Jackson was their choice as revealed in the state's popular vote. In a letter to Scott, published in the Missouri press and written probably more for the people than to Scott, Benton in the name of the people protested Scott's intention to vote for Adams; significantly, Benton added that this action would mean "lasting separation."

Scott's decision was not an easy one. Both the pressure exerted upon him by Clay to secure his support for Adams and the efforts of Benton to force him to vote for Jackson angered Scott, but he finally cast his vote for Adams—the winner.

Benton's stand for Jackson, as it coincided with his advocacy of direct election of the President and a more liberal land law, marked the final turning point of Benton's career and placed him in a position to bid for the leadership of the forces building up behind the popular Jackson; the same actions placed him in opposition to an elite class that had dominated Missouri politics. To many Missourians, Barton's choice of Adams connected him with the more conservative forces of the political *status quo* and with the economic interests of a northeastern-centered business class, interests Benton charged as representing the revival of a northeastern federalism.

On the basis of the final results of the elections of 1824, the Barton-Scott faction had seemingly emerged triumphant in Missouri politics. Barton had been re-elected to the Senate by a substantial majority; Scott was back in the House; and Adams was President, with the national patronage in the state sure to be dispensed through the two Missourians. Benton had not misgauged the depth of Missouri sentiment, however, or the growing strength of the Jacksonian movement. Reaction to Scott's vote was not long in coming, and an upcoming special election brought an important change in Missouri political life.

Gov. Frederick Bates's unexpected death from pleurisy in

August, 1825, made it necessary to hold a special election to fill that office.

Lt. Gov. Benjamin H. Reeves had resigned and the president pro tempore of the Senate, Abraham Williams, became acting governor; but since more than eighteen months remained in the term the constitution required a special election to fill the vacancy. Four men announced for the office: John Miller, registrar of the land office at Franklin since 1817; David Todd, judge of the first circuit court of Missouri, which encompassed a large part of central and northern Missouri; William C. Carr, St. Louis lawyer; and Rufus Easton, former territorial judge and delegate to Congress. Strong public sentiment against any caucus or factional affiliation, especially in rural areas, led the candidates to display an independence from any such connection. "A Voter" declared in the Jackson *Independent Patriot* that there would be no objection to a candidate because he was supported by Benton, Barton, or Scott, but if any candidate was a "tool" of these men, or of a faction, "We will not support him."

Benton actively supported Miller, but the candidate's friends denied strongly that he had been picked by Benton and instead stressed that Miller had made an independent decision to run before he knew that Benton would back him. With Barton and Scott both campaigning for Todd, the race displayed strong elements of a Benton-Jackson versus Barton-Adams alignment. The press presented the campaign as primarily between Miller and Todd, although Carr actually ran second to the victorious Miller. The newly established St. Louis *Missouri Advocate* proclaimed the election an endorsement of Jackson, a rebuke to the administration party of Barton and Scott, and proof that Benton was correct in supporting Jackson over Adams. John Miller's victory did place the state's political patronage in the hands of a Jackson-Benton man, and whenever possible Miller appears to have used that patronage to build the Jackson party power in the state.

In the elections of 1826, Edward Bates defeated Scott in his effort to return to his seat in the House of Representatives. Scott's effort to justify his vote for Adams indicated his recognition of the extent of popular opposition to that action. Such a burden, he lamented, should not have been assigned to the House when a popular referendum would have been better. He insisted that he wanted to vote the will of the people, but that he had been unable to determine it. In a positive defense of his vote, Scott pointed out that he could not have affected the outcome, because Adams already had the election sewed up, and it was to the best interests of Missouri to be on the winning side. Scott also pointed out that the Northeast had generally more capital, more manufacturing, more trade, and more enterprise than the South, and that the promise of a prosperous future for Missouri lay in economic ties with the Northeast rather than with the South. Given the southern orientation of Missouri in 1826, this explanation had little appeal to Missourians even though it contained more truth than many of them recognized or wanted to admit.

Bates, an ambitious politician, took advantage of Scott's problem and announced for Congress as a no-party, nonfactional candidate. He took a compromise position on the American System, supported state control of public lands, urged a strict interpretation of the constitution, and agreed to the right of instruction. Some Barton men thought that Bates had gone too far to appease the Jacksonian voter, and since they had no candidate of their own the Jackson men supported Bates partly to punish Scott. In Congress, however, the already established political principles of Bates caused him to emerge quickly in opposition to Benton and in support of a position closer to Barton's. He revealed himself as a conservative and a nationalist; the Jacksonian connections had been only temporary.

When the General Assembly met to elect a senator upon the expiration of Benton's first term, there was no one in the state who could seriously challenge his re-election, and he collected forty of the fifty-six votes cast. This substantial majority showed that Benton now held far greater support than in 1820. Opposition to Benton centered in the southeastern counties of Jefferson, Ste. Genevieve, St. Francois, and Madison, where Scott still retained influence.

During the campaign, Benton's supporters made an effort to reduce the "refining process" of indirect elections by insisting that candidates for the General Assembly pledge themselves in advance to vote for Benton. Many did—further indication of Benton's strong popular support throughout the state. The editor of the *Missouri Intelligencer* reported that, although it would be gratifying to have a Howard County man elected, there was no one available who could do the job as well as Benton. Benton's strong exertion in Washington to provide federal support for the Santa Fe trade had not gone unnoticed in the center of that trade. If Missourians were crazed with the brilliance of Benton's "land bubble," as the opposition cried, the people nonetheless believed in and voted for his program. Nor were the voters unaware of Benton's interest in electoral college reform and more democratic government. A master at being his own press agent, Benton promoted the use of favorable news items, some of which he actually originated to project a favorable image before the people.

As the economy started an upward swing, Missouri entered a period in which national elections and national questions created more excitement than state affairs. When Governor Bates died in office, his term had been too brief to influence the course of state policy, although his inaugural address indicated that he would have kept state action to a minimum. He criticized earlier legislative efforts to break the grip of the depression and denounced them as the "application of empirical palliatives, which soothe for a time and at length render the disease more systematically fatal."

Newly elected Gov. John Miller differed little from his predecessor on the subject of relief legislation. He pledged, in his inaugural address on January 20, 1826, strict adherence to the constitution and told the General Assembly that no attempt should be made to discharge debts by legislation or to interfere with the obligation of contracts. Miller stated in his first biennial address that he had always considered the loan office act "as impolitic and unconstitutional." As the chief Jacksonian state official, Miller disassociated himself from relief legislation and paper issues. Nor did Miller propose any significant legislation by the General Assembly in his first message, other than a request for consideration of the most effective use of school lands to advance public education, which he praised as the cornerstone of free republican government. Miller expressed concern about securing help from the national government through a more liberal land sale policy, a release of lead and iron ore lands, support for improvement of the Missouri and Mississippi rivers, and aid to the growing Santa Fe trade.

In his second inaugural address, Miller continued to press for the establishment of a system of public education; he strongly recommended immediate sale of the school lands for this purpose. He opposed the federal government's policy of leasing mineral lands because such action created tenancy, and, to the Jacksonians, this was unrepublican. With about $20,000 available in the 3 per cent fund created by the sale of public lands, the Governor recommended construction of bridges, believing the amount to be inadequate for any effective general road construction. Miller did recommend that a premium be paid for the best ton of water-rotted hemp produced in Missouri, to encourage production of a crop that he thought could be of great benefit to the state.

The General Assembly did even less than the Governor requested. Since the 1824 law providing for the leasing of school lands remained in effect, there was little increase in school funds. Not until 1832 did the General Assembly authorize the sale of the township grants subject to approval of three-fourths of the people of each township involved. Likewise, the General Assembly failed to approve a distribution of the limited 3 per cent fund. The state's policymakers, reluctant to assume a direct role in major economic or social development, left Miller to look to the national government for assistance. Speaking to the General Assembly, he pleaded for Congress to complete the national road to its terminus in Missouri, to graduate the price of public lands, to open mineral lands to public sale, to levy tariffs on items in competition with Missouri products, to reform the electoral college, and to provide protection for the Santa Fe trade—a good national Jacksonian program for Missouri.

In the 1826 congressional election, no one had announced as a straight-out Jackson man. Two years later the increased prestige of Jackson's name and the growth of the movement in Missouri resulted in two candidates entering the race under the Jackson banner—William Carr Lane, a politically ambitious St. Louis doctor and mayor of the city, and Spencer Pettis of

Cole County, who enjoyed the support of Howard County political leaders in the process of forming a powerful faction in
Missouri politics. With two candidates in the race, there was
danger of a split in the Jackson vote that would result in the
re-election of Bates, now clearly recognized as an Adams supporter. No party organization had been developed to nominate
candidates, but consultations constructed around Benton—recognized as the Jackson leader in the state—resulted in the selection of Pettis as the Jacksonian candidate. Lane, obviously
unhappy, withdrew from the race and later joined the Whigs.
Supporters charged that Benton had picked Pettis because he
knew that Pettis would not withdraw, and that above all else
Benton wanted to avoid a split in the Jackson ranks. The
charges may have been true in part, but the growing need to
recognize central Missouri's demands for national representation and for allaying popular suspicion of a St. Louis control of
state politics was probably instrumental in the decision to run
Pettis.

The followers of Jackson and Benton worked hard to secure
Pettis's election. Carrying their campaign directly to the people,
those working for Pettis were described in the *Missouri Intelligencer* as indefatigable in their efforts to get men to the polls.
Bates tried to disassociate himself from any connection with
the factions being formed in the 1826 congressional campaign
for the upcoming presidential election, but the *Missouri Intelligencer* naturally involved him by accurately describing the
campaign as one between the Jackson and Adams parties. Pettis
won the contest with over 60 per cent of the vote.

Other state elections also produced victories for the Benton-
Jackson forces. Benton boasted that the legislature was filled almost exclusively with his friends. No other candidate came out
for governor, so Miller was re-elected without opposition. The
strong unity and zeal among the Jacksonian leaders, coupled
with their success in marshaling the vote of the people, contributed greatly to the state-wide victory; Jacksonianism had
effectively identified its opposition with the Adams party.

Jackson's election as President promised to cap the Democratic victory, and his supporters marched double time toward
that goal. The 1828 national elections in November reflected the

alignments and issues of the August state elections and consequently a great victory for the Jackson group. With Jackson and Adams the presidential candidates, represented in the state by Benton and Barton respectively, the election was an important encounter between the diverging forces in Missouri politics, and its outcome did much to give form to Missouri's party system. Benton's twin measures of cheaper land and popular election of the President helped the Jacksonian candidates. These issues had been pushed heavily from the national level into state politics, and Barton had been increasingly forced to defend the unpopular side of both. Less clear-cut was the question of Henry Clay's American System—at this point essentially a protective tariff for American industry and national internal improvements. A leading newspaper, the *Missouri Intelligencer*, stated that Jackson was opposed to the American System and that the presidential campaign represented a contest between friends and enemies of the American System, but no such precise division existed. The supporters of Adams advocated the American System as a positive program, and the Jackson men did not openly oppose it. Taking a very cautious position without much positive commitment the Jacksonian victors had avoided a direct attack against all aspects of internal improvements by the national government, protective tariff, or the then existing Bank of the United States. Missouri's 1828 elections had contributed to the defining of political parties in the state, but the elections failed to define a majority position in the state on the important national issues.

The 1828 campaigns, especially for the presidential election, had triggered intensive grass-roots political activity throughout the state. Operating essentially as political parties, both groups had county organizations, and both held a state meeting to promote their respective candidates. The Jackson leaders convened a state rally in Jefferson City on January 8, 1828, the anniversary of Jackson's victory at New Orleans. Despite bad weather and winter roads, delegates attended from fifteen of the thirty counties. The rally took the form of an unofficial convention as it nominated a presidential ticket and agreed upon a slate of electors. Further, the convention organized a state committee as well as district and county committees to plan and conduct the campaign. The Adams men followed a similar pattern with a meeting in Jefferson City on March 3, 1828. The Adams leaders boasted that they had representations from twenty counties, but the Jacksonians responded that this larger representation was based more on the financial resources of the Adams supporters than on his popular support.

In political organization and operation the Jackson people were the more aggressive and enthusiastic, even permitting women and aliens, whom they undoubtedly hoped would become naturalized "Jacksonians," to attend their mass meetings. The distribution of a printed Jackson ballot by the party workers may have helped to consolidate the vote for Jackson. The Adams men throughout the campaign emphasized their "respectability," while the Jackson men emphasized the "masses." By election day in 1828, the Adams men in Missouri had little hope of defeating the growing strength of the Jackson forces. Jackson's victory was impressive; he carried every county in the state and defeated Adams by a margin in excess of 2 to 1. The Jacksonians took over; they could now make governmental policy and bestow political favors at both national and state levels.

The campaign machinery was not continued after the election as a permanent political party organization. The rank-and-file members were not ready for the long, constant, and sometimes dull routine of between-elections party work, and some leaders, including Benton, actually feared too much party organization and machinery might be a hindrance to a more direct expression of popular democracy.

Because effective party organization failed to develop in Missouri before the mid-1830's, national party labels as applied to groups or individuals in the state immediately following the 1828 elections were often confusing and sometimes misrepresented the actual situation. In a positive sense, however, there was by class interest and leadership a consistency in politically active groups that started no later than 1824, and that carried forward to form the two-party system of Whigs and Democrats as it stood in 1840.

Those who backed Adams in 1824 and again in 1828 were generally Clay supporters in 1832. The National Republican label was not popular in the state, but the supporters of Clay and the American System, more commonly labeled anti-Jackson or simply the Opposition, were clearly the Missouri movement representing the forces and interests of the National Republican party; they were to make up Missouri's organized Whig party of later years. With the usual qualifications against absolutes, this pre-Whig group included large property-holders, creditors, political conservatives, and supporters of national power for positive action as in the American System. At first symbolized by David Barton, Whig leadership was passing to Edward Bates at the turn of the decade.

The second group was composed of those who continued to back Jackson after his defeat in 1824. Antiadministration men, the Jackson party, the Democrats—whatever the label—these were the men of the coming Democratic party, which formalized in the mid-thirties. These forces—more agrarian, less nationally power-minded, more democratic politically, less favorable to the American System than their opponents—were rallied by Benton under the banner of the hero general of New Orleans, who came to symbolize western virtues and ambitions. These were the fairly well-formed political positions, without formal organization or platform, that squared away for the final rounds in the fight for political control after the Jacksonians scored heavy pointage in the early rounds.

When the Jacksonians took over in 1828, the interests of the fur traders and of the Spanish land claimants no longer occasioned much interest, since public policy in both instances had, for all practical purposes, been resolved with increased protection for traders and abolition of the factory system. Under a liberal policy, the majority of land claims reached settlement. Three major decisions under the law of 1824 providing for court action on remaining claims went against the large claimants on grounds that the Spanish official who issued the concession had no authority to do so; as a result, other similar cases were dropped. In the interest of the claimants the General Assembly sent memorials to Congress requesting a new commission, which Congress finally created in 1832, but the action appears to have had little political consequence. On the basis of the commission's recommendations in 1835, Congress confirmed about 350 claims, rejected 150, and left another 700 uninvestigated, doing nothing about the remaining claims until after 1860.

National land policy continued to be a major political concern in Missouri. No other public question was so close and of such direct interest to as large a number of Missourians. Internal improvements, currency, banking, and the tariff were more distant, indirect, and perhaps difficult for the people to understand; but, as the Jacksonian *Free Press* stated, "Touch the Land question; and you touch their interest in a tangible shape. The Public Land they can see, and feel, and clear, and plough, and sow, and reap, and mow." The newspaper did not add that for many Missourians, including general farmers, public land was something they hoped to buy cheaply and sell at high profit to newcomers. Members of the business community also favored a land policy that would attract settlers, for settlement meant larger markets.

Benton's proposal to graduate downward the price of land continued to be highly popular. In 1829 the Missouri General Assembly passed a resolution that praised Benton's graduation bill, instructed Senator Barton, and requested Congressman Bates—then a lame duck representative—all to support the graduation bill. Barton, the only western senator to vote against the bill in 1829, recognized the rising tide of popular support for Benton's plan when he referred in the Senate to the array of supporting petitions and commented that "graduation hung like a guillotine over his neck." Barton admitted that he represented a minority in his state, and his suggestions to substitute for graduation a reduction in the minimum price per acre from $1.25 to $1.00, and to meet the need of the poor by outright donation to those who would settle the small tracts from any public domain that was still unsold after five years, just did not satisfy Missourians. The advocacy by Bates of a similar land policy in the campaign of 1828 undoubtedly contributed to his own defeat in that contest.

Neither did Missourians share Barton's fear of increased land speculation under graduation. Barton acted against a growing opposition on a subject he believed was misunderstood by the people, until he bowed to instructions of the General Assembly and voted for graduation in 1830. Barton cited the support for graduation in his home state as an example of the inflaming of popular passions and hopes on unsound programs for political power and votes. His fear of popular democracy was thus confirmed as his bitterness toward his Senate colleagues increased. The bill did not pass, but Missourians continued to demand graduation, with Governors Miller (1825–1832), Daniel Dunklin (1832–1836), and Lilburn Boggs (1836–1840) stressing its importance in their messages to the General Assembly. The Jacksonian opposition in Missouri generally maintained a discreet silence on Benton's land proposal. The measure's popularity precluded their open opposition, in spite of their disapproval of the proposal. Even Barton had limited party support when he voted against the bill in the Senate.

Land debate in the first session of the Twenty-first Congress produced some extensive political ramifications. When Sen. Samuel A. Foot of Connecticut introduced a resolution to inquire into the expediency of limiting the sale of lands to those that had already been offered for public sale, Benton vigorously attacked the Foot resolution in his best political techniques. Speaking in the Senate, but really through that body to the people, Benton took a more definite stand against protective tariff, extensive national internal improvements, and the Bank of the United States, charging that all three had operated to the benefit of the Northeast at the expense of the West. Now, he contended, that same section was proposing to strangle western development by cutting off immigration through a high and restrictive land sale policy out of fear of western political power and economic growth. With great flourish Benton accused the Northeast of seeking to retain poor people to work in factories and to make paupers by law, rather than letting them acquire land in the West and become independent freeholders. As the spokesman for western interests, his stand reaped a genuine political harvest in Missouri. The Foot resolution led to the famous Webster-Hayne debate over the nature of the Union, but Benton avoided taking a position on either the nationalism of Daniel Webster of Massachusetts or the doctrine of state sovereignty advocated by Robert Y. Hayne of South Carolina.

Barton never joined in the attack upon the Northeast. As a supporter of the American System he charged that Benton and other Jacksonian leaders were raising sectional and class disputes to gain votes. Speaking in the course of the Foot debate, but not very specifically about the subject, Barton revealed his basic distrust of direct popular democracy because it was too easily misled; and he stated his defense of a select group, his support of national power, and his faith in a strong independent judiciary. The positions of Missouri's senators had revealed clearly the nature of political divisions between the Jacksonians and the pre-Whigs in Missouri.

The only major office at stake in the Missouri elections of 1830 was that of United States senator. Throughout the campaign Jackson men united to oppose the re-election of Barton. After the elections for members of the General Assembly, even his friends recognized the outcome to be a defeat for Barton, who wisely declined to run again. As Barton's popularity declined, Edward Bates began to emerge as a leader of this pre-Whiggery, but he inherited a responsibility of leadership without an organized party to lead. Bates, in something of a comeback, had worked hard in winning a seat in the state senate in 1830 over a Jackson candidate.

The common desire to defeat Barton did not extend to any similar agreement within the Jackson party concerning his successor. Six prominent names were placed before the General Assembly for the position of United States senator, and Benton called them all "true" Jackson men.[3] When Alexander Buckner was selected, both political sides claimed a victory. Although the *St. Louis Beacon* presented Buckner as a Jackson candidate, the *Missouri Intelligencer* hailed his election as a victory for the American System and the Barton party. According to the latter, in the absence of any anti-Jackson candidate the Jackson men planned to give complimentary votes on the first ballot and then concentrate their support on Miller on the second; but the decision of the Clay-Adams faction to support Buckner foiled the plan when he was elected on the first ballot because of the

3. William H. Ashley, Alexander Buckner, Gov. John Miller, John O'Fallon, Spencer Pettis, and Robert Wells.

scattering of Jackson votes. The explanation is plausible. Buckner, a self-declared Jackson man, was not an opponent of the American System and consequently was acceptable to the Clay-Adams party. Bates had been actively working to line up all shades of opposition to Benton and the Jacksonians behind Buckner. Having been close to Barton, and considering Benton an egotistical, irresponsible demagogue, Bates threw his support to Buckner as a practical and realistic way to advance the American System, which he thought was in the best interests of the nation.

As a senator, Buckner voted to recharter the Bank of the United States and spoke in favor of the existing protective tariff. It appears that the anti-Jackson men had, in effect, won a victory. Two points stood out in the confusion surrounding Buckner's election. First, the Jackson men had great strength, but they lacked organization to identify candidates with Jacksonian programs. Second, Jackson's name was politically attractive, and the system of running a "Jackson" man with "Opposition" alliances offered exciting possibilities for the minority party.

In the regular election for a representative to Congress in 1831 the issues were probably more clear-cut than in any previous election.[4] Bates and other anti-Jackson leaders organized an unstructured convention that nominated Barton on a platform pledged to support the American System. His opponent, the incumbent Spencer Pettis, strongly supported Jackson and Benton's land policy, while he clearly opposed the Bank of the United States, federal internal improvements, and protective tariffs. Pettis won an impressive victory with a majority of nearly 2 to 1, and as a result, the Jacksonians acted with a greater assurance that they now understood the will of the people.

A short time after the election, Thomas Biddle killed Pettis in a duel that had its origins in the latter's campaign criticisms of the Bank of the United States and of Thomas Biddle, who managed its branch in St. Louis.[5] To fill the resultant vacancy,

4. The General Assembly had changed the election date for the representative from 1830 to 1831.

5. Thomas Biddle was the brother of Nicholas Biddle, president of the Bank of the United States. Starting with Pettis's criticism of the bank

Governor Miller called a special congressional election for October 31, 1831. A regular party organization was still lacking, and confusion reigned among the Jackson men. Several candidates entered the field by self-announcement, while unofficial committees, public meetings, and newspapers nominated others. All of the aspirants professed to support Jackson, but their stand on the American System differed. The *St. Louis Beacon* supported William H. Ashley as a "true and loyal Jackson man," but it also published a letter from Ashley, which stated that he favored the re-election of Jackson, the rechartering of the bank, internal improvements at federal expense, and protection of home industry. The popular former fur trader and general of the state militia was a perfect candidate to run as an avowed Jackson man who supported the American System, and Bates gave Ashley the Opposition's endorsement. Recognizing the danger of splitting the Jackson vote between candidates, Jacksonian spokesmen finally arranged a state-wide convention, which nominated Robert Wells, a known advocate of lower tariffs and the limitation of national internal improvements, who announced his opposition to the bank at the convention. This "true" Jacksonian won the nomination over Ashley, his strongest convention opponent. Ashley refused to withdraw from the race and won the special election by a margin of less than 100 votes out of the almost 10,000 votes cast. Benton wrote to his friend Finis Ewing that the Opposition was boasting that they would dissolve the Jackson party by running Jackson men against Jackson measures; he emphasized that the future test must go beyond stated support of Jackson to a clear acceptance of Jacksonian principles.

In response to the defeat of Wells, the Jackson men made a greater effort to consolidate a party ticket and to isolate any candidate not in sympathy with Jacksonian policy from the magic of Jackson's name. A state convention held in November, 1831, nominated a state ticket for 1832 headed by Daniel Dunklin for governor and Lilburn W. Boggs for lieutenant governor.

---

and Biddle, the controversy erupted into violence when Biddle attacked the sleeping Pettis in his hotel room. Pettis challenged Biddle to a duel, and the terms set called for pistols at a distance of five feet, to compensate for Biddle's nearsightedness. Both men were mortally wounded.

Dunklin, a Potosi lawyer, had been elected lieutenant governor in 1828; he was a solid Jacksonian and a logical candidate for the position of chief executive. Boggs had established a general store in Franklin in 1818 and later operated a merchandising business in Sibley, which he moved to Independence in 1826. He had been serving in the state senate since 1826.

John Bull of Howard County ran against Dunklin. Bull claimed to be a Jackson supporter, but he favored the program of the Opposition, and the Jacksonian convention successfully separated Bull from Jackson's image. The notorious and colorful John Smith T, who added the T for the sake of individuality—hardly necessary in view of his frequent confrontations with the law—also sought the governorship in 1832. Having come to the territory in 1804 and settling at Ste. Genevieve, he had engaged in lead mining, land speculation, public affairs, and dueling. Credited with killing fifteen men, John Smith T has been described as being "as polished and courteous a gentleman as ever lived in the State of Missouri," and as "mild a mannered man as ever put a bullet into a human body." John Smith T's candidacy must have added some color to the gubernatorial campaign, but his credentials for that high office apparently impressed few Missourians, since he pulled only slightly over 300 votes. Dunklin became governor as the Jackson party swept both the state and national elections in 1832, except for the enigmatic Ashley, who won re-election to Congress over Wells. The General Assembly gave Benton an impressive margin in returning him to the United States Senate for a third term. He received the vote of the full representation of 22 counties, 4 split their vote and he lost only 7; 68 per cent of the votes cast in the House went to him, and that vote represented approximately 70 per cent of the population of the state. Jackson easily defeated Clay in the presidential race.

The elections of 1828 had done much to stamp a firm impression of Jacksonianism on Missouri politics, and with the elections of 1832 the party of Jackson, which officially adopted the Democratic title in 1835, assumed a primacy in the state that it continued to hold until the Civil War.

In the fall of 1833 approximately 70 per cent of Missouri's

eligible voters were within the Jacksonian orbit, and the Democratic party carried every major election until 1860. The vocal and active minority continued to provide opposition. Some issues remained unresolved within the Democratic party, which yet needed a more effective organization to offset Opposition candidates posing as Jackson men, but the period of Jacksonian supremacy was clearly under way in Missouri.

# CHAPTER IV

# THE YEARS OF
# JACKSONIAN SUPREMACY

As the Jacksonians were consolidating their power in Missouri, debate intensified over the American System and its related philosophy of government. A program designed to promote national economic growth and development, the American System called for a protective tariff to foster and protect American manufacturing. American factories would then create an expanded domestic market for western raw materials. The plan also envisioned the construction of a national system of internal improvements, financed at least in part from tariff revenues, to move finished products and raw materials across the nation. After 1828 a privately owned national bank to supply a national system of exchange, currency, and credit for an expanding and prosperous economy became a part of the package.

Nonetheless, dissatisfaction with the Bank of the United States, with the existing level of tariffs, and with the increasing national aid to internal improvements produced considerable doubt concerning the merits of the system. Tariffs appeared too much like taxes and seemed designed to benefit only the northeastern manufacturing interests. The Westerners, eager and needing to sell their products in world markets, feared that such economic nationalism would hamper international trade. Although the West badly needed additional internal improvements, many Jacksonians feared an excessive exercise of national power and worried about equality of distribution with the more populated Northeast.

Since statehood Missourians almost universally had supported protection for locally produced items, but they had declined to embrace clearly the principle of protection as a national policy. Most merchants generally favored higher tariffs as a means to raise revenue for internal improvements, but most consumers and farmers, as well as the majority of Missourians, increasingly looked upon the tariff as a special interest, high price mechanism.

For a time, Benton continued to reflect his earlier indecision. He supported a tariff on Missouri-produced items such as lead, iron, fur, and hemp, a tariff to raise revenue in order to pay off the national debt, and protection for products vital to the nation, but he opposed any duties on necessities and all inequitable protection favoring special interest groups. Just prior to the end of Benton's second term he attacked the Northeast and expanded his opposition to the principle of protection. In a later speech against the Tariff of 1832, Benton demanded a reduction in duties, attacked the protective principle as a creator of monopolies and of high prices beneficial only to the few who owned the manufacturing establishments, and also charged that the tariff restricted world markets for the West, reduced western income, and moved western money to the East. Benton reluctantly voted for the Tariff of 1832 because it did reduce some duties on necessities below their existing levels, but by remaining opposed to protection he succeeded in committing the Missouri Jacksonians against that concept.

Missourians were also debating the national government's role in internal improvements at the turn of the decade. Missouri needed improved transportation facilities, but it lacked either public or private capital for their construction. Businessmen generally supported national construction, but a growing concern developed, especially among the Jackson men, about the constitutionality of such action and about its effect upon state sovereignty. By 1832 Benton had shifted his position, as he abandoned the broad national government internal improvement programs that he had advocated as the aspiring editor-politician of the *St. Louis Enquirer*. He still favored the completion of the National Road to Missouri, but he opposed the extensive national action being advocated by the National Republicans, as he sought to limit congressional action to clear-cut national systems and to guard against any encroachment upon the soil and sovereignty of the states by national officials. Since river improvement could be justified as national in scope, Benton and his party endorsed federal work on Missouri's major arteries of transportation. Missouri's geography proved advantageous for political purposes. To help solve Missouri's capital shortage, Benton introduced a bill in 1832 to grant Missouri 500,000 acres of public land for internal improvements. The bill did not pass, but the proposal enhanced the Jackson party's image in the state.

One of the most heated issues during Jackson's administration concerned the Bank of the United States. Chartered by Congress in 1816 for a period of twenty years, the bank was a center of power for the entire national economy. The bank's authorization to issue notes, and its system of branch banks, gave it virtual control over the nation's currency and credit. The states could, and most did, charter banks, but their lack of resources and limited service areas placed them at a great disadvantage in competing with the Bank of the United States. With the exception of its very early period and its last years, the bank provided the nation with a system of commercial banking services, supplied a relatively stable and adequate currency, and checked speculation and unsound note issues of many local banks; but the Jacksonian aversion to government-sponsored special privileges made the bank a prime target for their attacks.

After only mildly criticizing the Bank of the United States during the 1820's, Benton led the assault upon this "enemy" of the people in the 1830's. Exhibiting characteristics of a basic Jacksonian theme, he charged that the bank was too powerful both economically and politically to be tolerated in a nation of equal laws. Benton charged that its special privileges and monopoly position were contrary to republican government; that its note issues created currency other than the gold and silver of the Constitution; that it operated for the benefit of the few against the many; and that it served the Northeast at the expense of the South and West. His position reflected a belief in hard money and a general hostility to the corporate device. Benton's antibank pronouncements in the Senate—as much for his local constitutents as for his congressional colleagues—apparently contributed to the desired effect, as Missourians fell into line against the bank.

Because of the complex nature of public issues, Missouri's political alignments failed to coincide with any clearly designated class lines. Over all, the division in Missouri over the bank question resembled the division on internal improvements and protective tariff. The Jacksonians led the attack upon the Bank of the United States, but many other individuals—including bankers who resented the competition—joined the fight for different reasons. The mercantile community's need for banking facilities and adequate currency caused them to look with favor upon the Bank of the United States and its St. Louis branch, established in 1829. The probank group generally represented the conservative class centered in the most heavily settled and developed regions of the state, especially St. Louis. Farmers who had less need for commercial banking services and currency than the merchants generally opposed the bank. Earlier unfavorable experiences with bank notes had left rural people with a great distrust of paper money, which they considered to be the primary activity of all banks. The Missouri agrarians listened with apparent approval to Benton's arguments for hard money and supported him in his attack upon the "monster Bank." Merchants, of course, preferred a stable currency, but, more than the farmers, they were in closer contact with economic conditions and could handle with fewer losses paper of depreciated value. With the largest number of Missourians and Missouri counties agrarian, the potential impact on politics was obvious. Criticizing Congressmen William H. Ashley and John Bull for failing to oppose the rechartering of the Bank of the United States, the editor of the pro-Benton *Jeffersonian Republican* reported that "a voice of popular discontent is beginning to be heard from the extreme western boundary, growing louder as it advances South, and spreading in every direction, portending the fate that awaits their [the people's] unfaithful representatives."

Just prior to the election of 1832, a bill to distribute the proceeds of land sales to the states came before Congress. Because this threatened to block Benton's graduation proposal, he attacked distribution as an adroit measure to keep the price of land high and to divert funds from the national treasury in order to justify a high tariff—both to the advantage of the Northeast. The distribution proposal apparently won little support in Missouri, and twice the General Assembly remonstrated against it. Congress, nevertheless, did approve in 1836 a Clay-sponsored Surplus Revenue Act providing for the distribution of the Treasury surplus in excess of $5 million to the states in accordance with their population. Sponsors of the bill intended the distribution to aid internal improvements, but Missouri put its share of the money into a permanent school fund, thereby benefiting more than most states, who lost their funds in the internal improvement speculation of the late 1830's. The Panic of 1837 ended all concern about a Treasury surplus, even though only one distribution had been made.

In the mid-1830's Missourians became increasingly interested in legislation for general pre-emption, and Benton associated it with graduation in his and his party's continued efforts to gain the support of the people. Finally in 1841 Congress approved a measure combining the pre-emption demanded by Benton with a part of Clay's distribution schemes. The Distribution-Pre-emption Act opened most of the public domain to pre-emption rights for quantities up to 160 acres; each new state was to receive 500,000 acres of public land for the construction of internal improvements, and 10 per cent of the proceeds of land sales was to go to the state in which the land was located, with the remaining 90 per cent, less administrative costs, to be distributed to the states according to population. Congress repealed the distribution provisions in 1842, but Benton had won pre-emption for Missouri and the West.

A number of internal policy questions also confronted Missourians during the 1830's. Following the Jacksonian victory in 1828, the first important political controversy erupted over attempts to amend the state constitution. Demands for constitutional change had remained relatively dormant since the unsuccessful attempts at amendment in the early twenties, but renewed demands to end the independence of the judiciary by making all court officers more responsible to the electorate appeared in the 1830's.

During its 1832–1833 session the General Assembly proposed amendments abolishing the governor's power to appoint judges, providing for the selection of supreme court judges by the General Assembly and the election of circuit court judges by popular vote, removing the power of selection of court clerks from the court and providing for their popular election, and abolishing the life tenure of judges and court officers with the substitution of a six-year term of office. Similar to the changes proposed in the early 1820's, these proposals reflected the national democratic movement of the period. Jacksonians supported the proposed changes while their foes opposed any action reducing the independence of the judiciary. Representatives from only five of the thirty-three counties voted against the amendments in the House when they were passed in the first stage of the amending process. Since the next General Assembly had the power to ratify or to defeat these amendments, they became an issue in the following elections. The Jacksonians, led by their newspapers, strongly endorsed the amendments, but despite their efforts the newly elected General Assembly failed to ratify them. The vote in the House, however, revealed the growing strength of Missouri's Democrats, who mustered 64 per cent in favor of the amendments—barely falling short of the two-thirds required by the constitution. The negative votes came from the counties of central Missouri and along the Mississippi River that represented the oldest, most heavily populated sections of the state that were furthest advanced beyond the frontier stage. Even though they held a substantial edge in the General Assembly, the Jacksonians still had to contend with a determined minority capable of coming together for a common cause.

Continuing their efforts to make legal procedure less abstruse and reflecting the common man's reasoning that justice was best served by common sense, the Jacksonians succeeded in enacting legislation in 1832 eliminating the existing requirement for a definite period of study for admission to the bar and instead placing the examination of candidates for the bar in the hands of lower-court judges. Additional efforts to secure constitutional changes got as far as a legislative submission to the people of a proposition to convene a constitutional convention in 1835, but it was defeated.

The election of 1832 placed a strong Jackson man, Daniel Dunklin, in the governorship. An ardent States' rights advocate, Dunklin expressed an almost overwhelming fear of national encroachment upon state sovereignty. He represented the Jacksonian hostility toward the Bank of the United States, the protective tariff, and any extensive role of the national government in internal improvements; he also favored cheap land and the graduation plan.

Early in his administration Dunklin spoke out forcefully

against a proposal to establish tollgates on national roads manned by federal collectors who would exact from each individual going to mill or church a sum of money as prescribed by the central power. In the nullification crisis of 1832 Governor Dunklin tempered his stand on States' rights with a recognition of proper national power. When the General Assembly considered South Carolina's request for support in her nullification of the Tariff of 1832, Dunklin outlined his views on the subject. If nullification meant disregarding a process or mandate of the federal courts, he was for it, because he saw no other way to check judicial encroachment on state power. Thus, Dunklin agreed with Georgia's opposition to Supreme Court decisions denying that state jurisdiction over the Cherokees, since he considered it an invasion of sovereignty. If nullification meant protecting the reserved rights of a state against usurpation by the federal government, he favored it; but, if nullification meant a single state at its pleasure could void a law passed by Congress because of an assumed abuse of power, he opposed it. Such action, the Governor told the General Assembly, would destroy the liberties, peace, and harmony of the country. Distinguishing between violations of a reserved right and an abuse of delegated power, Dunklin rejected the latter as a legitimate area for nullification.

Missouri rejected South Carolina's call for support. Despite the widespread sentiment favoring States' rights within Missouri, the attempts to nullify the Tariff of 1832 failed to create a rupture in Missouri's Jacksonian ranks, and likewise it did not produce a States' rights wing of Whiggery in the state comparable to the one that developed on the national scene.

Missouri statutes had designated the county court as the chief administrative and quasi-legislative arm of county government. However, the Jacksonians disliked the provision empowering the Governor to appoint the three county court judges who, in turn, appointed other administrative officials. In securing legislation making the judges and other county officials elective by the voters of the county, the Jacksonians advanced their cause of increased popular democracy.

Approximately three months before the end of his term, Dunklin resigned his office to accept the appointment tendered by Jackson as surveyor general of Missouri, Illinois, and Arkansas. His administration had been relatively inactive, but the forte of the Jacksonians was not aggressive government, and Dunklin did not have to face the variety of problems that confronted his successor.

A much more organized party system came into existence in Missouri after 1835. Basic political alignments remained unchanged, but the Democratic party experienced increased internal division as a Boonslick faction organized to gain control of the party. The Democratic division encouraged Whiggery, which also underwent some change in leadership as a structured party emerged in the state.

The campaign confusion, some of it planned, between candidates and programs forced the Democrats to create a party organization. To concentrate the vote on a ticket of true Jackson men running on true Jackson principles, Jacksonian members of the General Assembly issued a call for counties to send delegates to a state convention, which met in Jefferson City in January, 1835. This convention adopted a platform and nominated a slate of candidates for the Democratic party, attaching for the first time the formal title to the Jackson men. The convention nominated Albert Harrison, a lawyer from Howard County, and George Strother of St. Louis as congressional candidates for the coming election.[1]

Looking forward to 1836, the convention named Lilburn W. Boggs for governor and Franklin Cannon of Cape Girardeau for lieutenant governor. The convention also passed a declaration that no other candidates should be considered as true Jackson men—a statement aimed particularly at William Ashley. During the campaign the Jackson papers launched a heavy attack against Ashley to separate him from Jackson's magic image, but he still won a congressional seat. The entry of James Birch further confused the election. Habitually clad in a swallow coat with brass buttons, Birch apparently tried to present an impressive, com-

---

1. With congressional districting under consideration, the General Assembly postponed the regularly scheduled 1834 election for representatives until 1835. Congressional districts were not, however, established until the following decade. It was not until 1872 that Congress set the date for the election of all national representatives.

manding image, but he has been described as the holder of the most inconsistent record in Missouri politics. Birch ran as a Jackson man, but the Democrats refused to support him.

Voters chose Harrison for the second seat in Congress, but the Democrats still felt that they had lost one seat because many voters still believed Ashley to be a Jackson man. Benton warned the people against the false claim of "no party" candidates and "false" Jackson men. In September of 1835 he made a major speech in St. Louis stressing that there *were* two parties that could be clearly defined. One, he said, contended that property and money should control, and the other—Jackson's Democratic party—defended the inalienable rights of the people to govern.

The elections in 1836 clarified the Missouri political situation. Although no formal Whig party existed in the state, the Whig newspapers put together a state opposition ticket headed by the independent Ashley for governor. In the campaign Ashley did not declare himself a Whig, and the ticket did not carry that label, but it was closely allied with the national Whig ticket. Opposition leaders differed concerning which of the Whig presidential candidates to support, but they agreed to place a White and/or Harrison slate of electors on their ticket.[2] The Democrats won. Van Buren carried the state in the presidential balloting. Boggs's defeat of Ashley was a sweet victory for the Jacksonians, and two old-line Jackson men, Albert G. Harrison and John Miller, won the seats in Congress by heavy majorities.

The Democratic party also retained firm control of the Senate seats with the re-election of Dr. Lewis F. Linn. The death of Senator Buckner during the cholera epidemic in 1833 had given Governor Dunklin the chance to put a sure Jackson man in the Senate, and Dr. Linn, a highly popular physician with political ambitions and a leader of the party in the southern part of the

2. National Whig leaders did not convene a party convention in 1836 because they feared that the diverse interest groups that made up Whiggery, bound together primarily by a common opposition to Jackson, might not be able to reach any agreement on either a candidate or a platform. Rather, there was a general agreement to allow each section to put up a candidate with the objective of throwing the election into the House of Representatives. The three Whig candidates who emerged were William H. Harrison of Ohio, Hugh L. White of Tennessee, and Daniel Webster of Massachusetts.

state, got the nod. Despite Linn's strong party affiliation, the Whigs failed to produce a candidate willing to challenge him in 1836. Abiel Leonard, rising Howard County Whig personality, refused to even entertain a suggestion that he stand for the Senate against Linn; consequently all factions accepted Linn for a new, full term.

As a senator, Linn always remained second to the more dynamic, aggressive Benton, although he did earn some individual recognition for his work in securing the Platte region for Missouri and the Oregon territory for the United States. Just how much Linn bowed to Benton or acted in honest agreement with him will probably never be determined, but the two voted the same 349 times and differed only 17 times—with the differences being on items of little consequence. It is clear that Missouri had two staunch Jacksonian Democratic votes in the Senate.

With support from the Democratic state convention, Lilburn W. Boggs won the governorship in 1836. A staunch disciple of Jackson, he expressed wonder and astonishment at the rapidity with which one grand stroke of public policy followed another throughout Jackson's administration in such rapid succession "that the brilliancy of the last seemed to shed a lustre on those which preceded it." Yet Boggs, more than Dunklin, reacted to Missouri's changing conditions with proposals calling for more positive state action in many areas. Under his administration the Democratic leadership appeared less inclined to embrace a laissez-faire policy within the state than has since been associated with that party. The Governor emphasized early the need for internal improvements, including railroads, and suggested the state could undertake the construction itself or act in conjunction with private enterprise. Recognizing the lack of capital in the state, he recommended the use of state credit to secure loans for construction capital. "The policy and utility of internal improvements by the States," he told the General Assembly, "remain no longer a matter of speculation. The experiment has been tested and the results have been flattering beyond the most sanguine hopes of its friends and advocates."

The legislature responded to the needs for economic and social expansion by granting corporation charters with considerable gusto. The General Assembly of 1836–1837 granted eighty-nine charters—a number in excess of the total issued by the six preceding bodies. Prior to 1836 state charters had been issued primarily to public institutions such as schools, towns, and charitable institutions, but the charters issued in 1836–1837 included twenty-nine for railroad and turnpike companies, fourteen for insurance companies, and six for manufacturing and mining companies. Although Jacksonians retained their fears about government-granted exclusive privileges, they now believed that charters could be written so that they protected the public interest and guarded against such special privileges. These early state charters contained such built-in limitations as stockholder liabilities, limited life, and even repeal provisions. None provided for state financial aid, not because the General Assembly so strongly opposed the principle of state aid, but because legislators were unwilling to create a large state debt for that purpose. The chartered transportation companies never did undertake any actual construction, as the Panic of 1837 ended all hopes for internal improvements for almost a decade. Elsewhere the experiment of state credit for internal improvements had disastrous results, with the accumulation of large state debts and a lack of improvements. Boggs was overconfident about state-financed internal improvements. Nationwide speculation in internal improvements had, in fact, contributed to the depression.

Since Jackson's 1832 veto of the bill to recharter the Bank of the United States meant that the bank's St. Louis branch would have to close by 1836, demands for a state chartered bank in Missouri increased greatly. Considerable confusion surrounded the issue, and disagreement existed within the Democratic party. The *Jeffersonian Republican* opposed a state bank, and its editor asserted that a majority of Missourians were against it; but the *Missouri Argus* in St. Louis, also a Benton supporter, backed the creation of a state bank chartered under sound commercial principles with appropriate safeguards for laborer and merchant alike. The need for currency and credit in St. Louis undoubtedly influenced the *Argus's* position. Some supporters of the Bank of the United States, opposing a state bank because they feared its services would make it more difficult to secure a new charter, created additional confusion in the bank alignments. During the debates on the issue in the mid-1830's, however, the strongest support for a state bank came from St. Louis, while the strongest opposition originated in rural areas. The power of banks to issue notes that circulated as currency concerned many Missourians whose aversion to banking superseded their desire for bank services. Cheap money was not favored in frontier Missouri, but Missouri was in the process of change, and changing economic needs made such policies increasingly inadequate for the state's economy—especially for a growing commercial class. Moreover, since land sales in Missouri amounted to almost $2 million in 1836, the prospect of securing the deposit of this money along with other federal funds in a Missouri bank had great appeal to an area already short on capital.

Benton began to modify his opposition to all banking institutions and by mid-decade had come to approve of conservative, commercial state banks. A good bank, Benton pointed out, could be distinguished from a bad one if it was confined to the legitimate objects of discount, deposit, and dealing in bullion and exchange. The opposition to all state banks, Benton charged, represented an improper respect for the power and rights of the state. Initially he opposed any bank charter conveying the power to issue notes or to handle the paper of any non-specie-paying bank, but in the end he agreed to accept provisions authorizing note issues of large denominations. Benton apparently recognized that the rural hostility toward banks had to give way to the needs of a more advanced economy, but he accepted only a limited departure from hard money. Impressed by the state's financial needs, Daniel Dunklin, who had opposed a state bank during his term as governor, also came to support a conservative bank.

With the stage set for action, Governor Boggs, reflecting the shift among Jacksonian leaders, called upon the General Assembly to charter a state bank in November, 1836. While expressing the traditional Jacksonian view that monied monopolies were antirepublican, he told legislators that the state's economy could no longer operate on a pure specie currency. Since dependency on the notes of foreign banks was undesirable, he suggested that a well-regulated, specie-paying bank with only limited authority to issue notes offered the most effective means of guarding against the evils of paper currency and establishing the means for sound financial transactions in Missouri.

In response to the Governor's recommendations, the General Assembly chartered the Bank of the State of Missouri in 1837. The charter's provisions carried out Benton's specifications for a good bank. The state owned one-half of the new bank's stock, capitalized at $5 million. The bank could issue only notes in excess of ten dollars, and the total issue for the first five years could not exceed 100 per cent above the paid-in capital stock; after five years the issue could go as high as 200 per cent. Rigid restrictions regulated reserves and the maintenance of specie payments, and interest rates were fixed with a maximum of 8 per cent. Loans on real estate were to draw 8 per cent annual interest, with such interest being due every six months and 20 per cent of the principal due every year. In essence, the bank policies did not appear to be as favorable to farmers as might have been expected. The General Assembly appointed the president of the bank and one-half of the twelve directors for two-year terms, and the financial resources of directors were subject to legal claim to satisfy losses resulting from an excess of note issue that had been approved by them.[3]

Not all Missourians depended upon legal authorization to issue paper currency. For nine years a group of counterfeiters in Camden County printed notes that circulated widely and appear to have been accepted as far east as Philadelphia. The "Bank of Niangua," as it was termed by its contemporaries, came to an inglorious end in 1841 when a vigilante group known as the "Slickers" successfully put the counterfeiters out of business.

As chief executive, Boggs faced a number of difficult situations including a bitter religious conflict, a boundary dispute, defense of the honor of Missouri's fighting men, and a severe depression, most of which were clouded with highly charged emotionalism.

3. Important to the chartering of the Bank of the State of Missouri, or any other state bank, was the decision of the United States Supreme Court in *Briscoe* v. *Kentucky* (1837) that notes issued by a state-chartered bank were not bills of credit forbidden by the Constitution.

A decade of religious conflict unusual in American history followed the entry of the Mormons into Missouri. When near open warfare erupted between the Mormons and Missourians in the late thirties, Governor Boggs issued an order resulting in the expulsion of the Mormons from the state.

Joseph Smith founded the Church of Jesus Christ of Latter-day Saints in western New York in 1830, but the church experienced little growth and encountered much hostility, forcing the Mormons to move from one frontier to another. A central theme in Mormon beliefs and actions was the concept of the gathering—the coming together of all adherents of the church to form the perfect community of Zion, and in the day of judgment only Zion would be saved. A small group of Mormons settled in Jackson County during the winter of 1830–1831, and Smith traveled there in 1831 to designate the area as the site for Zion. He then returned to church headquarters in Kirtland, Ohio, to organize a Mormon migration.

With their conventional religious beliefs and loosely structured society, Jackson Countians looked with suspicion and hostility upon the newcomers and their authoritarian church organization. The doctrine of the gathering and the exposition by Mormon leaders of a divine plan for the church to own all of the land in Zion appeared to the old settlers to dictate their own extinction in the area. The aggressive proselytizing of the newcomers, along with their criticisms of the old faiths, further angered the Jackson Countians, in addition to the fact that most of the older residents were of southern background, and they were unhappy about the prospect of so many Yankee neighbors, especially since their attitude toward slavery remained uncertain.

Animosity between the peoples led to individual acts of violence against the Mormons, but the major confrontations did not come until 1833. The Mormon newspaper, *The Evening and the Morning Star*, shattered an uneasy peace when it published an article directed toward a small number of free-black converts allegedly planning to emigrate to Jackson County. The article called attention to the Missouri law requiring a free Negro to have a certificate of citizenship from another state before he could enter Missouri. When the opposition charged that the paper was providing specific information to encourage the migration of free blacks, the editor instead insisted he was trying to discourage their coming. This controversy produced two widely circulated documents designed to build a popular case against the Mormons. The "Secret Constitution," passed at a meeting of several hundred persons on July 30, 1833, characterized the Mormons as fanatics and knaves, classified their growing members as the lazy, vicious dregs of society, ridiculed their direct communion with and revelations from God, and charged them with abolitionist activity and with seeking to appropriate all of the land for themselves. A set of resolutions passed at the same meeting set forth the conditions that no additional Mormons could settle in the county; that those in the county who pledged to leave would be allowed time to sell their property; that the *Star* had to be closed; and that those who failed to comply with the conditions could learn from "their brethren who have the gift of divination . . . the lot that awaits them."

A committee immediately carried the demands to the Mormon leaders who, after being denied more time to consider, rejected them. The men at the mass meeting then razed the newspaper office, destroyed the store of Gilbert and Whitney, and tarred two Mormon leaders. Three days later some 500 well-armed men visited the Mormon settlements threatening to whip the leaders to almost certain death and to burn out the entire Mormon community unless all agreed to leave the county. The Mormons could do little but bow to the pressure and signed an agreement promising that one-half would be out by January 1, 1834, and the remainder by the following April 1.

Upon advice sent by Smith from Kirtland, the Mormons petitioned Gov. Daniel Dunklin for protection. In his reply the Governor expressed sympathy for any group that suffered conditions described by the Mormons, but asserted that legal redress was available through the courts. As a result the Mormons employed the law firm of Doniphan, Atchison, Rees, and Wood of Liberty.

When it appeared that the Mormons were not making proper plans to move, the anti-Mormon zealots went into action. A small band destroyed ten houses and whipped several men in the Whitmer settlement in late October. A court magistrate refused to issue a warrant against the attackers and also stated his disregard for Governor Dunklin's response to the Mormon petition. Early in November a raid on a Mormon settlement on the Big Blue resulted in an exchange of shots in which two raiders and one Mormon were killed. A partially organized operation against the Mormons followed as raiders roamed the county driving the people from their homes and destroying their property.

The violence directed against the Mormons brought forth some public support for them as newspapers across the state, including such important ones as the *Missouri Intelligencer* and the *Missouri Republican*, condemned the forced dispersal. Governor Dunklin suggested a court of inquiry, but the Mormons believed that any impartial judicial action was impossible and feared for the safety of their witnesses. In February of 1834 a few Mormons announced they would testify before a Jackson County grand jury, but when they were advised by a state attorney that it would probably be impossible to get a conviction, the Mormons changed their minds.

The more militant leaders of the church apparently finally pushed Smith into action. It is not clear if or just how Smith intended to use the little army, designated as Zion's Camp, which he led from the East in May, 1834. The "army" was ill-equipped, had limited supplies, and slightly over 200 men when it entered Missouri, but its approach terrified the people of Jackson County, who took defensive measures while increasing the depredations against the local Mormons.

Alarmed by events, Governor Dunklin stepped up his efforts to get the two sides to reach a compromise, and leaders arranged a meeting in Liberty on June 16. The Jackson County delegation offered to buy all Mormon properties at double the value set by arbitrators selected by both parties or to sell to the Mormons on the same terms. The Mormons did not, as all knew, have the money to buy, and they had announced that they would not sell. Nevertheless, the Mormon delegates agreed to consider the proposal and gave their pledge that Smith's army would not enter Jackson County.

After the meeting in Liberty, a ferry crossing the Missouri River after dark with seven Jackson County citizens, including some members of the delegation, suddenly sank, killing the owner of the the ferry, two of his employees, and two Jackson County men. There was an outburst of charges against the Mormons for sinking the ferry, while the Mormons viewed the event as the working of God's vengeance. Since the boat was never examined, the cause of the accident remains unknown.

The expected Mormon rejection of the proposal made at Liberty came on June 20. Three days later Smith started Zion's Camp toward Liberty, but he redirected its course after a warning of adverse consequences from Mormon attorneys. That night cholera struck the marchers and soon dispelled Zion's Camp, whose members dispersed among the Mormon settlements.

The Mormons had lost, and they moved across the Missouri River into Clay County. The amount of land the Mormons owned in Jackson County is unknown and its ultimate disposition somewhat unclear. A church official deeded slightly over 1,000 acres to Alexander W. Doniphan in 1838 in settlement of legal fees, with other land later sold through an attorney.

The residents of Clay County received the Mormons with considerable compassion, probably because a general understanding existed that their stay would be temporary. As new church members arrived and the signs of an intended permanent residence increased, however, the people of Clay County began to react against the Mormons. Resolutions repeating essentially the Jackson County charges against the Mormons and requesting them to leave were drawn up in 1836.

This time the Mormons decided to move to unsettled lands to the north. Sponsored by Doniphan, their lawyer and friend in the General Assembly, the legislature created Daviess and Caldwell counties out of the northern area of Ray County. Although not officially stated it was understood that Caldwell County was for Mormon settlement with the local government to be under their control. They quickly founded Far West as the county seat, and by the fall of 1838 it had about 3,000 residents. Morman settlers soon filled Caldwell County and began to take up land in neighboring Carroll, Clinton, Daviess, and Livingston counties. Soon the distrust, fear, hate, and violence between the Mormons and others again appeared.

A schism within the Church of Jesus Christ of Latter-day Saints over internal policy and over a cautious or militant stand against hostile Missourians made it even more difficult to maintain the peace. Sidney Rigdon, an intemperate and doctrinaire authoritarian, rose to great power, and his actions drove some of the best leaders from the church.

A fight occurred at Gallatin in Daviess County on election day, August 6, 1838, when the Mormons were told at the polls that they could not vote in Daviess County. The Mormons involved may have been members of the Danite organization looking for a confrontation.[4] In addition, Daviess County Whigs, having heard that the Mormons were going to vote Democratic, reportedly were planning to prevent them from voting at all.

After the Gallatin melee, a rumor circulated that the Adam-ondi-Ahman colony was to be destroyed. Sampson Avard and Sidney Rigdon organized a force to resist the attack, and Smith accompanied the group to the colony. Finding no danger there the men marched to Gallatin, where leaders demanded and secured from Justice of the Peace Adam Black his pledge to respect the legal rights of Mormons. As a result of this action Smith was arrested, tried, and bound for $500 to keep the peace, but there was to be no peace.

By the fall of 1838 general violence had developed into a near state of civil war. Armed bands of Missourians stole Mormon livestock, fired their haystacks and storehouses, whipped the men, and drove families from their homes. With Smith's augmentation of the Danite organization into the Armies of Israel, plus their legally organized militia, the Mormons appeared more willing than ever to test violence as a defense of their cause. When Carroll Countians sent demands to the Mormons to leave DeWitt, Smith sent 200 newly arrived Canadian converts to reinforce the town, which the old settlers then placed under siege. Conditions worsened in DeWitt so that Smith moved the residents to Far West. A deepening sense of despair gripped the Mormon community as internal differences widened. Under pressure from the militants, Smith announced in mid-October that his people would have to fight, since all

---

4. There is little information available about the Danites, but this semisecret group was led for a time by Sampson Avard, a known advocate of violence in defense of the church.

other efforts to secure their rights had failed. Rigdon was enthusiastic. A Mormon band attacked Gallatin, almost deserted by news of their coming, looting the town and burning some buildings, and similar assaults occurred in other areas.

Before the month of October was over Governor Boggs directed Gen. John B. Clark to use the state militia to restore order. The Mormons, the Governor instructed General Clark, were to be treated as enemies and "must be exterminated or driven from the state if necessary for the public peace." Although there was considerable violence and a lack of personal and property security, the chief executive was receiving much false information and apparently assumed the Mormons were at fault.

The Mormons gathered in Far West for a final stand, but their situation became hopeless as state militia units commanded by Maj. Gen. Samuel Lucas, an old enemy of the Mormons, surrounded the town. Smith saw no reasonable course of action other than to accept the stiff terms stated by General Lucas. Certain Mormon leaders, including Smith and Rigdon, were to surrender and stand trial for treason; all Mormon property was to be confiscated to indemnify claims for damages; all arms were to be surrendered; and there had to be an immediate mass migration of all Mormons from the state—the alternative was annihilation.

Immediately following the surrender, Doniphan, in the dubious position of being both the attorney for the Mormons and the commander of a militia brigade, received an order from General Lucas to execute the Mormon leaders. Doniphan refused to carry out the order, advising Lucas the execution would be "cold-blooded murder" and if carried out he would hold him responsible in a court of law. Lucas reconsidered.

Under duress, the Mormons signed away their property. Looting started the day after the surrender, and Far West was literally stripped. Over fifty men arrested at Far West were charged with treason, murder, arson, burglary, robbery, larceny, and perjury. They were taken for a hearing before Judge Austin A. King in Richmond, where the judge released or admitted to bail all but ten of the prisoners. In Far West, Brigham Young organized the Mormons for a move to Illinois. Approximately 15,000 made the trek during the winter of 1838–1839, and Young had to flee from Missouri authorities in mid-February.

With the frenzy declining rapidly and publicity lending question to the actions of the old settlers, an increasing public sympathy for the Mormons made the prisoners almost an embarrassment to local officials who were unsure what to do with them. Finally, in early April, 1839, Smith and his fellow prisoners were taken to Gallatin for trial. There lawyers gained a change of venue to Boone County, but the group was never to come to trial. With a jug of whiskey and a few hundred dollars properly distributed, the prisoners "escaped" while enroute to Boone County and joined their fellows in Illinois.[5]

Missouri was also involved in a controversy over its northern boundary. The population movement in the 1830's had created some jurisdictional problems, since Missouri's northern boundary had never been surveyed. In 1836 the Missouri General Assembly proposed the creation of a joint commission, with members appointed by the governor of Missouri, the governor of Wisconsin Territory, and the President, to survey the boundary. The only one to act was Governor Boggs, who appointed Missouri's commissioners, who in turn employed Joseph C. Brown to make the survey. Brown had difficulty in identifying the rapids of the Des Moines River as a boundary point stated by Congress, but he did determine such a location and established a line at 40° 44′ 60″, which the Missouri General Assembly subsequently accepted as the state's northern boundary. In creating the territory of Iowa in 1838, Congress simply defined its southern boundary as the northern boundary of Missouri, while authorizing the President to have the line surveyed by a joint commission composed of representatives from both Missouri and Iowa. Missouri declined to participate this time, but Maj. Albert Miller Lea directed a new survey. In his 1838 report Lea designated four lines, any one of which he believed could be the line described by Congress in 1820. Farthest north was the line surveyed by Brown for Missouri, and Missouri obviously preferred

5. The often discussed doctrine of polygamy was not a subject of controversy during the troubled 1830's, but it did become an issue in the next decade.

this one. A second line lay approximately nine miles south and ran along an old Indian boundary line that had been drawn in 1816. The national government had recognized this line in Indian treaties as the Missouri boundary, as had the Missouri legislature prior to 1836. Iowa, at least in the beginning, chose to agree on this line. A third line, still farther south, ran parallel to the rapids in the Mississippi River at the point where the Des Moines River flowed into that stream, and this was probably the boundary intended by Congress. Despite Brown's finding to the contrary, there were no rapids in the Des Moines River; those in the Mississippi had in earlier times been known as the rapids of the Des Moines River. A fourth line was related to another Indian cession, running slightly south of the old Indian boundary, but it was never brought into the contention between the two states. The survey apparently had settled nothing.

Efforts of two sets of officials to control the disputed area soon created trouble. Boggs ordered all officials of Missouri's northern counties to execute the laws of the state up to the line designated in Missouri's survey and, if necessary, to use the militia. In turn, Robert Lucas, governor of Iowa Territory, issued a proclamation warning Missouri officials to stay out of the area north of the old Indian line. Local officials were caught in a squeeze, and Sheriff Uriah Gregory of Missouri's Clark County was the first victim. Gregory went north to collect taxes, but encountered such hostility that he scurried back to safe territory and asked Jefferson City for instructions. Missouri refused to back down, and Boggs issued a proclamation to all county officials to continue performing their duties in the disputed area. Sheriff Gregory tried again on November 20, 1839; this time the sheriff of Van Buren County, Iowa, hauled him off to jail, although within a short time Iowa officials released him on his own recognizance.

A Missourian's cutting of three bee trees in the disputed area triggered a ridiculous but deadly serious set of reactions. An Iowa territorial court rendered a judgment of $1.50 against the bee tree cutter, and, since the man had gotten back to the safety of unquestioned Missouri soil, rumor had it that Iowa authorities and hostile citizens were awaiting his return in order to collect.

## NORTHERN BOUNDARY DISPUTE

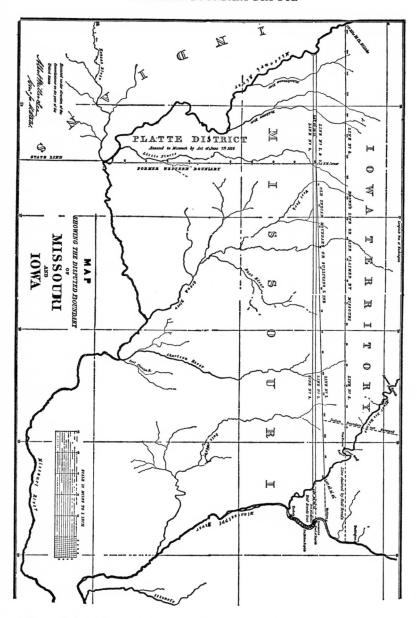

Missouri's boundary dispute concerned which of four possible northern boundary lines surveyed by Maj. Albert Miller Lea in 1838 was the one originally designated by Congress. Not until 1851 did the United States Supreme Court accept Line No. 1 (*above*) as the Missouri-Iowa border.

In response to Boggs's call nearly 800 militiamen from Clark, Knox, and Lewis counties assembled in Clark County to defend Missouri's territorial rights. When Governor Lucas suggested that Congress establish the line, Boggs responded that he would not let Congress change the boundary of the sovereign state of Missouri. Lucas then called out the Iowa militia, and approximately 300 men were mustered in Van Buren County. A real fracas seemed certain. On December 2, 1839, the Clark County court ordered the sheriff to collect taxes in the disputed area with militia support, but fortunately, the court revoked its order before any action was taken. With something less than a high regard for their respective governors—to the unhappiness of a few hotheads who were spoiling for a fight—cooler heads convened a committee from the two militia groups to talk peace. Other peace moves got under way when the Clark County court sent a committee to visit the Iowa legislature. A responsive legislature appointed a committee that returned to Clark County, where discussions led to the adoption of resolutions on December 24, 1839, requesting the two governors to submit the boundary question to Congress and to suspend military operations. The officers gladly complied with the resolutions by sending their troops home. Missouri's Governor Boggs, unimpressed with the compromise resolutions, declared that he had no authority to suspend military operations that were necessary in the faithful execution of the state laws and that Congress had no right to detach any portion from the constitutional limits of the state. The Governor appears to have conveniently forgotten that the boundary he claimed was the one that had been marked by Missouri, but the militia field commanders suspended the military operations. The line remained unsettled, however, and jurisdictional disputes continued to plague the area during the administrations of Governors Thomas Reynolds, M. M. Marmaduke, and John C. Edwards.

This unhappy episode, known as the Honey War, took its name from a comic poem published in the *Palmyra Whig and General Advertiser.* Although "The Honey War" reflected a Whig bias against Boggs, satirist John L. Campbell undoubtedly mirrored much of the popular criticism of the conduct of the authorities, as the following verse indicates:

Now if the Governors want to fight,
Just let them meet in person,
And when noble Boggs old Lucas flogs,
'Twill teach the scamp a lesson.
Then let the victor cut the trees,
And have three bits of money,
And wear a crown from town to town,
Anointed with pure honey.
And then no widows will be made,
No orphans unprotected;
Old Lucas will be nicely flogged,
And from our line ejected.
Our honey trade will then be laid
Upon a solid basis;
And Governor Boggs,
Where'er he jogs,
Will meet with smiling faces.

"The Honey War" was not great poetry, but sung to the tune of "Yankee Doodle" it undoubtedly helped many Missourians express their sentiments about the borderline "bee tree" fiasco. The mobilization of the militia for the Honey War cost the state about $20,000 that it could ill afford.

In June, 1844, Congress finally initiated action to settle the controversy by providing for a commission composed of three members—one appointed by the President, one by Missouri, and one selected by Missouri and Iowa—to locate the boundary, with the decision of the majority of the body to be final. The Missouri General Assembly accepted the plan, but the newly elected Governor Edwards vetoed the legislature's action in January, 1845, on grounds that the General Assembly had no power to assent to conditions that might alter the constitutionally established territory of the state. He did indicate that Missouri might accept a settlement by a proper court case.

Starting in 1845 the three parties moved toward a judicial settlement. After an unexpected delay, Iowa was finally admitted to the Union in December, 1846, and the dispute could then be heard by the United States Supreme Court as a case between two states. The Missouri petition asked for the northernmost line marked by the Missouri survey. Iowa, however, nearly doubled the area in dispute by moving her claim from the old Indian line to the southernmost line intersecting the rapids in the Mississippi River. In the decision handed down in February, 1849, the court declared that there were no rapids in the Des Moines River and dismissed all reference to such for a boundary line. The court held that the old Indian line was the correct line according to the original enabling legislation, and it appointed commissioners to survey and mark the boundary. The report of the commissioners was accepted by the United States Supreme Court on January 3, 1851. The decision may have been a practical compromise; it divided the disputed area about evenly, and it officially established a line that had been generally recognized for years. Missouri's claim to the line surveyed by Brown simply was not valid.

Missouri had better luck in securing an extension of her western boundary. The straight line of Missouri's western boundary running due north from the juncture of the Missouri and Kansas rivers left an attractive and fertile area of land between the boundary and the Missouri River recognized as Indian territory. This easily accessible area, known as the Platte region, contained some of the nation's most productive brown loess soil. Reflecting traditional attitudes Missourians could not see why such fine soil should be a home for Indians who seemed to get increasingly hostile and who did not cultivate the great resources available to them. Furthermore, finding it inconvenient to cross Indian land to use the Missouri River, it was easy for Missourians to argue that the river should be the natural boundary for the state.

The national government's policy of removing all Indians west of the Mississippi River complicated Missouri's desire to acquire the coveted area. The United States had negotiated a treaty in 1830 at Prairie du Chien in which a number of Indian tribes ceded to the United States a large area, including the Platte country. Since the treaty and the Indian removal laws authorized the President to use the Platte region as an area for permanent assignment of Indians, Missourians feared the Platte region was on the verge of being closed indefinitely to white settlers.

In 1831 the Missouri General Assembly sent a memorial to Congress requesting the cessation of Indian removals to the

Platte region. As a new senator, Lewis F. Linn made Missouri's interest in the Platte acquisition a major project. His efforts resulted in the addition of an amendment to an Indian removal treaty of 1833 closing the Platte region to Indian reassignment. He also secured a report from the chairman of the Committee on Indian Affairs favoring the westward extension of the Missouri boundary. During the summer of 1835 a militia muster held near Liberty prepared a memorial to Washington, and, as more positive action, a group resolved to move into the Platte region and settle there. They did, but United States troops removed them. Missouri's campaign to annex the Platte country attracted widespread support, and the efforts of Missouri's representatives in Congress paid off when that body agreed in June, 1836, to make the Platte region a part of Missouri as soon as all Indian titles to the land could be extinguished. Once again the unfortunate Indians had to give way before the relentless westward movement of the settlers. National authorities moved between 800 and 900 Iowas and about 500 Sacs and Foxes across the river into Kansas. Smaller bands quickly bowed to governmental pressure and agreed to treaties of cession before the end of the year. In March, 1837, President Van Buren officially declared the extension of the Missouri northwestern boundary to the Missouri River.

The addition of the Platte region to Missouri raised the question of the extension of slavery into an area north of 36° 30', which Congress had designated as free territory at the time of Missouri's admission into the Union. Benton, not one to underestimate his own ability or accomplishments, wrote that the task was a challenge to the diplomatic skill of Missouri's representatives, but he did credit northern statesmen with "magnanimous assistance" that was just and generous to their slaveholding brethren. Senators dealing most closely with the Platte annexation realized that it technically violated the Missouri Compromise, but none seemed interested in contesting it. Since northern politicians knew the action would not affect the balance of power in the Senate, they probably viewed support for Missouri's wishes as a way of gaining the good will of Benton, Linn, and others.

Governor Boggs, considering the frame structure that served

as both capitol and executive residence as inadequate and dangerous, recommended to the General Assembly that a new capitol be constructed at an estimated cost of $75,000, and the legislature authorized that sum. Ironically, before the new capitol was completed the Governor's fears were realized when the old building burned, destroying all official records. If this foresight gained any support for Boggs, it was offset by the problems of financing the new construction. The $75,000 estimate fell far short of the need. In 1838 Boggs asked for an additional $125,000, which the legislature approved, although it meant a significant increase in the state debt, since $70,000 of the first authorization had had to be borrowed. At the end of Boggs's administration the building remained incomplete, and another $50,000 was necessary to finish the construction. The increasing costs that plagued the Boggs administration resulted in a legislative investigation. Although the committee reported no corruption had been involved and that the construction was sound, it did declare that Boggs violated the law in borrowing money from the Bank of the State of Missouri after efforts to sell bonds authorized for construction failed.

When President-elect Martin Van Buren asked Benton in 1837 if some volunteers might be raised in Missouri for the two-year-old Seminole Indian War, Benton assured him that they could. The men of Boone, Callaway, Chariton, Howard, Jackson, Marion, and Ray counties responded to the call, with Benton's encouragement, and a volunteer regiment was raised with Col. Richard Gentry of Columbia commanding.

Six hundred men left Columbia, but only 432 stayed with the outfit long enough to debark from New Orleans for Tampa. Because of the loss of a number of horses at sea, Gen. Zachary Taylor ordered those without horses discharged, leaving less than 300 of the original volunteers. The Missourians participated in the 1837 Christmas Day victory over the Indians at Lake Okeechobee, but they suffered heavy casualties and lost Colonel Gentry. After the costly victory, great suffering, and long march home, Missouri tempers boiled when General Taylor, the national commander at Lake Okeechobee, charged the Missouri volunteers with incompetency and cowardice. A committee appointed by the General Assembly reported that the Missourians had indeed fought with honor and deserved praise for the performance of a duty made more difficult because they were not given proper support by the Regular Army.

The Panic of 1837 added to the problems of the Boggs years even though Missouri did not feel its full impact until after 1840. The extensive speculation in land, internal improvements, and the hasty economic expansion—all stimulated by unsound banking and political financial policies—contributed to the economic collapse in the late thirties. In June of 1836 President Jackson issued the Specie Circular to curtail land speculation by requiring specie payment for public land. Land prices consequently fell. The distribution act that same year forced the banks holding government funds to release them for payment to the states starting on January 1, 1837. This compounded the difficulties of already hard-pressed banks, many of which had overextended their note issues. State banks, with little specie, could not make new loans nor meet the specie payments on their own notes. Notes depreciated, banks suspended specie payment, and some went broke. The expenditure of the distribution receipts by the various states on questionable internal improvement projects added to the problems. By the summer of 1837 the panic was on: business was at a near standstill; markets were hard to find; prices were low, debts could not be paid. Many states found themselves under heavy obligation for bonds expended for internal improvements that had yielded only limited results.

In general Missouri escaped trouble in the late thirties and weathered the full depression cycle better than most other states. Several factors contributed to Missouri's rather unique position. The past decade had been a period of relatively sound economic growth and development. There was an increasing migration from the East, and the new immigrants frequently brought money with them that stimulated a demand for Missouri goods. The Santa Fe trade brought hundreds of thousands of dollars in specie into the state. The heavy deposits of the national government in St. Louis for purchases to supply frontier military posts and for Indian agencies, the income derived from the far western fur trade, and the business of supplying the immigrants going to the Far West all contributed to Missouri's advantageous position. Moreover, lead mining and tobacco production in the state both expanded, since the depression had a limited effect on the market for those products.

Missouri's sound banking system and the absence of speculative internal improvements projects also contributed greatly to the state's relatively good economic condition. Missouri's only state bank, the Bank of the State of Missouri, conservatively managed under its very restrictive charter, went through the panic without a depreciation of its notes. On the other hand, the state needed transportation facilities, the business community needed currency and credit, and the economy needed a boost. Missouri may have been relatively better off than her sister states less because she did nothing than because they did things so badly.

The bank's conservative management drew criticism for failing to supply adequate credit and currency to meet the needs of normal commercial operations. In late 1839 the officials announced that to protect the institution the bank would not receive notes of other state banks that had suspended specie payment, and that it would not expand its own issues. St. Louis businessmen especially disliked this restrictive policy, and they moved to circumvent it in order to secure the needed currency. Many of them removed their deposits from the bank in 1841 and gave their support to the operations of a number of chartered companies, most commonly insurance companies, which handled out-of-state bank notes, issued notes as a form of currency, and carried on an illegal form of general banking. The city of St. Louis issued its own script, and several other cities followed suit. Consequently a flood of currency, much of which could not be redeemed in specie and therefore lost purchasing power, was circulating throughout the state. Although deposits from the national government and from the Santa Fe traders who favored the strict specie policy somewhat offset withdrawals of unhappy businessmen, the bank still had to restrict its operations.

Most of the banks across the nation had been able to resume specie payment, but when they ceased again in 1842 Missouri found itself in the mainstream of the depression. By summer the state faced a drastic decline in the prices of commodities, jobs were scarce, and script depreciated. Newspapers were filled with notices of bankruptcies, the courts were loaded with cases, and sheriffs' sales were common as men lost their property for failing to pay taxes. The forces of progress were not, however, to be stayed. There were losses, but Missouri, like the nation, came out of the depression by the mid-forties.

A short time after his term as governor expired, Boggs was the subject of an attempted assassination. The former governor had opened a store in Independence, where he also established his residence. On the evening of May 6, 1842, as Boggs was reading in his home, an assailant shot him from outside a window. The buckshot from the assassin's gun inflicted a serious head wound, but Boggs fully recovered. Since his administration had been a troubled and controversial one and because he was currently a candidate for the state Senate, some contemporaries attributed the attempted assassination to the ex-governor's political enemies.

The first of two men arrested for the crime was identified by only a surname, Tompkins. Prominent citizens and leading newspapers indicated that there was ample evidence to put Tompkins at the scene of the crime, but either the evidence proved inadequate or witnesses failed to respond, because a jury acquitted the accused.

In the summer of 1842 officials of the Mormon church came under suspicion for the assassination attempt. An excommunicated Mormon, John C. Bennett, announced that he had proof that Joseph Smith had planned the assassination of Boggs, and that Orrin Porter Rockwell, Smith's personal bodyguard, had fired the shot. Allegedly Smith had marked Boggs as an enemy of the church to be punished for his anti-Mormon activities. When Missouri's Gov. Thomas Reynolds requested the extradition of Smith and Rockwell from Illinois, state officials refused to release Smith, and Rockwell escaped Illinois authorities. Missouri authorities subsequently arrested Rockwell in St. Louis as he was trying to get back to Nauvoo, Illinois, and took him to Independence in March to stand trial for attempted murder. Public hostility against Rockwell became so emotionally charged that a mob bent on hanging attempted to take him from authorities. The handling of charges against the accused was of questionable procedure, and the actions of authorities unclear. With the lack of any sound evidence placing Rockwell at the scene of the crime, a grand jury refused to indict him. Local officials returned him to jail where, after being held for several months, he escaped. Authorities recaptured and indicted him for jailbreaking. Tried on this charge, he was found guilty, but the judge gave him only a five-minute jail sentence. Alexander W. Doniphan, his reluctant defense attorney, advised Rockwell to leave Missouri at once, and he complied.

Hostility toward the Mormons and later violence in Utah involving Rockwell helped keep alive a popular belief that justice had not been done in regard to Rockwell's release. Unanswered questions and the lack of evidence still today make it impossible to support a theory of Mormon conspiracy.

State elections in August of 1838 had continued the Democratic successes in Missouri and forecast continued Democratic control, but there were signs of internal party conflict. Despite the successes in bringing together an association of candidates and programs, the party had failed to create an effective and continuing organization for making platforms, selecting candidates, conducting campaigns, and compromising internal differences. Even Benton was opposed to a centralized, permanently structured party organization, fearing that if the party became too organized a select few might gain control and stifle the popular will. He opposed caucuses and nominating conventions, but this may have been because of his established position of power and his personal techniques. When he worked with political instruments he did so reluctantly, and then only when he considered them necessary to offset the "counterfeit" Jackson men. Benton's major role was in securing a definition of issues and in forcing candidates to openly state their position, and when party organization did develop in more structured form after 1838 he was not really a part of it.

Men espousing the old Republican tradition dominated the early Democratic party organization and controlled the important Jefferson City convention in 1835. Known generally as the Central Clique, this group of central Missouri Democratic politicians had its headquarters in Fayette. They held Benton up as their idol, preached hard money, and monopolized the important state offices. Some of the men had mercantile connections, but they were predominately Southerners and slaveholders, who stood apart from the urban-commercial interests of the state. This central Missouri power structure supported Benton and his program until the growing controversy over the slavery question split the party's ranks.

Divisions among Democrats over banking and currency, together with the weakened image of Jackson's heir, Martin Van Buren—resultant from the Panic of 1837—strengthened the Whig hopes and determination to defeat Benton for re-election in 1838. Whig leader William E. Campbell believed that the pressure of the times had proven Benton's hard-money proposal to be a "humbug." The *Jeffersonian Republican* declared that the Whigs had at last come out, party lines had now been drawn, and never before had such exertions been made to defeat Benton.

The election of a senator in 1838 provided an opportunity to test the apparent increase in Whig strength against the personal influence of Benton, who was seeking his fourth term. Nevertheless, Benton was re-elected in 1838, but by a lesser margin than in either 1826 or 1832. The Whigs for the first time made an effort to concentrate their strength behind a single candidate, Abiel Leonard of Howard County, who received thirty-six votes to Benton's fifty-five. Leonard was not active in his own behalf nor pleased that members of the General Assembly had put up his name without his consent or knowledge. James S. Rollins later explained to Leonard that the Whigs had been forced to place a candidate in nomination to consolidate their strength in order to prevent the unanimous re-election of Benton, but he assured Leonard his name had been put up in good faith, and that he was the party's first choice for the Senate seat.

Benton's vote was most impressive on account of the total number of counties that he carried, wherein rests a noteworthy aspect of Democratic party strength and the cause of important political controversy in the coming decade. Of the total fifty-five counties voting, Benton received the vote of the full delegation in thirty-six, with seven divided, and Leonard won the full vote of twelve. An important common characteristic of a substantial portion of the Benton counties was the late date of their organization. Twenty-three counties had been organized since 1832; twenty-one of these voted for Benton, and with the exception of Warren they had been carved out of areas that had shown Benton strength in the past. Most of the new counties were in the less developed frontier areas, and it was the more nearly self-sufficient, noncommercial agrarian class to which Benton and his democracy of hard money and cheap land continued to appeal. In a reverse pattern, counties that supported Leonard in the General Assembly were those in the older sections of the state with the most substantially developed economy. When the General Assembly was in the process of organizing more counties in 1840 William Campbell, bitter about the county balance, wrote to Leonard that the state was on the verge of having the rotten borough system fastened upon it. New areas of the state had been settled and population had reached the point where new county organization was justified, but the Democrats had rushed things a bit in the interest of party power.

Dominating the Democratic party convention of 1840, the Boonslick politicians created a party organization and controlled it themselves. They created a nine-member state central committee with all members residents of Howard County and empowered that group to fill its own vacancies. They also organized county and township committees that were responsible to the state committee. Making up the party ticket the convention picked candidates from the central part of the state. Thomas Reynolds, a Fayette lawyer, editor, and clique leader, received the gubernatorial nomination while Meredith M. Marmaduke, a farmer of consequence in Saline County, won the second spot on the ticket.

Differences between outgoing Governor Boggs and incoming Governor Reynolds reflected a potential division within the party. The inaugural address of the victorious Reynolds might well have been drawn from the same well as the doctrines of the old-line, agrarian, States' rights, limited government Republicanism of John Taylor of Carolina. In his call for strict economy and in his warning against centralized government, Reynolds differed little from the preceding governors, but his opposition to any expenditure for internal improvements, and his uncompromising stand on hard money no longer represented the views of large numbers of Missourians, and he seemed retrogressive in the midst of a changing economy.

In the mid-decade, a younger group of politicians such as

Henry S. Geyer, Abiel Leonard, William Campbell, and James S. Rollins—who opposed what they thought were obstructionist tactics of older leadership—had begun to work on organizing a more viable and aggressive Whig organization. Because he was disappointed with Whig developments and in part because of illness, Edward Bates dropped, at least temporarily, from politics and devoted full time to his law business.

The Whigs held their first state convention in 1839, where they put together their first complete party ticket for the 1840 elections. Leonard, who acted as chairman of a newly created Whig state committee, assumed an active role in directing the affairs of the party. When the Whig party jelled, it created an organization for the already existing Jackson opposition. Composed largely of men attached to the American System, the party supported an active national program to promote economic development, with a special emphasis on commerce and industry. Missouri's Whig party did not have a strong pro-Southern slaveholding wing comparable to the national party. Most Missourians with intense States' rights views remained within the Democratic party structure. Nor did the state have a significant anti-Masonry movement that came under the Whig umbrella.

The Whig party did emerge as representative of a middle class, and not as a party of aristocratic capitalists or large landholders to be contrasted with a Democratic party of small farmers and workers. The Whig party did have a larger membership of men with wealth and of those from professional and educated groups than did the Democratic party. Farmers were numerous in both parties, but the agrarians shaped the nature of the Democratic party more than was true of the Whig party. The same was true of the less skilled occupational groups. There was, however, an air of aristocracy and snobbishness about Whiggery that distinguished it from the appeal to the masses so effectively made by its opposition, and an important index that set Missouri Whigs apart was that of wealth. The leaders of both parties were relatively well off financially, although the Whigs had an edge. The difference was greater at the middle level of party policymaking, and among the ranks the gap between the two parties was noticeable. Sectionally the party strength of Whiggery was located in the counties along the rivers where the economy had advanced furthest from a frontier stage.

In general Whig leaders seemed reluctant to sacrifice time from private interest to run for office. Perhaps their aristocratic tendencies made it hard for them to perform the distasteful tasks of campaigning for the common man's vote. Politically more conservative, the Whigs were also more prone to have nativist attitudes, while the Democrats eagerly sought the foreign vote.

As an organized party the Whigs remained a minority. Despite the favorable conditions in 1840 the Missouri Whigs still had problems. Their leaders—who still preferred Clay—were not happy over the selection of Harrison as the presidential candidate. Moreover, the Missouri Whigs did not readily accept the new Whig Log Cabin and Hard Cider campaign technique of emotionalism, and at first they failed to understand its symbolic mass appeal. Whigs held their first log cabin rally in a well-to-do St. Louis area with formally dressed Whigs prominent among those in attendance. Demonstrating the Whig reluctance to run for office, Joseph Bogy, the party's candidate for lieutenant governor, a member of an old French family in Ste. Genevieve, announced that he would not campaign, and his terms were accepted. When Thornton Grimsley and Woodson J. Moss, the 1840 convention's nominees for Congress, dropped out of the race, Leonard, after some difficulty in finding willing candidates, put George Sibley, former factor at Fort Osage and founder of Lindenwood College, and E. M. Samuel, a Clay County merchant, on the ticket. Gubernatorial candidate John Clark stayed in the race; not a top leader, he later broke from the Whig party to become a southern Democrat.

The Democratic party slate easily carried the state in 1840. Going against the national trend, Missouri gave a majority to Martin Van Buren, who lost the presidential race to the Whigs' William H. Harrison. But Missouri's Democratic party and Missouri politics in general were not to sail freely on untroubled waters. New public questions and the intensification of old ones stemming from an increasingly charged emotionalism and from changing economic interests were to create many a political storm in the ensuing two decades.

# CHAPTER V

# URBAN AND COMMERCIAL DEVELOPMENT

The Panic of 1819 adversely affected the fur trade, but a rapid recovery continued that business as Missouri's most important single commercial activity during the early years of statehood. Most of the actual trapping or trading was done far beyond Missouri's boundaries in the remote regions of the trans-Mississippi West by men who were not necessarily Missourians, but Missourians organized, supplied, and directed a large part of the western fur trade from their headquarters in St. Louis. Each year the warehouses of the St. Louis firms received large shipments of furs coming down the Missouri River for processing and distribution in world markets.[1]

A few large companies monopolized the highly organized operations of the fur trade. Most of the literally thousands of individuals who roamed the West as traders and trappers were either employees of or dependent upon the big concerns for supplies and markets for their peltries. Supporting them was a host of unrecognized historical figures who manned the boats and posts and performed many other chores as company employees in the extensive operations. Only a large organization with considerable capital and efficient management could gather the trade goods, keep fieldmen supplied, and operate a transit system to transport hides to world markets. Hostile Indians frequently required that the traders also be organized to defend themselves.

The association of traders organized by William H. Ashley and Andrew Henry in 1822, which later became known as the Rocky Mountain Fur Company, soon superseded the long-

1. According to the *St. Louis Directory*, fur accounted for $600,000 of that city's $2,000,000 commercial volume in 1821. This figure may have been too large, because a St. Louis newspaper placed the value of fur in 1824 at $270,000. A commonly cited, conservative estimate of the annual average value of fur handled in St. Louis from 1808 to 1847 is between $200,000 and $300,000.

dominant Missouri Fur Company. An imaginative and aggressive leader, Ashley introduced the annual rendezvous bringing the St. Louis traders and the fieldmen together, thereby replacing the necessity for costly fur forts. Ashley was able to retire, a rich man, in 1826. Many important St. Louis traders were active in the Rocky Mountain Fur Company. John Jacob Astor's American Fur Company, which controlled most of the Northwest trade, initially supplied trading goods and marketed furs for the St. Louis traders. Astor's company, however, established its Western Department in St. Louis in the early 1820's, entering directly into the Rocky Mountain trade. The coming of the American Fur Company created great resentment among the established St. Louis traders and was followed by several years of intense competition. A complex series of company reorganizations, combinations, sales, and closures culminated in 1834 with the Rocky Mountain Fur Company's reorganization as part of the American Fur Company giving that firm a near monopoly on the trade. In the same year, however, Astor sold the St. Louis operation to Pratte, Chouteau and Company, long-time leaders in the Missouri trade. The processes of consolidation absorbed rather than ousted the St. Louis traders. The fur trade continued to be a very flourishing enterprise for another decade after Astor sold out in St. Louis, but by the middle of the 1840's western immigration began to deplete the fur sources, and the 1850's witnessed a substantial drop in the fur business.

The Santa Fe trade also contributed greatly to Missouri's economic development in the years following statehood. As the most important settlement in the northern part of the Spanish Southwest, Santa Fe offered prospective traders furs, silver, and livestock. Also, because of its isolation from North American trading centers, Santa Fe's potential markets long had attracted American traders, but Spanish authorities blocked any trade with the United States. When Mexico gained her independence from Spain, Mexican authorities were willing to relax the old trade restrictions, and Missourians took quick advantage of the potentially profitable opportunity.

Whether accident or good luck, it was William Becknell, a Franklin trader, who made the first successful trading contact with Santa Fe in 1821. In June he advertised for men to join him in an expedition to the southwest Rockies "for the purpose of trading for horses and mules and catching wild animals of every description." At that date the Mexican War for Independence could have hardly figured in Becknell's plans, and although the party of thirty did not leave from Arrow Rock until September—about one week after Mexico declared her independence from Spain—the traders could not have been aware of this, nor could they have predicted the war's outcome. Moreover, the limited supply of trading goods carried by Becknell's party indicated that its objectives had not been altered from those outlined in the original announcement. Near Raton Pass in November the party made contact with a small Mexican army force from which they learned that Mexico had declared its independence and that the traders would be welcome in Santa Fe. Rushing to that settlement, Becknell's party disposed of their limited goods and returned to Missouri in January with a handsome profit and reports of the trade's potential. At least three Missouri groups traded with Santa Fe in 1822; Becknell led the most important party, which set both the pattern and the route for future trade. The early traders may have earned profits as high as 100 per cent, but as the trade leveled off a profit of between 20 and 50 per cent was more common.

Unlike the western fur trade, the Santa Fe trade was carried on by a sizable number of small independent traders. The relatively small amount of capital required to buy a wagon outfit and a load of trading goods, plus the advantage of an open, free route, worked against the development of the large, more monopolistic organizations. A caravan organization solved the problem of Indian defense. After 1822 large numbers of wagon caravans departed from Franklin, and later Independence and Westport, headed for Stanta Fe. In the early years actual traders constituted the bulk of the caravan members, with only about one-third of the group working for hire. Later the percentage of employees increased, but the trade continued to be conducted by small businessmen.

Wagons soon replaced packhorses and mules as the main carriers. Likewise the Conestoga wagon made in Pittsburgh and the Murphy wagon made in St. Louis later gave way to the larger prairie schooner built in Independence and Kansas City.

Wagons often weighing as much as 5,000 pounds were drawn by six yoke of oxen, which animals came to be used almost exclusively in the trade. Caravans varied in size, with one in 1824 having twenty-five wagons and another at late as 1856 consisting of thirty-six. Departures for the five-month trip were most common in May, and the returns were late in September or early October.

Estimates place the total value of goods taken into the Southwest at more than $3 million during the years from 1822 to 1843, with an annual average of nearly $200,000 after 1828. The business of outfitting the caravans created a boom for Missouri businessmen—especially in the west central part of the state, where they equipped traders for the trip and supplied them with a wide range of trading goods. Commodities most commonly carried by the traders included a wide range of cotton goods such as coarse and fine cambrics, calicoes, domestic shawls, handkerchiefs, shirting, cotton hosiery, woolen items, and smaller amounts of tools, cutlery, looking glasses, and other miscellaneous items.

Traders exchanged these goods in Santa Fe for furs, horses, jacks, jennets, mules, and silver bullion. To advocates of hard money like Benton, the silver bullion made trade particularly valuable. Benton stated that the trade brought $180,000 worth of silver into the state in 1824; historians have since estimated the value to have been between $100,000 and $200,000 annually.

The unsettled relations with Mexico and then the Mexican War in the mid-1840's cut off this southwest trade. When the annexation of the great Southwest was accomplished, a new era in trade with that region began. While less dramatic, the volume of goods nevertheless reached amounts far in excess of the earlier Santa Fe trade, and the trail and its trade helped strengthen the tie between the new territory and the United States.

An increase in settlers moving west created additional opportunities for Missouri businessmen who supplied wagons and outfitted them. The limited migration that started toward Oregon in the late 1830's turned into a tidal wave with the California gold rush. In the spring of 1849 an estimated 1,000 immigrants passed through St. Louis each week, and approximately 12,000 wagons had departed from western Missouri by June 1. Initially

St. Louis played a key role in outfitting the steady stream of immigrants heading westward, but gradually this business moved up the river to new towns offering the advantages of extended water travel before switching to the more difficult land route. As the towns of Franklin, Independence, Westport, St. Joseph, and Kansas City developed to serve as outfitting and supply stations, St. Louis businessmen shifted to the role of wholesale suppliers to the new western towns. Missouri farmers producing the goods used to supply the travelers also profited from this great migration.

Despite the importance of the western trade and migration, the towns most involved in these activities had a more permanent and far-reaching impact in developing Missouri's society. The towns, their promoters, and the services offered by the townspeople spearheaded the opening, settling, and developing of new regions and served as the economic, social, and political centers of their surrounding areas. Located out of necessity on the rivers, the towns maintained steamboat landings to receive eastern goods and to ship local products. In addition small-scale manufacturing also developed for processing local raw materials to meet the needs of the settlers as well as other markets.

St. Louis is a classic example of a town literally set down in a wilderness. Founded as a fur trading headquarters long before many farmers settled in the area, this city of some 5,000 persons stood ready in 1821 to supply the commercial and business services necessary to open and develop the new state. From statehood on, St. Louis easily maintained its position as the state's largest city in population, wealth, trade, and manufacturing. Located on the confluence of the Mississippi and Missouri rivers, it became Missouri's major link to the rest of the nation. Through this city, Missourians exported their products to southern, eastern, and world markets, and imported the merchandise needed in the rapidly developing western sections of the United States.

The town of Franklin was established just prior to statehood at the gateway to Missouri's famed Boonslick country. During the 1820's this frontier town of more than 1,000 inhabitants served as the focal point in the region, which had lost much of its frontier appearance and had assumed the characteristics of a completed, stable society by 1830. Serving as the location of the county seat and a federal land office, Franklin was an important political center; its newspaper was a major source of information for the people of the region. The town contained a variety of shops serving a wide area and a varied clientele. Tailor shops, bakeries, a confectionary shop, and several general stores handled merchandise including textiles, hardware, building materials, household furnishings, clothing, groceries, and liquor. Craftsmen and professional men filled the major needs of the trade area. There were carpenters, masons, painters, plasterers, shoemakers, cabinetmakers, saddle makers, blacksmiths, barbers, doctors, at least one dentist, and several lawyers. The town was an adequate center for the processing of local products, containing sawmills, gristmills, brickyards, rope walks, distilleries, and tobacco-processing establishments. Just as the people of the Boonslick country depended on Franklin, it relied in turn on St. Louis for its supplies from the East. Missouri River floods destroyed Franklin in the late twenties. Thereafter other towns, including Boonville, Columbia, Fayette, Independence, Lexington, and Rocheport, all established in the 1820's, supplied the essential services to the growing region.

Within a few years after its 1826 designation as the county seat of Jackson County, Independence developed into a major trading center for supplying goods for the Great Plains and the Southwest and for outfitting immigrants going west. Similar to other developing towns, Independence served its clientele with several general stores, blacksmiths, wagonmakers, saddle and harness shops, druggists, jewelers, hatters, gunsmiths, tinners, and whitesmiths. The local leaders actively publicized the town's advantageous location, attempting to attract more immigrants by newspaper advertisements and personal letters. In 1844 the town had a reported population of over 700 residents, but with the growth of Westport and Kansas City in the late 1840's Independence declined as an outfitting center, because it was not located directly adjacent to the Missouri River.

The growth of both Westport and Kansas City reflected the influence of geography. First opened for settlement in 1825 by the Osage and Kansas Indians' cession of their lands, this key western river location in west central Missouri attracted settlers interested in supplying the needs of the western fur traders and army posts, the Santa Fe traders, and the Indians. In 1833 J. C. McCoy, proprietor of a general store, divided Westport into lots in conjunction with the promotional activities of Maj. John Campbell. From Westport a road was built to a natural landing place on the river near the Chouteau trading post, which had been established a decade earlier.

In the late thirties, lots were laid out in the present area of Kansas City, known at that time as the Town of Kansas because of the proximity of the Kansas River. From 1838 until 1843 disputed land titles and disagreement over objectives between the members of the Town of Kansas Company delayed the town's development. Most of the promoters were involved in mercantile operations and envisioned the land purchased by the company in 1839 as a steamboat landing and base for caravans to New Mexico, rather than as a city site. By 1844–1845 many of the company members had sold to their partners, who had greater interest in real estate development and town building. By 1850 the company had ceased to exist, but the growth of a city was at hand.

Officially organized in 1850 and chartered three years later, the City of Kansas was soon serving as a western terminus for Indian trade, prairie commerce, and emigrant outfitting through its warehouses and general stores. As the decade of the 1850's progressed and the Kansas Territory was opened for settlement, the City of Kansas, by then called Kansas City by many people, moved toward a more general commercial development. Efforts were made to organize joint business enterprises and community projects. Instead of concentrating on western merchandising, more of the city leaders consciously shifted to real estate and banking. Charles E. Kearney, for example, owner of the largest prewar wholesale grocery house in Kansas City, invested in bottom land near the town that later became the city's first industrial site. Physician Francis A. Rice wisely invested in another city addition and also promoted railway connections for Kansas City. Older families such as the Chicks and McGees helped broaden the city's economic base, while newcomers such as Thomas Swope and Kersey L. Coates adopted a more speculative interest in land development.

The city leadership organized as the chamber of commerce actively promoted Kansas City during the late 1850's. Robert T. Van Horn, the aggressive editor of the *Kansas City Enterprise*, which was later enlarged as the *Western Journal of Commerce*, took an active role in extolling the city's virtues. The chamber sought government mail contracts, petitioned for navigational improvements on the Kansas River, sought state charters for local insurance and banking companies, and promoted additional schemes for urban growth and commercial advantages. The drive to secure railway connections soon superseded other promotional interests, as the city's leaders decided that railroad transportation held the key to future growth. Time would prove the wisdom of their action.

In 1858, at the request of the chamber of commerce Charles Spalding published the *Annals of the City of Kansas*. A book intended to "sell" Kansas City to the nation and dispel the myth of the "American Desert," it glorified the city's commercial and manufacturing growth and predicted future greatness. The wisdom of its leaders, the *Western Journal of Commerce* explained, had led the city to undergo a two-year improvement campaign that produced amazing results. The *Journal* reported in 1859 that the city had a population of 8,000, along with mercantile houses, expanding trade, four major streets through the bluffs with cross streets, the best levee on the Missouri River, a proposed bank and insurance company, and the natural center of the meat industry. The booster spirit must have overstated the population, since the census of 1860 reported only about 4,400, but there had been real growth, and the chamber's spirit was not out of control with predictions of a bright future.

St. Joseph, where Joseph Robidoux had established a trading post in the mid-1820's, also experienced rapid growth. Serving as a supplier of meat and staples to the military establishments of the Great Plains and the mining settlements farther west, St. Joseph added to her established wealth as an outfitting post. As early as 1845 the town contained twelve mercantile establishments, three hotels, and numerous mechanics of all trades offering services to those moving west.

Cities and towns played a key role in Missouri's society, even though they contained only a small percentage of the total population. At mid-century less than 12 per cent of all Missourians were living in urban areas with over 2,500 inhabitants, and in 1860 this urban population was only a little more than 17 per cent. Omitting St. Louis, only about 6 per cent of all Missourians made their homes in cities or towns of over 250 inhabitants in 1850, and as late as 1860 Missouri contained only twelve cities counting near or more than 2,500 residents, and these, considering that Independence did have access to a landing, were all river cities.[2] The next twelve largest towns were between 1,000 and 2,000 population, with eight of them having river locations.

By 1830 both rural and urban types of society were forming in Missouri. The frontier was large enough to allow both developments, each complementing the other, but the urban society was more aggressive and dynamic. By far Missouri's largest city, St. Louis contained the most highly developed institutions and the tone of an urban society, but at the same time it typified the society that was developing to a lesser degree in the small cities. St. Louis had a well-defined business community early, and the city's rapid growth sharpened class lines. The business community was being split between the first prominent merchants and the emerging manufacturers. Professionals were gaining prominence, while the laborers were expanding their political and economic power. Particular residential areas obviously reflected the presence of upper-class families, while others lived under unsatisfactory housing conditions. The various backgrounds of residents gave St. Louis a diversified quality and a rather cosmopolitan outlook, but actually city leaders often imitated eastern manners and methods, depending on past experiences to answer their questions rather than on their own innovation. Cities naturally dominated cultural activities because rural society had little leisure time, and the population was still too sparse. Yet, as specialization occurred in agriculture, the rural society benefited from urban institutions and leader-

2. According to the United States census, the twelve were: St. Louis, 77,860; St. Joseph, 8,932; Hannibal, 6,505; Kansas City, 4,418; Lexington, 4,122; Carondelet (joined to St. Louis in 1861), 3,993; St. Charles, 3,239; Independence, 3,164; Jefferson City, 3,082; Cape Girardeau, 2,663; Boonville, 2,596; and Louisiana, 2,436.

ship and added impetus to the transformation of Missouri from an unrefined wilderness to a rich, economically and socially diversified society.

St. Louis experienced many common urban problems. City streets were poor, housing inadequate, crime rates high, fire prevention and fire fighting services short, protection of public health ineffective, and dissident opinion polarized. The rudeness and vulgarity present on the levee, intensified by the transit rivermen, plagued the city.

Throughout the territorial period the mackinaw, a flatboat forty to fifty feet long designed for downstream traffic, the smaller bullboat constructed from buffalo hides stretched over a pole frame, and the keelboat, the most efficient of non-steampowered river craft, served Missouri's most basic transportation needs. Soundly constructed, the keelboat was used for both down- and upstream traffic. Utilizing a variety of power sources including oars, poles, sails, and the cordelle, the keelboat was capable of moving twenty tons upstream; moving at a rate of ten to fifteen miles a day, a trip from New Orleans to St. Louis often took months.

The introduction of the steamboat on the western rivers greatly improved transportation facilities for the western region and tremendously speeded Missouri's growth and development. Steamboats had operated earlier in the East, but it took several years to adapt them for the shallow water, strong currents, and other hazards of rivers like the Mississippi and the Missouri. The first steamboat to reach St. Louis was the *Zebulon M. Pike*, which arrived from New Orleans in 1817. In 1819 the *Independence*, constructed in Pittsburgh for very shallow water, docked at Franklin only thirteen days out from St. Louis. In June of 1819 a military and scientific expedition under Maj. Stephen S. Long steamed out of St. Louis in four boats to explore parts of the trans-Mississippi West. Long's flagship, the *Western Engineer*, was a fantastically designed craft with a bow resembling a serpent's head and its smokestack so situated as to give the appearance of smoke pouring from the mouth of "Long's Dragon." Designed with the intention of scaring the Indians, this strange monster under the white man's control apparently

succeeded in that objective. On the whole, Long's use of steamboats was only minimally successful, but steam power had come
up the river and a new era was dawning. A few years after
Long's trip, steamboats regularly made runs to Independence,
St. Joseph, and Westport. Fur traders made especially effective
use of the new mode of transportation in the early years. In 1831
the American Fur Company's *Yellowstone* successfully traveled
1,300 miles up the Missouri River. The steamboat facilitated the
shipment of goods needed to supply the Santa Fe trade and
western army posts. Service broadened until they were carrying
people to western Missouri and all variety of goods into, within,
and from the state.

Arrival of the steamboat did not immediately displace other
water vessels, but its greater efficiency soon had it dominating
river traffic and quickening the tempo of economic life by
greatly reducing upstream travel time. Early steamboats made
the trip from New Orleans to St. Louis in ten days, and they
moved freight at only a fraction of the cost of shipping by land
or even by keelboat. In the decade of the 1840's steamboats increased in number, size, and speed as the aggressive rivermen
geared to handle Missouri's growing needs, along with the demands of the thousands of immigrants headed for the Far
West.

In 1832 St. Louis docks received 532 steamboats; in 1845 the
number reached slightly over 2,000 and soon thereafter jumped
to more than 3,000 annually. The tonnage carried by these
steamboats docking at St. Louis grew from 174,000 tons in 1834
to 716,000 tons in 1844 and then reached approximately 1,500,000
tons in the mid-1850's. Kansas City reported 729 steamboat
arrivals in 1857. In 1849 there were 58 steamers operating on
the Missouri River, and by 1858 at least 60 packets and about
40 transits regularly plied the river's waters. Rates varied, but at
mid-century it cost 25¢ per 100 pounds to ship goods from St.
Louis to Glasgow; above that point the rate increased to 35¢;
whiskey could be shipped at a cost of 50¢ a barrel. Rates did,
however, more than double in the 1850's. Passenger fares varied
from time to time and according to accommodations. In the
1850's cabin passengers traveled in plush quarters with meals

for from 1¢ to 2¢ per mile; deck passengers carried their own food and paid less. The cost of the fare did not appear to hinder immigrants nor any others who had reason to travel.

The size of the boats also varied, but at mid-century a common steamer was about 250 feet long with a 40-foot beam that could carry 300 or 400 passengers plus up to 700 tons of freight. Speed was increased with a record set in 1849 of three and one-half days from New Orleans to St. Louis. In the early 1840's the *John Warren* made the round trip between St. Louis and St. Joseph in one week, and the *Highland Mary* left Kansas City one day at noon to arrive in St. Louis at 6:00 P.M. the next day, after stopping for the night.

Most steamboats, having been constructed and equipped more for passenger service than to haul freight, were generally ornate structures designed to capture the fancy of potential passengers. A keen sense of rivalry drove owners to strive for supremacy in both style and speed. Men of status traveling via cabin class with accommodations equal to the most plush hotel were on the same boat carrying deck passengers with wagon and team. The gambler was always on board, and speculators and promoters worked their ventures among passengers of all ranks including midwest farmers, far-western emigrants, and professional and more conservative businessmen. The key man on the steamboat was the pilot, who had to keep the boat in the channel, free from all hazards. A skillful pilot sometimes received as much as $1,500 per month for his services. Captains were paid much less, but they frequently owned a part of the boat and shared in the profits.

As a business, steamboating was carried on by relatively small operators who were able to gather the small capital outlay required. In the Golden Age of the 1850's a large steamboat cost between $50,000 and $75,000, which, while a considerable sum of money, was not beyond the reach of many individuals or small partnerships. The large number of operators and the intense competition that developed worked against any large company, monopolistic formations, as did the decision of the United States Supreme Court in *Gibbons* v. *Ogden* (1824) that curtailed the authority of the states to grant special privileges on interstate rivers.

In spite of its contribution to the economic development of Missouri, the steamboat was not the complete answer to Missouri's full transportation needs, and steamboating had its problems. Approximately 2,000 miles of waterways ran within the state, but many of the rivers lacked adequate water to accommodate a steamboat, leaving the adjacent regions continuing to depend on the older type of craft. The fairly regular operation of steamboats to Warsaw, 200 miles up the Osage from the Missouri, was the deepest penetration into the state from the two major river arteries. Large areas of the state had no usable streams.

Both the Missouri and the Mississippi rivers had their limitations. Both were more difficult to navigate than most eastern rivers. The Missouri provided boatmen the greatest challenge they had yet faced; full of snags, sand bars, shifting channels, and rapid currents, it ran through areas whipped by winds, rain storms, and blizzards that produced great floods in the spring and summer followed with ice blocks in the winter. In addition to these hazards high bluffs, crumbling banks, and large flood-prone lowlands restricted the number and location of satisfactory docks. The Mississippi River was only a little better. The rivermen, however, harnessed the two rivers to serve the growing state.

Frequent accidents caused by natural hazards, boiler explosions, and fires also plagued steamboating. Of the many dangers in the pre–Civil War years boiler explosions were probably the most serious and frequently resulted in heavy human casualties. In 1842 an explosion on the *Edna* killed forty-two persons, most of whom were German immigrants. Ten years later the *Saluda*, carrying a large number of Mormons, had an explosion that killed over 100 passengers. Snags took a heavy toll of steamboats, but sand bars, ice, and fire also contributed to heavy losses. After only two losses in the 1820's, the Missouri River went on to claim almost 100 steamboats in the three decades preceding the Civil War.

Land transportation developed slowly in early Missouri. Road construction and maintenance remained costly, and the few existing roads at the time of statehood were little more than poorly cleared paths. The wagon, cart, and stagecoach had only limited value as carriers. Although the state constitution charged the General Assembly to encourage internal improvements, the first legislature continued the territorial policy of assigning primary responsibility for road construction and maintenance to local units by requiring county courts to maintain state designated roads free of obstructions with stumps to be no higher than twelve inches and to construct a crossing for horsemen or carriages over streams. The First General Assembly failed to provide state funds or to authorize any road taxes, but it did make all males from sixteen to forty-five years of age subject to road work and assessed a fine upon those who failed to comply, with payments on such fines going into the local road fund. County officials could also call for a man to bring his team and fine him for failure to respond. This system for the support of public roads was quite unpopular among the farmers because they believed the merchants received the greatest benefit and the farmers made the greatest contributions. Even with a rural dominance in the General Assembly, a major change in road policy was slow in coming.

In the following years, the General Assembly started the development of a loose state system of roads by planning inter-county routes and designating existing roads along those routes as state roads, or ordering the counties to build new roads to augment the state plan. By 1834 there were sixteen such state roads. The job of finance, construction, and maintenance remained primarily a county function. In 1835 the General Assembly imposed a county road tax on nonresident real estate owners and on city licenses, but the tax could be worked out at the rate of seventy-five cents a day. The state's distribution—according to population—of the 3 per cent fund granted by the national government from the sale of public lands located in the state provided the counties with their first financial assistance for road building.

Road mileage increased to over 400 miles of designated state routes by mid-century, but the generally poor condition of these roads made them difficult to use as arteries of commerce. Even in central Missouri, newspapers complained that wagoners refused to haul goods over the roads. The need for more roads to open new areas was evident to most Missourians, with a special interest in short roads connecting the hinterland with the state's major waterways. Discussion concerning the state's role in internal improvements failed to produce any noticeable changes in the existing system. Public support was lacking for additional state or local taxes, and southern and Jacksonian emphasis remained on local control. In 1839 the General Assembly did establish a state board of internal improvements to exercise a general supervision and control over all state internal improvement funds and over all state-approved roads, railroads, and water projects, but the depression prevented the board from taking any significant action.

The economic recovery in the mid-forties rejuvenated interest in internal improvements. Local governmental units remained responsible for roads, but some aid was forthcoming from the 500,000 acres of land granted to the state by the national government in 1841. Legislation in 1845 provided for the distribution of money received from the sale of this land equally among the counties—a real boon for those with small populations. The principle of local control overrode the advantages of a state-wide planned road system when the same legislature also allowed almost complete local autonomy in the actual expenditure of these funds, which apparently were inefficiently handled. Finally in 1855 the state legislature acted to establish an improved financial base for roads by authorizing county courts to levy a small tax for road purposes, but county response was limited and little additional revenue was forthcoming.

Privately operated toll roads offered an alternative to the public-supported system. The General Assembly chartered some road companies in the late 1830's, but none of them became operative. A decade later, revived interest in the operation of private toll roads resulted in the chartering of several road corporations. Sponsors of the then current plank road craze optimistically hoped to provide an all-weather, hard surface system at a cost substantially below that of gravel or macadam. Unfortunately their eagerness to secure a cheaper form of construction apparently caused almost all concerned to overlook the impracticability of the wooden surface, which experience in the East had already demonstrated to be unsatisfactory. The state actually chartered forty-nine companies, but only seventeen ever built any road mileage.

The plank road was usually constructed by laying eight-to-twelve-foot 2½-inch black oak planks crosswise over three oak sills laid lengthwise with the road. Technically unsound, the planks warped and pulled out of the sills and wore out quickly. Plank road travelers had a rough ride even when the roads were functioning at their best. Promoters of toll roads soon realized their limited possibilities in meeting the state-wide transportation needs. Most toll roads were short and designed to connect a local area with existing transportation routes. The longest and the most famous of Missouri's toll roads was the Ste. Genevieve, Iron Mountain, and Pilot Knob road extending forty-two miles from the Mississippi River. A fairly successful operation, this road was converted from planks to macadam. Provisions in the toll road company charters that fixed the charges collected from road users reflected an important public policy of economic regulation in the public interest.

As vital as waterways were to transportation, they sometimes created an obstacle in the movement of people and goods by land. Those streams that could not be forded required some means of crossing. Missourians built few bridges over major streams before 1850, relying primarily on ferries, which were usually operated as private business enterprises. State and local authorities regularly took steps to encourage the establishment of ferries and bridges and to regulate their services and rates in the public interest. The county court most frequently granted the licenses and established a maximum rate schedule for ferry operations.

For the smaller streams, local authorities included the construction and maintenance of bridges in the local road program, but most of the bridges were poorly constructed. The state authorized the counties to levy a bridge tax, but this was done only infrequently; part of the cost for bridges was sometimes raised by subscription. The potential business at key water crossing points led to the construction of a considerable number of private toll bridges, many of which were wooden covered bridges like those constructed in the 1850's. Like other similar internal improvement operations, licenses or charters granted to construct and operate a toll bridge included provisions for public regulation of the rates charged to users.

Often overlooked in early transportation developments is the first overland communications system to the Southwest. Following the outbreak of war with Mexico in 1846, the War Department organized a pony express to improve communications with military operations in the field. After the war, the pony express continued to operate monthly service from Leavenworth, Kansas, to Santa Fe. When the pony express was unable to handle the demand, the postmaster general contracted in 1850 with the Independence firm of Waldo, Hall and Company for a regular monthly wagon mail run from Independence to Santa Fe. Shortly thereafter the firm added regular stages to the run, thereby marking the beginning of regular overland wagon traffic across the plains.

In the decade just prior to the Civil War, Missourians were involved in two dramatic, national transportation operations. Missouri's strategic location made the state the logical base for launching a freighting business to serve the growing western settlements. Alexander Majors, an experienced Missouri freighter, formed a partnership with William B. Russell and W. B. Waddell in 1855. Known as Russell, Majors, and Waddell, the firm had its headquarters in Lexington and developed an effective large-scale operation that nearly monopolized the freight business on the Great Plains. In 1858 the Lexington firm was operating approximately 3,500 covered vehicles with 40,000 oxen and employing 4,000 men. The freighters carried consumer goods and supplies to distant mining camps, army posts, ranches, and other frontier settlements, and they brought back a variety of products, including hides, furs, and precious metals.

Attempts to establish regular communications with California created intense national debate over the location of a route. Congress finally authorized the postmaster general to select a contractor who was privileged to pick a route starting from some point on the Mississippi River to run to San Francisco. The southern postmaster general selected two experienced contractors, John Butterfield and William G. Fargo, who formed the

Overland Mail Company, more commonly known as the Butter-field Overland Express, establishing its eastern terminus in Missouri. The first load of mail for California left St. Louis on the Pacific railroad on October 16, 1858. At Tipton the mail was placed on a Concord stage, which headed southwest along a route that had seventeen relay stations in Missouri before it passed from the southwest corner of the state on the long overland haul to California. The stage took twenty-four days to reach its destination.

Recognizing the potential of steam-propelled railroads to open new lands and to develop further trade and commerce in existing areas, various states, localities, and individuals rushed to secure the benefits of this new development for their regions. The national race to build railroads during the 1830's, even before many technical problems had been worked out, produced great financial losses. Several states advanced large amounts of public funds to encourage these poorly managed and highly speculative ventures. Few railroads were actually built, but many states suffered heavy losses and were left with a large public debt after the Panic of 1837 ended the first steam railroad boom.

Interest in railroad construction generated considerable early excitement in Missouri. A group of St. Louis leaders organized a state convention in April, 1836, which attracted sixty-four delegates from eleven Missouri counties. This convention proposed that two railroads be constructed from St. Louis—one to Fayette in central Missouri and the other to run southwest to the mineral regions. The convention also recommended that the state subscribe to 50 per cent of the railroad stock, even if it was necessary to borrow for that purpose. Further, the convention expressed the hope that Congress would make a land grant to support the proposed railroads. The newspapers of both political parties strongly supported railroad building efforts, although many Democratic papers refused to endorse any state subscription of stock in the companies. A belief that Missouri could not afford to allow other states to outstrip her in railroad construction was repeatedly stressed by newspapers and other spokesmen including ex-Governor John Miller.

In its 1836–1837 session, the General Assembly chartered eighteen railroad corporations, but none of them received financial assistance from the state. None had started construction when the depression of 1837 temporarily ended interest in railroad building.

Fortunately Missouri escaped the internal improvement misfortunes of the 1830's. With an underdeveloped, extractive economy the state still lacked the private capital necessary for such undertaking. Moreover, Jacksonian reluctance to use state funds to aid private companies, especially to create debts for that or any other purpose, remained strong. State aid meant higher taxes, always a point of opposition, especially in view of the state's limited tax base. Aside from the financial considerations, additional resistance to railroad construction came from those who continued to look upon Missouri's river system as the key to the state's future economic growth and well-being. In late 1840, with some benefit of hindsight, the *Missouri Argus*, a Democratic paper in St. Louis, expressed great pride in the fact that Missouri had avoided the early internal improvements rush and was without state debt, in contrast with the neighboring state of Illinois. The "progressive" policy in that state, the *Argus* reported, had produced a debt of over $13 million, with an annual interest cost of $790,000 to construct a grand total of twenty-four miles of railroads.

By the mid-1840's, however, a renewed surge of interest in railroad construction gripped Missouri. The depression had passed; increased economic growth had made financing more feasible; and a continued growth demanded better transportation facilities. In addition, Missourians hoped to acquire the eastern terminus of a proposed national trunk line to the Pacific. Ready to embark upon a program of steam-powered land transportation, the General Assembly chartered the Hannibal and St. Joseph Railroad Company in 1847. Actual construction began after many problems and delays.[3] The original charter provided no financial aid to the company, but Missourians

3. Missouri's first-known railroad connected Farmville, a village about one-half mile north of present-day Henrietta, with the Missouri River just opposite Lexington. Built between 1849 and 1851, it was composed of rails cut from virgin walnut and white oak and was operated by mule power. This early operation, like similar ones elsewhere in the country, proved inefficient and offered no real solution to Missouri's need for economical land transportation.

rapidly moved toward acceptance of a policy of state aid.

A national railroad convention held in St. Louis in 1849 further aroused interest within the state. Of the nearly 900 delegates attending the convention, 453 came from Missouri. Organized to promote support for national construction of a railroad to the coast, the convention revealed the sectional struggle over its location and thereby emphasized its value to any area.

By 1851 the forces had so jelled in support of railroads that the General Assembly launched a program of state aid to railroad construction. In that year the legislature provided for a state bond issue of $3.5 million. These bonds were loaned to the Hannibal and St. Joseph road and to the Pacific Railroad Company—the latter had completed its corporate organization in 1850 and was to build a line from St. Louis to Jefferson City and then to a point on the western boundary of the state. The companies were to sell the bonds to secure capital for construction and pay the state interest at 6 per cent annually, with the bonds to be repaid in full as decided by the General Assembly at any time after twenty years. The state took a first mortgage on the railroads as security. No bonds were to be turned over to a company until it had raised $1.5 million in capital, at which time the state would turn over $50,000 worth of bonds; for each additional $50,000 the company expended for construction it would receive an additional $50,000 worth of bonds, until the total amount authorized had been used. These loans established the pattern for later ones. Public interest in securing railroads prompted many local communities to provide additional public financial aid. Often, as in the case of the Pacific Railroad Company, the railroad promoters were public-spirited citizens who honestly believed that they were doing a public service. When problems later developed, with resultant private and public financial losses, some Missourians had second thoughts about their public support.

Once the state embarked upon this course, it advanced more and more aid through state bonds. Costs constantly increased and overran estimates, but most Missourians deemed the roads essential to develop the state and to enable it to retain its position in national commerce. By 1861 the General Assembly had incorporated 104 railroad companies, only a few of which completed their proposed roads, and many never began construction. Only seven of the lines, however, received state aid, and they were the only companies that laid any significant amount of trackage during the 1850's. In 1852 the General Assembly authorized a second bond issue in the amount of $4.75 million for aid of the North Missouri, the St. Louis and Iron Mountain, the Pacific, and the Southwest Branch of the Pacific. The North Missouri road was chartered to run from St. Charles up the divide between the tributaries of the Mississippi River and the Missouri River to the northern boundary of the state. The St. Louis and Iron Mountain was to run from St. Louis to Pilot Knob in the mineral area; the Southwest Branch of the Pacific was to build from Pacific, Missouri, along a route south of the Osage River to the southwest boundary of the state.

Construction progress was slow as costs exceeded estimates by as much as 30 to 100 per cent. Difficulty selling the state bonds made it necessary to offer them at a discount, and proposals for a third state bond issue to finance continued construction generated considerably less enthusiasm. Having already extended itself into railroad financing, the General Assembly faced a dilemma. To grant additional aid would tax further the state's limited financial resources. Moreover, the risk involved made new loans increasingly unpopular with many taxpayers. On the other hand, unless the state provided the added funds, the railroads seemed certain to remain uncompleted, thereby causing the state to lose its earlier investments and depriving it of railroads. The problem was further compounded by charges of waste and corruption, which caused the General Assembly to appoint a commission in 1855 to make an investigation before it granted any additional assistance. The commission found less than 100 miles of railroad in operation. Only the Pacific, which had completed its road to Jefferson City, had made any substantial progress, but the Hannibal and St. Joseph and the St. Louis and Iron Mountain did have a considerable part of their roads under construction. Slightly more than one-half of the authorized bond total of $8.25 million had been issued to the companies. The commission reported that there had been no graft in salaries, engineering expenses, or in the contracts for either work or materials, and it recommended additional state aid to finance completion of the railroads; the General Assembly authorized another $11 million worth of bonds.

One new company included in this distribution, the Cairo and Fulton, proposed to build a road to run from the mouth of the Ohio River to the Arkansas border. The state authorized its final loan in 1857 for a total of $5.7 million. The last of the seven roads receiving state aid—the Platte County, which was to operate from a terminus on the Pacific road at Kansas City to the Iowa line—received a share of this 1857 bond issue.[4]

Local units of government also advanced financial support. Since a rail connection would give a boost to any community, competition was keen because leaders also realized that a town or community without a railroad might die, while its neighbor located on a railroad would grow and prosper. When soliciting bids, railroad promoters sometimes capitalized upon local uncertainties by playing one town against another. Of the approximately $12 million in stock sold by Missouri's railroad companies prior to 1860, counties bought 54 per cent, municipalities took 12 per cent, while individuals purchased 34 per cent. Considered a sound investment in part because of its rich land grants, the Hannibal and St. Joseph sold nearly 80 per cent of its stock to individuals, and many of its large stockholders were in Boston and New York. Most of the financial aid given to the railroads by local government required the issuing of bonds and resulted in heavy indebtedness for many communities involved.

Missouri railroads also had the advantage of federal land grants. In June, 1852, Congress granted to the state all of the even-numbered sections of land in a strip six sections in width on each side along the proposed route of the Hannibal and St. Joseph and the Pacific railroads. If any of the sections were legally occupied, the federal government allowed the company to select equivalent areas elsewhere, within fifteen miles of the road. The government stipulated that the companies could not

4. In the final tally, the state had authorized loans of state bonds up to the total of $24,950,000, of which $23.1 million had been released by 1860. Of the allocation, the Pacific loan of $7 million was the largest. The North Missouri received $5.5 million; the Southwest Branch of the Pacific, $4.5 million; the St. Louis and Iron Mountain, $3.6 million; the Hannibal and St. Joseph, $3 million; the Platte County, $700,000; and the Cairo and Fulton, $650,000.

sell the land for less than double the minimum price of public lands and that the roads must carry without charge all federal property and troops, along with the United States mail, at a rate set by Congress. Later the Cairo and Fulton and the Southwest Branch of the Pacific received similar federal grants. By 1860 the Pacific had sold nearly 78,000 acres of its land at an average of about $2.50 per acre, while the Hannibal and St. Joseph had received about $350,000 for just over 33,000 acres—better than $10.50 per acre.

Even with these large-scale land grants and financial aids, railroad construction remained painfully slow. The Hannibal and St. Joseph broke ground amid great excitement with a big barbecue on November 3, 1851, probably unaware of the effort required to build a railroad. Actual construction did not begin until 1853 and on June 1, 1857, only thirty-four miles of track had been completed. But this was probably the best financed and managed of the Missouri concerns, and construction soon accelerated, with final work completed in 1859. The Pacific had built only some five miles of track by the end of 1852; by 1860 the road remained unfinished, but it had reached Smithton, located 189 miles west of St. Louis. By the end of 1860 Missouri had slightly over 800 miles of operative railroads.[5]

The major disaster of Missouri railroad building in the pre-Civil War years occurred on the Pacific road in November of 1855. After completion of the road to Jefferson City, an excursion train of ten passenger cars departed from St. Louis for the capital city to honor the event. Tragedy occurred when a partially completed bridge over the Gasconade River collapsed; the train fell into the river and killed several passengers.

Despite the excitement and support generated for railroad ventures in the 1850's, many Missourians remained convinced that rivers would continue to play a dominant role in the nation's commerce and trade. In fact, Missouri originally planned its railroad system so that it could fit in with the existing waterways.

5. The completed Hannibal and St. Joseph was the largest with 206 miles of track, and the Pacific's 189-mile operation to Smithton was second. Others were, in descending order: North Missouri, 168 miles; St. Louis and Iron Mountain, 86; Southwest Branch, 77; Platte County, 44; and Cairo and Fulton, 26.

By connecting rivers and supplying transportation from outlying regions to a river, the railroads would be part of a greatly expanded transportation system.

The wisdom of public financing of the railroads has been widely debated, but it does appear that railroad construction would have been long delayed if it had been necessary to wait for full financing by private capital. Perhaps new methods of economic research may one day reveal the loss from such a delay or discover that the roads were not actually needed at the time, but Missourians apparently accepted the principle that public aid was essential to a program that they believed benefited the state. While supporting state aid to private concerns, which aid they expected to be repaid, Missourians generally opposed actual state construction, ownership, or operation of the railroads at the time. Unfortunately, the railroads handled the financial aid badly, and great losses caused even the major companies to default in the 1860's.

Telegraphic connections with the East via Louisville first reached Missouri in December of 1847 and Chicago a short time later. Until technical problems could be resolved, telegraph messages had to be ferried across the Mississippi at St. Louis. Attempts to use aerial suspension to cross the river failed; the extreme tension would break the wire, or it was often snapped by a boat. River currents, which made it difficult to hold a line in place, ended the first underwater effort. In 1852 underwater wires encased in gutta-percha and then covered with lead proved more successful, but firmly fixed river connections did not exist until Western Union Telegraph Company laid a still heavier cable in 1859.

New Yorker Henry O'Reilly had promoted the plans and organized the company that brought the telegraph to St. Louis. After the line reached St. Louis, towns to the west requested service. When O'Reilly initiated plans to extend service into other areas of Missouri, Taliaferro Preston Shaffner, who also held a Samuel F. B. Morse patent, blocked his efforts. In March, 1850, Shaffner had brought a telegraph line from Nashville to Cairo, Illinois, where it spanned the Mississippi to Cape Girardeau and then ran into St. Louis. Shaffner started building westward later in 1850 and opened telegraph service to Jefferson

City in January, 1851. Chartered in 1851 as the St. Louis and Missouri Telegraph Company, Shaffner's organization extended service to Kansas City in July and to St. Joseph in the fall of 1851. The company initially seemed successful, but poor construction and inadequate maintenance resulted in increasingly poor service and resultant financial problems. The company changed hands in 1856, after which the Pacific Railroad Company agreed to rebuild and maintain the line along its right of way from St. Louis to Jefferson City in exchange for free telegraph service. Financial problems continued to plague the company, and it passed into the control of the Western Union Telegraph Company in 1859 with the advent of the era of consolidation.

As on other frontiers, the lack of capital, machinery, and labor combined with the limited market to restrict manufacturing in early Missouri. Commerce and trade not only provided more lucrative opportunities for businessmen, but frequently created a vested-interest class, some of whom opposed the development of local manufacturing as competition to their established business.

Missouri's early manufacturing involved the relatively simple processing by which local raw materials were converted into finished goods for local consumption. Most early production was done in the household, by individual craftsmen in a small shop, or in a small locally operated mill, ropewalk, or other similar enterprise. In some instances primitive manufacturing operations begun in order to meet local needs in isolated areas closed when an increased population and a better transportation system made it feasible to import more finished merchandise from eastern firms. Before 1820, for example, the town of Franklin had several shoe and hat manufacturers, but during the decade of the twenties these shops closed as local merchants began to import these items from the East. On the other hand, as the local markets grew and as transportation improved, local firms processed an increasing amount of local raw materials for home consumption and for export. Early in the decade the Boonslick country produced sizable amounts of flour, meal, rope, and pork, much of which it shipped to southern markets via the Missouri and Mississippi rivers.

Missouri's manufacturers gradually expanded the size, scope, and complexity of their operations to take advantage of an increasing raw material production and a growing demand for goods in the rapidly expanding state and western markets. Just when a factory system arrived in Missouri would be impossible to say, but the evidence suggests that some factory production was under way by 1840, with an increasing transition from pre-factory production methods after that date. With the passing of the Panic of 1837, iron foundries in St. Louis made a quick transition from the older handicraft shop methods of production to factories with new machinery and a large labor force brought together under one roof.

Missouri's capital investment in manufacturing according to the 1840 census was approximately $2.7 million, with the value of its manufactured products for that same year over $3.8 million. The reported over $8 million invested in retail stores, however, indicates the continued predominance of trade and commerce. The 1840 census reported leather goods, machinery, headwear, cordage, carriages and wagons, tobacco, lumber, whiskey, and malt beverages as Missouri's leading manufactured products.[6]

The next two decades witnessed important growth in the manufacturing sector of the Missouri economy. On the broader scope of the Missouri scene this reflected an increased migration of people from the North, an increased economic activity within the state that had more in common with the North than with the South, and a new balance between agrarian and business forces within the state. Missouri's almost 3,000 manufacturing establishments ranked the state fourteenth in manufacturing among the states in 1850. A slight increase in the number of establishments by 1860 to over 3,000 maintained the state's national ranking. The increasing capital invested in manufacturing was more startling. Jumping from less than $3 million in 1840, the capital investment reached $8.5 million and a rank of thirteenth in 1850. This figure more than doubled to a total of over

6. Although the United States censuses of 1840, 1850, and 1860 are recognized as inaccurate and incomplete, they are the only source for any state-wide economic statistics. It would be reasonable to assume that the statistics are somewhat less than the true figures, but that the figures are nonetheless indicative of Missouri's economic conditions.

$20 million in 1860, although the state dropped to a rank of sixteenth in the nation. In 1850 the value of manufactured products was $24 million, and in 1860 the figure reached $42 million, with the state ranking tenth and eleventh respectively. Manufacturing employed about 20,000 working Missourians on the eve of the Civil War.

As late as 1860 there was still a close correlation between Missouri's extractive resources and its manufactured products. Mills scattered throughout the state produced flour and meal annually worth almost $10 million. The state's sawed lumber was valued at over $3 million in 1860, while refined sugar, pork, and beef products all approached $1.8 million. Manufactured products with a value of over $1 million included tobacco, machinery, soaps and candles, cordage, and malt liquor; distilled liquor was extensively produced. Stoves, clothing, footwear, tinware, copperware, and ironware, saddles and harnesses, brick, wagons and carriages, pig iron, and bar, sheet, and boiler iron all exceeded the $500,000 mark. With eighty-six establishments turning out a production worth over $300,000, Missouri was the second-ranking state in wool carding. Primarily dependent upon raw materials produced within the state, Missouri's industry nonetheless was becoming quite diversified.

Producing some two-thirds of the total value of goods, St. Louis was clearly the manufacturing center of the state. Outside of St. Louis the leading manufacturing counties, in order of value of products, were Howard, Jackson, Buchanan, St. Charles, Marion, Pike, Cooper, and Lafayette. Meat packing in St. Joseph placed Buchanan County in the top group of manufacturing counties. Commercial meat packing in Kansas City was primarily a local operation before the Civil War.

Some Missouri manufacturing became fairly sophisticated, and some products found wide markets. Flour and meal were exported in large quantities, as were Missouri rope and bagging. By the mid-1850's, however, some hemp producers were switching to general farming as iron ties and wire replaced rope and as steam power replaced sails. Some relatively large Missouri companies engaged in the tobacco business. The Swinney and Lewis Tobacco Company, operating in St. Louis and Glasgow, was said to be the largest tobacco establishment in the Midwest in 1850. The Lewis Tobacco Works at Glasgow employed between 400 and 500 persons, most of whom were Negroes, including the firm's 125 slaves. Fire destroyed the Glasgow works in 1860 with an estimated loss of between $150,000 and $200,000. The Lewis brand was a commonly known and popular label throughout the United States, and Missouri plug and fine-cut tobacco was also exported to Europe in large amounts.

There were rich deposits of iron ore in Missouri, but exploiting them efficiently remained a difficult task. The heavy ore could not be transported long distances, so ironworks had to be constructed at nearby sites, which also provided timber for fuel and water for power. Several small ironworks sprang up early adjacent to the iron fields southwest of St. Louis to produce pig iron and bars primarily for St. Louis manufacturers. They did, however, manufacture such common items as plowshares, axheads, hoes, nails, horseshoes, kettles, skillets, and simple machinery to meet the needs of the immediate vicinity. The demands for iron played a major role in the development of transportation from the mineral areas to St. Louis, but the improved transportation, in turn, reduced local production of iron commodities, since products of improved quality could then be secured from the more efficient urban manufacturing centers.

A successful ironworks required a substantial outlay of capital, a large supply of skilled and unskilled labor, and an efficient and economical system of transportation—not one of which was available in Missouri's mineral regions. The owners of an ironworks in Washington County operating from the early 1820's to 1840 ran it like a plantation, although they did not use slave labor, supplying the needs of workers with a company store.

Missouri's most important iron manufacturer in the early decades was the Maramec Ironworks, located at Maramec Spring some seventy-five miles south of St. Louis. Founded in 1826 by Thomas James, a merchant-capitalist from Chillicothe, Ohio, the company's operations typified the manufacturer role in the development of the West. Established in an undeveloped part of Missouri, the company was the major force in opening the region and in shaping both its social and economic development. It brought settlers and workers to the area, provided a major market for local products and employment for the area's residents, functioned as a major wholesaler and retailer of consumer goods, and carried out quasi-banking operations. The area's transportation developed to meet the company's needs, and the company, a paternalistic operation, helped to provide schools, churches, and other general civic improvements.

Since iron production required some of the most advanced technology, large amounts of capital, machinery, skilled labor, and capable management, Thomas James must be given credit for daring innovation in his successful operation of the company. When the firm's management passed to a son, William James, in the 1840's the Maramec Ironworks increasingly specialized in supplying industrial users with iron while decreasing its production of items for the local trade.

Some investors expressed interest in the iron ore deposits of Iron Mountain in the mid-thirties, but significant production did not get under way for another ten years. A major national publication, *Hunt's Merchant's Magazine*, told its readers that the deposits of iron in the Iron Mountain and Pilot Knob fields were large enough to supply the needs of the world for a hundred years.

Techniques of lead mining and processing changed little from the late Spanish period until the Civil War, with Jefferson, Madison, St. Francois, Ste. Genevieve, and Washington counties continuing to provide the bulk of Missouri's lead output. With a high-grade ore very near the surface, virtually anyone could extract and smelt the mineral with relative ease. As a result, most of the southeast mines were shallow diggings manned by farmers on a part-time basis. Shaft mining was rare. A shortage of capital and inefficient methods of smelting kept most operations small and confined mining operations to only those areas with high-grade ore. By the 1850's an attempt to exploit the poorer ore had gotten under way, but any significant changes in this procedure did not come until after the Civil War. Nevertheless, despite the relatively primitive character of lead mining operations, Missouri's southeastern lead production supplied a raw material of great importance to the business economy of St. Louis.

In the decade preceding the Civil War a significant amount of lead began to come out of the southwestern part of the state.

Settlement had been relatively slow in southwestern Missouri until the discovery of rich lead ore created a mining boom. Although exposed lead ore had been used for shot by the early settlers, it was not until mid-century that the extensive subsurface ore was found; miners began to converge upon the area, and even local farmers began to devote more time to mining. The big find was in 1854 at Granby in Newton County, where about 300 mining shafts had been opened by 1860. Transporting the lead from distant fields to market was a major operation. Wagons hauled the pigs to Spring River, where flatboats carried them down the Grand to the Arkansas and on to the Mississippi River before they reached New Orleans. An alternate route was by wagon north to the Osage River and down that waterway to the Missouri. Large quantities of zinc existed in conjunction with the lead ore in the southwest, but zinc's commercial value remained undiscovered prior to 1860.

The national government's policy of leasing mineral lands broke down in Missouri, and the system created a continuing conflict between some Missourians and the national government. The leasing policy, begun early in the eighteenth century, had been designed to guard against wasteful exploitation and monopolization of lead and to ensure an adequate supply for military needs. Since all leases had expired by 1822, federal officials sent Lt. Martin Thomas to Missouri to negotiate new leases and to administer the leasing law in the state. They also instructed Thomas to mark new lead lands and to keep unauthorized people away from the lead. Thomas, a competent and conscientious officer, negotiated thirty-eight leases in his first year in Missouri; he also removed some illegal occupants and by 1828 had marked over 400,000 acres of lead lands closed to public entry. A rising tide of opposition and ill will directed toward leasing prevented Thomas from eliminating trespassing, and further attempts to remove the intruders would only have aroused Missourians all the more. While some advocated that the lead lands be turned over to the state, most favored their public sale. Senator Benton, damning leasing policy for creating all of the ancient evils of tenantry contrary to good republicanism, pressed for their sale. Barton questioned leasing, but, in part because he feared speculation and monopoly, he moved more cautiously toward change. Since it involved only a few Missourians, the leasing issue never became a major political one in the state. Ultimately both senators supported a memorial from the General Assembly requesting the sale of the lead lands, and Congress gave its approval to such a policy in 1829.

The existence of coal had been known from the first part of the century, but little was extracted from the earth before mid-century. Except for blacksmiths, the major early consumers of coal, most Missourians used wood as their primary fuel. The limited commercial production of coal began around 1840, with operations centered in the counties along the Missouri River from Callaway and Cole westward to Ray and Lafayette. Preliminary surveys in connection with railroad promotion revealed extensive coal fields in many parts of the state prior to 1850; coal production in Missouri increased steadily after that date when, in response to the growing demands of railroads and industry, new fields were brought into production, making Missouri one of the major bituminous coal producing states.

Missourians freely used the abundant timber supply—a valuable commercial resource—for fences, buildings, and fuel, and were producing timber products valued at several million dollars annually before the Civil War. As it had been since territorial years, the Gasconade River valley continued to be an important lumber exporting region, with much of its output destined for St. Louis. Great quantities of plank and timber also came out of the Ozark region, where many settlements grew up in conjunction with timber processing.

In common with a general public policy in Missouri, St. Louis probably practiced the most extensive regulation of commercial and manufacturing operations in the state. A considerable number of city ordinances designed to protect the customer against fraud and unfair competition practices and to safeguard the public health were passed. Present-day residents of St. Louis might be surprised to learn that in 1848 the *Western Journal* warned that unconsumed smoke from new industries had created air pollution hazardous to the people's health. The newspaper's call for preventive action was unsuccessful.

As on most underdeveloped frontier regions, labor remained a scarce item for several years. Gottfried Duden's 1826 letter written while in Montgomery County reported that the ordinary wages of male workers, white or black, were from $8 to $10 per month with board and from $12 to $14 per month without board. Referring primarily to wages for farm laborers, Duden reported that they had been twice as high a few years earlier, and he advised Germans against coming to Missouri as laborers because a continued increase in population would produce lower wages. Duden remained confident, however, that wages would not fall to the low levels of Europe because of the easy availability of farm land. His estimates, however, may have been too pessimistic with regard to wages in the towns.

State-wide labor statistics and indexes of relative values with which to assess accurately the pre–Civil War status of laborers are lacking still today. The demand for labor, especially in the construction trades, created by the state's rapid economic growth placed workers in an excellent bargaining position. St. Louis attempted to recruit workingmen with promises of good wages and steady employment, and St. Louis workers probably received more than their counterparts elsewhere in the state. Certainly they received more than farm laborers. Wages in that city advanced in the mid-1830's until in 1836 common laborers received $1.75 per day, carpenters $2.25 per day, and ironworkers $3.00 per day. Hours were long, but not all workingmen objected. Master craftsmen appear to have held considerable pride in the right to set their own work schedule, which often amounted to as much as fourteen hours per day. Most workingmen and mechanics, however, had demanded the ten-hour day, and some had won that concession by 1836 without apparent difficulty. Several labor societies existed in St. Louis, with their organized action in behalf of wages and hours apparently dating from 1837.

The full impact of the depression that hit the nation in 1837 did not reach Missouri for some time, but the depression years, with the resultant contraction in construction and business, lessened the favorable position of the individual workingman and produced Missouri's first organized labor movement. Unemployment in St. Louis in 1837 brought a reduction in wages for general laborers to $1 per day; in general, the wages of all workingmen and mechanics dropped by 50 to 75 per cent. The workers protested, and the journeymen organized for common action to secure pay raises. The cabinetworkers won a 20 per cent pay increase, but did not get the written contracts they demanded. The plasterers organized in 1837 in their attempt to secure a pay increase from $2.00 to $2.50, and the journeymen carpenters struck for the ten-hour day in 1837. Some were successful; others were not. Thus, by 1840 Missouri's labor force had organized to use collective bargaining with the strike as a major weapon, but they had not yet employed the boycott, union label, or picketing. Unconnected to national labor movements, Missouri's earliest attempts to organize workers remained local efforts. Conditions, of course, were not conducive to well-developed collective bargaining. There were no large employers, and a large part of the workers were really independent craftsmen rather than company employees. Information on labor activity outside of St. Louis is sparse, but probably the city was the only place in which any organized effort took place or was really possible.

In the opening years of the 1840's the workingmen of St. Louis came more under the influence of the national labor movements, and they turned to political action in the effort to gain two of their major goals—a universal ten-hour day and an improved mechanics' lien law. Both Whigs and Democrats, the former with greater reluctance, tried to attract the workingmen's vote in 1840. Neither party ticket, however, satisfied the workers, who brought out the Independent Mechanics' and Workingmen's slate with two candidates for the state House of Representatives from St. Louis. The labor ticket lost, but the workingmen continued their efforts to exert pressure for favorable legislation.

A meeting of workers in the summer of 1840 prepared a petition to the General Assembly requesting a law for a ten-hour day and an improved lien law. The committee to which the petition was referred in the 1840–1841 session reported that no change should be made in the existing law, which was limited to a contractor's lien on buildings that he constructed. The General Assembly rejected the committee's report and approved legislation extending the lien right to subcontractors for materials furnished and for work done on buildings. Labor groups kept up their campaign until a new law passed in 1843 provided that all persons, including every mechanic, artisan, and working-man, should have a lien upon buildings for payment of labor or material on such buildings. The workingmen's effort to secure the ten-hour day by law failed. The House of Representatives defeated a proposal for a ten-hour day by a 63 to 13 vote in 1841. Six of the seven St. Louis representatives—all of whom were Whigs—voted for the proposal, but Missouri's rural, agrarian power apparently remained more hostile to such "radical" meas-ures than did conservative Whiggery. The General Assembly did act in 1840 to bring about one change favored by St. Louis laboring groups when it abolished the property and tax quali-fications for voting and office-holding in that city.

The political efforts of pre–Civil War labor were short-lived. After a weak effort in 1842 the St. Louis Mechanics' and Work-ingmen's party died following its failure to muster the strength to put a ticket in the field. With the return of generally good economic conditions after 1842, the workers' organization with-drew from active political activity and ceased, for several years, to be even a strong economic force. Mutual aid and benefit societies became the major organized activity of the workers, although even in social affairs the labor societies appear to have declined in the years just before the Civil War. In 1854 St. Louis factories paid their workers from $2.00 to $2.50 per day, while the wages of other workingmen averaged about $12.00 per week. When the depression of 1857 brought unemployment and a substantial reduction in these wage rates, there was no or-ganized response from the laborers.

The changing economy of the forties increased the needs and pressures for a major change in Missouri banking practices, even though the hard-money Benton Democrats resisted most innovations to the end. The Bank of the State of Missouri was a sound operation, but its conservative management continued to dissatisfy many businessmen. Its highly restrictive note issue was increasingly unpopular, especially with the St. Louis com-mercial community. The General Assembly enacted legislation in the 1840's preventing any state corporation, with the exception of the Bank of the State of Missouri, from issuing notes or en-gaging in any other banking practices. State laws also restricted the circulation of notes of non-Missouri banks. Despite this legislation, some businessmen found substitute methods to provide all banking services except the issuance of notes.

One such approach was to organize savings banks. In 1847 the General Assembly granted a charter to the Boatmen's Savings Institution in St. Louis authorizing it to receive deposits and to make loans, but it could not issue notes. The General Assembly decided that savings institutions were not within the restrictions of the constitution or existing law. The savings bank proved a profitable operation, with no less than twenty-five of them organized by the mid-fifties.

Opponents of the antibanking legislation found an important loophole in the existing statutes. Since the prohibitions against providing banking services applied only to corporations, by mid-century a number of individual and partnership banks had been established to conduct general banking business, excepting the issuing of notes. Fifteen of the state's nineteen nonincorporated banks operated in St. Louis. During the depression of 1857 several of these banks closed, but a number of them did later reopen. With the formation of new banks under more liberal legislation by 1857, there were over forty private banks in the state by the end of the decade.

The banking legislation of 1857 stemmed from the continued internal agitation and the influence of general national practices as all parts of the nation struggled to create a satisfactory banking and currency system. Missourians could see that under general incorporation legislation other states had developed a system of free banking, which was generally understood to mean that the right of entering the banking business was open to all persons on equal terms and that banks might issue notes without restrictions other than a general liability that would be incurred by the issuing institution.

The legislative session of 1854–1855 worked out a proposed amendment to repeal the 1820 constitution's strict one-bank limitation and to authorize the General Assembly to establish banks, up to ten in number, as might be deemed necessary for the interests of the state. Although the amendment permitted an extension of banking services and note issues, it was not free banking, since the amendment did not provide for general incorporation and limited the total number of banks. The proposed amendment created only limited debate as it easily carried both houses. With assurances from Gov. Trusten Polk that the public overwhelmingly supported the proposed change, the General Assembly acted quickly on the banking question in its 1856–1857 session. It ratified the amendment as required by the constitution, passed with only token opposition a new general banking law, and offered ten charters to banking organizations.

In addition to the limitations set by the constitutional amendment, the 1857 law attempted to provide for state-wide needs while safeguarding the public against unsound banking practices and note issues. St. Louis was the home for eight of the ten chartered banks, but by requiring those corporations to establish branch banks at specified locations the General Assembly assured services throughout the state. The law established regulations on the sale of stock and reserved for the state the right to purchase such stock; limited note issues in relation to the amount of paid-in stock; required that specie reserves be maintained and that all notes had to be redeemable in specie; ruled that notes could not be issued in denominations of less than five dollars; set rules to govern loans; and established an office of state bank commissioner to supervise the operation of the banks under the law. The General Assembly selected Claiborne F. Jackson, a hard-money man from central Missouri, as the state's first commissioner. Missouri obviously was not a free-banking state.

Despite the restrictions imposed by law, Missouri banking was soon in deep trouble. Partially because of the national depression of 1857, all but one of the newly chartered banks suspended specie payment, and Missouri currency, which had at an earlier time ranked among the best in the United States, was by 1859 one of the worst. The basic distrust of the old-line Benton men for private currency had not been unfounded.

# CHAPTER VI

# LITERATURE, THE FINE ARTS, AND RECREATION

While they were engaged in the tasks of economic development, Missourians were also pursuing an active interest in the
creative arts and in recreational activities, from which they enriched their society and their personal lives.

In any discussion of Missouri literature certain basic limitations require recognition at the outset. For the purposes of this
book only a limited number of authors and works was included,
and the selection was complicated by deciding just what con-
stitutes Missouri literature. As a general rule this discussion includes only those authors who actually resided in the state and
who wrote about the Missouri scene. It is this literature that best
reflects the society and history of the state. Like other frontiers
Missouri attracted her share of traveling missionaries, adven-
turers, and scientific and general observers who recorded their
experiences. Few of these works had literary merit, but their
extent indicates a wide interest in writing, and their content has
enhanced understanding of the period. Much of this work—
descriptive and in the form of personal experience—nonetheless
merits inclusion in a consideration of Missouri literature.

In 1819 the natural scientist Henry Rowe Schoolcraft published *A View of the Lead Mines of Missouri*, a book of lasting
value for historical reference. As noted earlier, Gottfried Duden's
letters, published in Germany in 1829 under the title *Bericht
ueber eine Reise nach den westlichen Staaten Nordamerikas*
provided vivid pictures of Missouri and of the opportunities that
awaited those who would migrate to the state. While his *Report*
was not literature in the strictest sense of the word, and his descriptions were too romantic and too optimistic, Duden's letters
are still a valuable source of material on early Missouri. One of
the most frequently cited observers of early Missouri life is
Timothy Flint. A Harvard graduate, Flint came to the Missouri
Territory as a missionary in 1816. For a number of years he

resided in St. Charles, but he also traveled widely throughout Missouri. His *Recollections of the Last Ten Years Passed in the Occasional Residences and Journeyings in the Valley of the Mississippi* . . . (1826), considered as an outstanding source on the plant life of the Mississippi Valley, was one of the earliest attempts to describe the life and people in frontier Missouri.

*The Far West* by Edmund Flagg, a lawyer-turned-editor of *The St. Louis Daily Commercial Bulletin*, was published in 1838. A journal of his wanderings over Missouri and Illinois, the work was not entirely original, since Flagg drew frequently from printed sources without identifying them, but his book did make available much information about the West. Like many frontier writers, Flagg employed a stilted style that resulted from an attempt to emulate English authors. A famous Catholic missionary, Pierre Jean De Smet, wrote extensively of his experiences in Missouri and other western regions where he did religious work with the Indians. Coming to Florissant in 1828, De Smet later made St. Louis his home. His book titles—translated from French—included *Letters and Sketches; with a Narrative of a Year's Residence among the Indian Tribes of the Rocky Mountains* (1843), *Oregon Missions and Travels over the Rocky Mountains, 1845–46* (1848), and *Missions De l'Amerique du Nord* (1849).

Closely related to the Missouri scene was John T. Hughes's *Doniphan's Expedition* (1848), in which the author, a member of that expedition, recorded the story of the army of Missourians during the War with Mexico. Josiah Gregg, not a Missourian, published the valuable reference work *Commerce of the Prairies* (1844) after accompanying a caravan to Santa Fe. The experiences of Missouri's famous Christopher "Kit" Carson— trapper, Indian agent, guide, and generally versatile man of the western frontier—reached book form by an indirect route. Carson, who was scarcely literate, dictated an autobiography to Jesse B. Turley, a Santa Fe trader, friend, and former Missouri neighbor. This manuscript was edited by Dr. DeWitt C. Peters and published in 1858 as *The Life of Kit Carson*. *Wild Western Scenes*, by John Beauchamp Jones (1841), was hardly quality literature, but it was popular and still stands as a valuable period work because of its frontier humor and local color. The author secured his material while operating a store during the early 1830's in New Franklin and Arrow Rock. His *Western Merchant* (1849) and *Life and Adventures of a Country Merchant* (1854) related his experiences as a Missouri storekeeper. *Western Border Life; or What Fanny Hunter Saw and Heard in Kansas and Missouri* (1856) has been regarded as perhaps the best portrayal of life in western Missouri and eastern Kansas during the period preceding the Civil War. The author was probably Fanny Hunter, a preacher's daughter who most likely had come west with abolitionists and conducted a school for a western Missouri family.

George Thompson based his book *Prison Life and Reflections* (1847) on his personal experiences as an inmate. The author, a self-styled abolitionist and a ministerial student, came to Missouri in the early 1840's to help carry out a plan for the escape of some slaves. Arrested near Palmyra, he subsequently was given a twelve-year prison sentence for his efforts to free the slaves. The book contained both prose and poetry and was intended to stimulate its readers to labor for the removal of human suffering; lacking in style it nonetheless presented a depressing treatment of prison life, death, and religion. The poetry in Thompson's book was later published under the title *The Prison Bard* (1848).

Sen. Thomas H. Benton achieved some prominence as a writer. At the close of his career in public office he authored a massive two-volume work with the long but descriptive title: *Thirty Years View: or, A History of the Working of the American Government for Thirty Years, from 1820 to 1850 . . .* (1854–1856). With 65,000 copies of each volume sold within thirty days of its publication, Benton certainly had the equivalent of a best seller. Highly critical of the United States Supreme Court's decision in the case of *Dred Scott* v. *Sandford*, Benton produced his *Historical and Legal Examination of . . . the Dred Scott Case, Which Declares the Unconstitutionality of the Missouri Compromise Act, and the Self-extension of the Constitution to Territories, Carrying Slavery Along with It* (1858). Benton was a tireless worker, and just before his death he completed the sixteenth volume, covering through 1850, of his projected *Abridgment of the Debates of Congress from 1789 to 1856.*

Missourians produced few novels prior to the Civil War, and none were of lasting value. Nathaniel Beverley Tucker's *George Balcombe*, published in New York in 1836, was probably the first novel written in Missouri. Although legend has it that upon his arrival in Missouri he set up his law office in a hollow tree, Tucker, a member of an aristocratic Virginia family, had established himself on a farm of southern dimensions in Saline County by 1830, following a successful career as a Missouri lawyer and judge. *George Balcombe* uses a Missouri setting and its plot revolves around two Virginia gentlemen in the West seeking to recover an estate from a villain who is the black sheep of a good family. Throughout the novel Tucker stresses a distrust of democracy and reflects the intellectual biases of his own class.

A decade passed before the appearance of additional Missouri novels. James D. Nourse, a St. Louis newspaperman, attempted not too successfully to portray the adventures of steamboat and frontier life in *The Forest Knight* (1846), a melodrama full of intrigue, duels, sinister villains, crime, fair ladies, and gentlemen. The hero in *The Unknown* (1849), by St. Louis attorney Pierce C. Grace, saves the genteel Lady Harriet and then turns out to be of royal birth himself. Set in London and Charleston, *The Unknown* reveals more about English than Missouri culture. The first known novel written in Missouri after mid-century cast the Jesuits as villains in a tale of horror, conspiracy, and murder. *The Mysteries of St. Louis* (1851) by Henry Boernstein made use of local material, but it reflected too much of the author's intense hatred of Roman Catholicism to have literary significance. Boernstein, a man of varied talents, had greater success in other areas such as promotion of the St. Louis theatre and as editor of the *Anzeiger des Westens*. Augustin Kennerly's *The Heiresses of Fotheringay* (1856), patterned after Sir Walter Scott's romances, and T. Addison Richard's *Tallulah, or The Trysting Rock* (1856) typified the florid but generally inferior literature of the mid-century.

Designed primarily to offer instruction in morality and religion, the works of two St. Louis authors—Anna T. J. Bullard and Sally Rochester Ford—omitted any trace of local or regional color. The Bullard novel, *Matrimony, or Love Affairs in Our Village Twenty Years Ago* (1852), was set in a village near

Boston and warned the reader against the evil resulting from improper conduct in love affairs. The Ford novel, *Grace Truman* (1852), was a near-religious tract emphasizing Baptist doctrines.

Only a few Missourians attempted biographies. Hugh A. Garland, a well-known St. Louis lawyer, produced a two-volume *Life of John Randolph of Roanoke* in 1850. He also wrote a *Life of Thomas Jefferson*, which was at the press at the time of his death in 1854. A fictionalized biography entitled *John Fitch; or The Inventor's Fate*, published in the St. Louis *Weekly Reveille* under the pseudonym of Joe Miller, Jr., was actually written by Thomas (or Thompson) Westcott.

Missourians produced few if any full-length books whose literary style or content distinguished them in any way or gave them claim to any long-time fame. Most Missouri novels, written in a style that was unnatural and florid, represented unsuccessful attempts of inferior writers to copy the widely read English masters. Generally moralistic in tone these early works of fiction often reflected an author's political and religious biases. The most valuable books probably were the travel accounts and the personal narratives describing frontier life. None of the authors were full-time professional writers; they came from all walks of life, but professional men, especially lawyers, appear to have been particularly inclined to write books.

Poetry seems to have been the most common form of creative writing employed by Missourians, but the voluminous outpouring from many pens was far greater in quantity than in quality. As a young man, and perhaps a poverty-stricken adventurer, Angus Umphraville had been in Missouri only a short time when his *Missouri Lays and Other Western Ditties* was published in 1821. In this first book of English poetry printed west of the Mississippi River, Umphraville paid tribute to the great English writers, and then issued the challenge:

> Why not Missouri claim
> Illustrious bards of equal fame?
> Why may she not with Albion vie
> In such a generous rivalry?

Umphraville never created any such rivalry.

After Umphraville's effort no book of verse was published for some twenty years, and only about ten such books came out prior to the Civil War. Students of Missouri literature refer to this early poetry as undistinguished imitations of the then current literary models. A few wrote on Missouri themes, but most of the state's early poets concentrated on such universal themes as love, death, and religion. Lacking the skill to handle the ornate and unfamiliar subjects they so frequently attempted to explore in their works, these poets overworked poetic diction and produced a nondescript verse. In spite of the large quantity of poetry produced, only three book-length efforts were published. John Russel, a self-described school teacher and apparently a picturesque St. Louis character, wrote a small book of repellent but historical poems entitled *A Mournful Elegy on the Unfortunate Victims Who Fell Sacrifices to the Ravages of that Fell Destroyer, The Asiatic Cholera at the Gravois Coal Diggins*. . . . Parley P. Pratt, an apostle in the early Church of Jesus Christ of Latter-day Saints went to prison for resisting attacks against the Mormons. *The Millennium and Other Poems* (1840) represented his attempt to describe the Mormon conflict in Missouri from their point of view. Critics call it poor literature, but it was concerned with a crucial event of Missouri history. George Thompson's *The Prison Bard*, mentioned earlier, also dealt with the emotion-laden slavery question.

Despite their generally poor quality, these poetical outpourings received some acceptance by Missourians. The books of verse apparently had some sale, and newspapers regularly carried large amounts of verse.

To satisfy the demands of prospective settlers and travelers for information about Missouri and to promote the state's resources and appeal, Missouri's publishers put out a number of gazetteers packed with a variety of geographic data. In 1823, Lewis G. Beck published *A Gazetteer of the States of Illinois and Missouri*, the first such work relating to Missouri. An outstanding early gazetteer was Alphonso Wetmore's 1837 *Gazetteer of the State of Missouri*. An interesting and readable book, this publication was more than the usual geographical dictionary. To enliven the regular fare found in gazetteers, Wetmore included stories of the West and bits of dialogue written in the frontier idiom. Here were the characteristics and expressions of "a real horse" of a man, or the threat to "row you up Salt River." Of six short stories included on western life, the best was probably the "Sketch of Mountain Life," which featured mountain man Gall Buster constantly coping successfully with a variety of exciting frontier dangers. Gall Buster typified the frontier character who would become a standard part of this important genre of Missouri literature.

Missouri writers made their greatest contribution to American fiction in their short stories and tall tales, with the short stories providing the best picture of Missouri society. Wetmore's light, humorous style, using material he gathered from travels and conversation with people, made him the most skillful author in the tall-tale form prior to 1840. Along with Wetmore, a small number of able young men in St. Louis developed a great interest in the rich folk stories built around frontier characters and situations. Their works contained the local color of western adventure, the odd character, the practical joker, the bumpkin, the mythical hero, the stories of danger, escape, and physical prowess all described in suitable frontier phraseology. The tall tale was rather rough, sometimes risqué literature with humorous exaggeration as one of its principal ingredients.

Short-story writers produced few books; their stories appeared in newspapers and periodicals including their principal forum, the St. Louis *Weekly Reveille*. John S. Robb, who wrote under the name "Solitaire," was probably the most important of this group of writers. His collection of stories published in 1847 with the title *Streaks of Squatter Life and Far-West Scenes* is one of the outstanding works of the period.

In addition to Wetmore and Robb, the St. Louis group of tall-tale recorders included Joseph M. Field, who wrote as "Everpoint" and "Straws," Solomon Franklin Smith, Charles Keemle, Matthew C. Field, and Noah M. Ludlow. Joseph M. Field had a collection of stories printed in the late 1840's as *The Drama of Pokerville: the Bench and Bar of Jurytown, and Other Stories.* Solomon Franklin Smith, an attorney, writer, and actor, wrote largely in anecdotes. He published his stories widely, and his book titled *The Theatrical Apprenticeship and Anecdotical Recollection of Sol Smith, Commedian, Attorney-At-Law, etc.* (1845) is indicative of the nature of his work. These young writers of the 1830's and 1840's created a native, humorous style in contrast with the earlier stilted attempts at emulating English literary conventions. Missouri tall-tale writers made one Mike Fink the hero of many of their tales. A real-life boatman on the Ohio, the Mississippi, and the Missouri rivers, Fink became a stock character in folklore and in fiction depicting western life, humor, and values. The legendary boatman was a "man's man," but he was also "half-horse, half-alligator"; he was all man, "save what is wild cat and extra lightning." Through folklore, Fink boasted that he could "out-swim, out-swear, out-jump, out-drink, and keep soberer than any man at Catfish Bend."

Missouri authors seldom wrote to champion social, economic, or political causes. Only a very few such as the abolitionist George Thompson hoped to effect any social change. Aside from an emotional concern in some of the less-effective writings for moral issues, Missouri writers generally avoided any involvement in reformist crusades or politics.

Many well-read men resided in colonial St. Louis, and the city contained numerous private libraries. At the time of his death in 1843, for example, John Mullanphy left a library of over 1,200 volumes, including books on history, travel, science, the classics, literature, and memoirs.

During the territorial period nearly every merchant offered books for sale, and in 1820 a store opened in St. Louis dealing exclusively in books and stationery. Newspaper advertisements show that by the end of the first decade of statehood an impressive variety of books was for sale throughout the state. The offerings contained a heavy percentage of works by the best of the eighteenth-century and nineteenth-century writers. The Bible, Homer's *Odyssey*, Milton's *Paradise Lost*, the plays of Shakespeare, the works of Goldsmith, Fielding's *Tom Jones*, and Defoe's *Robinson Crusoe*, along with volumes by Byron, Moore, Pope, and Scott, were among the more popular books stocked by early booksellers. Through their general stores the Aull brothers sold the people of western Missouri a wide selection of standard works for a wide range of reading interests. A bookstore in Boonville in 1845 advertised over a hundred school-books and other titles on a great variety of subjects including medicine, agriculture, encyclopedias, fiction, gazetteers, history, household hints, morals, poetry, and theology. Missourians also often purchased books directly from eastern and foreign dealers. Newspaper usage and the popular oratory of the time indicate widely varying degrees of familiarity with the major works of literature.

The contents of personal libraries in pre–Civil War Missouri varied greatly, but books in the field of religion, history, and practical topics predominated. Literary works by English and American authors were about equally divided in most libraries, although the contents of smaller collections revealed that the frequently assumed common acquaintance with the great masters of literature may be questionable. Book ownership was certainly not exceptional, and evidence indicates that more than one-third of the families in pre-1860 Missouri possessed some books.

As would be expected, individuals in the older, more prosperous areas of the state had most of the larger collections, with the number of families holding over fifty titles increasing after 1830. There was not, however, a clear relationship between wealth and the number of books owned. In contrast with smaller holdings, larger libraries reflected lesser emphasis on religion and a greater interest in secular subjects including the classics, literature, and scientific and philosophical treatises. Private libraries contained numerous books of verse with a much heavier concentration of English than American works. Available evidence indicates that book preferences in Missouri reflected national tastes.

The State Library founded at Jefferson City in 1833, the state's only true public, tax-supported library, held approximately 3,000 volumes at mid-century. Missourians also formed numerous private organizations to operate semipublic libraries. Through the sale of stock for membership these associations most frequently raised capital to purchase books that members could use. The libraries were most generally opened to others on a fee or rental basis. These associations, however, served primarily persons with the financial means necessary to support their reading interest, and their holdings appear to have been heavily weighted toward the moral and informational titles.

The St. Louis Library Association organized in the mid-1820's sold membership shares for $5 each; within less than one year it had acquired over 1,000 titles. Books were available to non-members for a rental fee. The association soon ran into some difficulties and transferred its operations to another organization in 1831, which expanded to serve minors and apprentices for a fee of twenty-five cents quarterly. The Panic of 1837 created financial problems that forced the board of directors to sell some books to pay debts. The association turned its remaining hold-ings over to the St. Louis Lyceum. In central Missouri a group organized the Franklin Library Company in 1819, only two years after the town had been founded, and residents of Fayette established a subscription library in 1826.

The organization of the St. Louis Mercantile Library, which became a nationally known institution, was probably the most important single library development in ante-bellum Missouri. A group of St. Louis merchants who believed that it was sound business to upgrade the educational and cultural level of the men of the business community and to take a positive role in a gen-eral community cultural improvement formed the Mercantile Library Association in 1846. The association, which opened its library to the mercantile community in April, 1846, reported a membership of 261 and a library holding of over 1,000 volumes at its annual meeting held in January, 1847. The association steadily grew, and by mid-century the library subscribed to the best literary, scientific, and professional journals, and the leading United States and foreign newspapers. From its holdings mem-bers could select from a wide variety of titles in history, belles-lettres, philosophy, jurisprudence, government and politics, and theology, along with a limited number of business manuals and vocational instructional materials. When the association moved into the new Mercantile Library Hall in 1854 it held over 10,000 volumes and had a membership of just over 1,000. In addition to its library the Mercantile Library Association regularly spon-sored a lecture series, which featured such notable personalities as Sen. Thomas H. Benton, the Reverend William G. Eliot, Edward Bates, James Shannon, president of the University of Missouri, and Ralph Waldo Emerson.

Community leadership often emphasized the moral uplift, virtue, and concrete economic advantages that came from the use of libraries. The editor of the *Missouri Republican* on January 13, 1850, expressed great satisfaction that young men were using the library in their leisure time and assured, as well as warned, that "The vigilant eye of the businessman can see as well into the drama shop or theatre as into the library, and it will not fail to sift the gold from the dross."

Reflecting cultural interests similar to those involved in the library movement and the production of literature were the lyceums and debating and literary societies that were becoming quite common throughout the state. Residents of Franklin founded one of rural Missouri's earliest debating clubs in 1825. These organizations brought many prominent speakers to Missouri and provided Missourians with opportunities for self-expression and participation in cultural and intellectual discussion. Debating such subjects as "Where Does Fire Go When It Goes Out?" the societies obviously had their entertainment as well as educational functions. These organizations also brought some drama to their communities with dramatic dialogues and colloquies at a time when most local residents considered the legitimate theatre with its scenery, costumes, and make-up to be immoral.

Students often engaged in debates. Their rather flowery analogies were seldom original, but they seriously tackled controversial problems such as the justification of war, whether conscience or law was the greater deterrent to individual action, slavery, and whether the Negroes or the Indians had been most wronged, with probably less caution than their elders. Student speakers in pre–Civil War Missouri were idealistic and certain of their positions; but, most generally, the speakers accepted and sought to encourage the common basic values of the emerging society.

Missourians seemed to prefer oral sources of information, rather than reading for themselves. With oratory considered an art form, Missourians turned out en masse to hear lawyers plead at court, preachers denounce sin, and politicians proclaim the virtues of self and party while they attacked the opposition. Eloquent speakers at holiday assemblies and miscellaneous other gatherings always attracted large crowds. With rolling voices and grand figures of speech, orators played to audiences who loved eloquence. The oratory of Missouri's public speakers, with its emphasis on moral values, religion, and patriotism, reflected the broader values of society. As they praised the nation and its people, orators stressed the ties between democracy and Christianity founded on the Constitution and the Bible. Missourians took their orators seriously as these public speakers fulfilled the expectations and embodied the beliefs of their listeners, and they viewed eloquence itself as a source of liberty and knowledge and as a guardian against evil and tyranny.

The theatre offered another form of entertainment for Missourians. Acting groups in St. Louis presented more than fifty different plays in that community in 1820. Although the number of productions declined in the early twenties as a result of the depression, the theatre made a strong comeback in the following decades.

St. Louis again naturally had the most developed theatre, with more professional actors than the state's smaller communities, and local drama groups and traveling companies both performed for the city's residents. Noah M. Ludlow and Solomon Franklin Smith established that city's first professional theatre company in 1835, and their firm dominated the St. Louis stage until mid-century. "Sol" Smith, a man of diverse talents, was a central figure in Missouri and Midwestern theatre. Born in 1801, Smith was a lawyer, a preacher, and as a youth a journalist in New York; he was also an actor and play manager, and in the early 1820's he became manager of a troupe playing Mississippi River towns. For a time considered one of the nation's leading actors, Smith also wrote with much humor about his life experiences and about people who amused him, although his work has since been described as one "eccentric writing about another." In addition to his diverse talents, Smith actively participated in Missouri's American political party in the 1850's.

The theatre fare for Missourians differed little from that of other Midwestern areas at comparable time periods. Alphonso Wetmore, a Missourian, published the highly successful play *The Pedlar* in St. Louis in 1821. A three-act farce containing a great deal of local interest and color, *The Pedlar* featured Nutmeg, a Yankee peddler with something like a "modern five-and-ten-cent store" in his pack, who successfully wooed Pecanne,

Old Prairie's niece. Missourians presented few plays written by fellow Missourians, or, for that matter, many American plays. Of all the known titles produced in rural Missouri before 1860, only twelve were by American writers, with British plays constituting the bulk of Missouri theatrical offerings. Shakespeare appears to have been the most popular single playwright, and he was more popular in St. Louis and with professional companies than in rural Missouri or with the amateur groups. Theatregoers preferred farces and melodramas to tragedies, and amateur groups especially liked light plays, with well over half of those produced being farces or comedies.

St. Louis theatre patrons were demanding of higher-quality productions. By the mid-thirties regular press and self-appointed critics were finding fault with all aspects of local theatrical performances. In an effort to meet the growing criticism, local theatrical groups began importing star performers to play leading roles. Jenny Lind became a St. Louis favorite, as did English actress Ellen Tree and her husband Charles John Kean. Eastern road companies also played the city, and St. Louis gained the reputation for being a good show town.

St. Louis was the western outpost for the first-rate actors and the better traveling companies. In fact, only fifteen small professional troupes are known to have played rural Missouri before 1860. However, local citizens throughout the state organized their own drama groups, which attracted many of the community leaders. The Thespian Societies, as they were invariably called, appear to have been organized by those who considered rehearsing and performing a more intellectual, cultured form of recreation than partying and carousing. The Boonville Thespian Society at one time had two future judges, the publisher of the local paper, the mayor, a doctor, a lawyer, and a merchant.

Theatre facilities were always a problem. The "Old Salt House," the only theatre building in St. Louis for several years after statehood, came under constant criticism. Charles Keemle, editor of the *Commercial Bulletin*, led a campaign based on civic pride as well as love for drama to raise funds for a new theatre, which opened in 1837 amidst claims that it was unsurpassed by any other in the United States. Rural Missouri communities depended largely on makeshift arrangements, although several amateur groups made a building one goal of their organization. Organized about 1838 the Thespian Society of Boonville first performed in a log theatre, but after two decades it erected the large Thespian Hall in Greek Revival style, undoubtedly the most ambitious building project outside of any in St. Louis.

The pre–Civil War theatre in Missouri faced considerable opposition throughout the state. The leadership of the Catholic Church opposed the "frivolous nature" of the prevailing theatrical performances, which caused the otherwise gaiety-loving and cultured French elements to remain aloof from theatrical productions. Religious opposition came from other sources as well. Shortly after mid-century, the Reverend William Greenleaf Eliot, the popular and liberal Unitarian minister in St. Louis, condemned the theatre as a bad influence on youth. The press generally gave the theatre favorable coverage, but a spirited controversy did develop in St. Louis between Charles Keemle and the reformer Elijah Lovejoy, editor of the *St. Louis Observer*. Lovejoy opposed the theatre on religious grounds, while Keemle supported it as a positive moral force. Many rural Missourians especially demonstrated a hostility toward the theatre performances, which they considered evil, and toward actors, whom they viewed as sinners. Societies and companies made a substantial effort to assure the public that their productions would not be offensive to anyone and that they would be of high moral standards; and indeed, many plays did contain a definite moral lesson. To help offset criticism, local Thespian groups frequently donated admissions to the support of some civil project like a public hall or a school.

At least one effort was made to legislate on the subject of the theatre. Rep. Charles D. Drake, speaking in 1860 in support of a bill to prevent certain practices on Sunday, attacked the "vulgar and obscene theatre" of the Germans and charged that their productions were indecent and offensive to all of "our ideas of propriety." Drake did not speak from first-hand knowledge, for he asserted that he had never attended a German theatre, but the evil, he said, was a matter of public record. The bill did not pass the General Assembly.

In addition to the dramatic productions, traveling wagon

shows and circuses also brought pleasure to many Missourians, although they were by necessity limited to the counties located on the Missouri or Mississippi rivers. No less than sixty-one circuses and menageries toured rural Missouri before 1860. The variety of their programs helped the circuses attract more Missourians than any other type of professional entertainment. Like the theatre, the circus faced criticism from staunch moralists in each community. They created antagonism because confidence men found the circus opened attractive fields for their operations, and circus promoters often failed to make adequate effort to curtail their activities. Local opponents also frequently protested that the traveling shows took money out of the community.

The river showboat was the most colorful of all prewar show business enterprises. At first the showboat offered primarily vaudeville or circus acts, but popular melodramas soon became an important part of their programing. The arrival of the showboat always generated tremendous excitement as showmen with steam calliope, bands, and parades enticed people to the performances.

Many other forms of entertainment were available to Missourians. The Negro minstrel gained popularity about 1850; professional dancers were also a part of the fare, with ballet being performed as far west as St. Joseph. A wide range of individual or team performers, including singers, dancers, readers, comedians, magicians, and ventriloquists, performed throughout the state, with the latter two especially welcomed by rural Missourians. Traveling lecturers were also common, with phrenology being one of their most popular subjects. Missourians could be quite gullible, too, as indicated by the newspaper advertisements of spiritualists, fortune-tellers, and a variety of traveling novelties and freaks.

Missouri had an abundance of newspapers; in 1820 the territory had five, and the number increased with every decade, despite a high mortality rate among fledgling publications. In 1850 Missouri counted fifty-four papers, and by 1860 the number had grown to 148, including fifteen dailies. Printer-editors with both altruistic and personal motives, governmental needs for publication of laws and other official actions, popular demand for information and amusement, and the desire of politicians and political parties to influence public opinion all contributed to the establishment of frontier newspapers.

Frontier publishers generally conceived of their function in the broadest possible terms. They often promised their prospective subscribers that they would include essays on agriculture, commercial, literary, moral, and religious subjects, news of foreign and domestic intelligence, proceedings of Congress, and coverage of the actions of the state government, and that they would keep their papers open to all who wished to express themselves on issues of public concern. An editor would proclaim the press and individually his own paper to be vital forces in a democracy and guardians of personal liberty. As an early editor, Thomas H. Benton equated the newspaper in America with the forum of Greece and Rome as a powerful institution to shape man's mind and to influence a proper course of public policy. The pioneer editors also considered belles-lettres, novelty, politics, and ideas to be news; most made an effort to put literary quality into their own writing.

Few editors were able to live up to the promises made in their prospectus. In general, Missouri newspapers did contain some works of local writers and of favorite national and international authors, as well as a large amount of foreign and national news, much of which was copied from eastern papers. The public printing took up considerable space, but politics overshadowed all other areas of coverage and undoubtedly played a key role in the expansion of the press. Congressional debates and the speeches of major political personalities frequently filled many columns of a single issue. As political parties took more definite shape and as contests became more heated, politicians increasingly considered the press an effective instrument to advance their cause and, consequently, a necessary instrument to combat the opposition. Election years usually produced new newspapers, most of which disappeared after the elections.

Newspapers devoted relatively limited attention to general affairs such as agricultural conditions, commercial and business development, religious life, and the ordinary community social relationships, nor did the Missouri press take a lead in promoting municipal or local improvements. While newspapers might present information in support of a civic project, they seldom initiated or acted as prime movers. Nathaniel Patten, considered by some historians as Missouri's leading pioneer county editor, wrote only four editorials on roads—a primary need of any frontier area—throughout his career from 1819 to 1835. There were, of course, exceptions. William F. Switzler through his *Missouri Statesman* in Columbia campaigned positively and aggressively on behalf of many programs of public interest including the University of Missouri, railroads, plank roads, street improvements, a courthouse, and fire protection. Switzler's paper, prominent in the forties and fifties, has been recognized as a leader in moving Missouri journalism out of its pioneer stage.

The early papers were rarely launched without some assurance of a revenue from public printing or from more direct political financing. Besides the revenue gained, the printing of official proclamations, laws, legislative journals, militia orders, and the like helped boost circulation. Victorious parties used government printing contracts to reward the faithful and to punish the opposition. The state government for several years distributed its printing throughout the state, but the procedures were far from satisfactory, and the work was not well done. In 1845 the General Assembly adopted a measure authorizing the legislature to name a single state printer to work under a system of specifications, inspection, and pegged prices. Those who supported the law as both a political reform and as a way to secure more efficient printing services were disappointed in its outcome, but further pre–Civil War efforts to establish a spoils-free system of contract printing by bids on a business basis failed.

To launch a newspaper was no easy task. With the average capitalization of newspapers between $1,500 and $1,700 as late as 1840, the capital requirement was not too great, but production was much more difficult. Irregular and undependable frontier transportation made it difficult for editors to secure a press, type, paper, and other necessary printing supplies. Even after a paper mill was established in Boone County in 1834 and a type foundry in St. Louis in 1840, publishers still had to secure much of their material from eastern concerns.

Profits were always uncertain. A printing historian estimated that a newspaper with a fair amount of advertising and 600 subscribers was marginal; on that basis, very few newspapers in the state could have shown a profit. An early common subscription price was $3.00 in advance or $4.00 at the end of a year. By the 1840's prices were $2.00 to $3.00 in advance and $2.50 or $3.50 at the end of the year. Publishers had to be willing to take payment in kind, although frequently they got neither money nor kind. Newspapers did serve more people than subscription lists would indicate, for they circulated from hand to hand—something the editors did not appreciate. Many newspapers failed for financial reasons, and the same editor would seek a new location to try again. It was the direct financial support given by politicians and parties or by public printing contracts that kept many newspapers operating.

Early editors were generally also printers, and one individual usually performed all of the operations in getting out the pioneer newspaper. With the development of the press as more and more of a political vehicle, a politician-editor would push the printer into the role of craftsman. The personality and role of Missouri editors in the early decades are difficult to assess. In general they were colorful men seeking recognition and influence, but because of their individualistic personalities, frequent moves, poor business management, and the changing processes of their business, most never achieved the status they so strongly desired. An editor had to be a brave man to face almost constant threats from opposing editors, politicians, and unhappy readers, but as a group Missouri editors remained staunch defenders for the freedom of the press.

The legal questions of libel and extent of freedom of the press have been historically complex ones. The Bill of Rights of the Missouri Constitution of 1820 carried the usual guarantee for freedom of the press. Prior to the Civil War, Missouri law limited the press only on coverage of the subjects of fornication and adultery, and incitement of Negroes to rebellion. In all cases of libel the "truth" was allowed as evidence, and a jury was to determine facts and apply the law under the direction of the court. In actual fact, the balance between freedom and libel was not well struck. There was a lack of restraint and some instances of irresponsible journalism, especially in periods of heated political campaigns; editors often printed information about individuals that was emotionally charged, vindictive, and derogatory—much of it false. The "truth" against such charges was, as it has always been, hard to prove in a court, and even then it was often too late to correct the damage already done. Few Missourians believed the occasional abuses as serious as the potential danger from greater legal restrictions upon the press. Since politicians were the primary subjects abused in the newspapers, perhaps Missourians considered them fair game.

The transition from a frontier to a modern press occurred gradually and at different rates in various parts of the state. Perhaps the change began in St. Louis as early as 1836 with the establishment of the first daily and was sustained and strengthened by the advent of the power press, a larger capital investment with more complex business organization and increased concern for profit as the end, the specialization of work, a greater self-imposed restraint, the improvement of transportation and communications, and a new emphasis on local news. These changes were most pronounced in St. Louis and other important population centers and least noticeable in rural areas, so that full transition remained incomplete by 1860.

Throughout the period a number of newspapers began production to serve special groups of people, organizations, or causes. In August, 1832, the first issue of *The Evening and the Morning Star* appeared in Independence. The paper, under the editorship of William W. Phelps, was an organ of the Church of Jesus Christ of Latter-day Saints, and a hostile mob forced its closing the following year. Just before the Mormons were driven from the state in 1838, a second Mormon press began business at Far West in Caldwell County. Elijah P. Lovejoy published a religious journal, the *St. Louis Observer*, in St. Louis in the mid-thirties. Lovejoy was a minister in the Presbyterian church, but the church had no official connection with the paper. An outspoken foe of slavery, he came uncomfortably close to espousing abolitionism for slaveholding Missouri, and a mob destroyed his press. While on the one hand the law proclaimed freedom of the press, unpopular and unorthodox journals did not flourish, and, on the other hand, papers such as the Catholics' *Shepherd of the Hills* published regularly and without harassment.

The *St. Louis Advocate* founded in 1833 became the first newspaper devoted to promoting the interests of labor. Temporarily reorganized as the *Missouri Argus* while under the editorship of William Gilpin, the paper followed a class conflict theme and damned American aristocracy. After Gilpin's brief stint as editor the paper adopted a more moderate stance.

Missouri also had a number of foreign language presses. The *Anzeiger des Westens*, a pro-Benton German paper, was started in St. Louis in 1835; the influential *Westliche Post* began publication in 1857. The *Volksblatt*, an important paper for a German area outside of St. Louis, was started in Hermann during the mid-forties. The German papers were the most successful and influential of the foreign language press, in part because of the large number of German-speaking Missourians. Most of the French journals were short-lived; *Le Revue de l'Ouest*, started by the French Literary Society of St. Louis in 1854, was probably the most successful.

Of Missouri's many pre–Civil War newspapers, some played particularly important roles in the state. The *St. Louis Enquirer*, one of the state's earliest papers, helped advance the political career of its editor Thomas H. Benton. The most important early paper in outstate Missouri, the *Missouri Intelligencer and Boon's Lick Advertiser*, brought out its first issue in April, 1819, at Franklin. Located on the edge of the Missouri frontier, this paper experienced the problems and hardships of a frontier press as it served the emerging society. The paper was moved from Franklin to Fayette and then to Columbia where its long-time editor Nathaniel Patten sold it in 1835 to a Whig buyer after both party groups had tried to purchase it. The paper finally passed to the ownership and editorship of William F. Switzler in 1841. Switzler renamed it *The Missouri Statesman* and made the paper one of the most influential in the state. The *Statesman* became a powerful supporter of the Whig party and joined the Democratic ranks after the party upheavals and reorganizations of the 1850's.

William Lusk, Sr., founded the *Jefferson Inquirer* in Jefferson

City in 1838. The paper's location in the state's capital city frequently won it the state printing contracts. An influential Benton paper that strongly supported his hard-money policies, the *Jefferson Inquirer* modernized relatively early and issued the first daily west of St. Louis in the 1840's. The *Daily Missouri Democrat* was an important later paper and the forerunner of the current *St. Louis Globe-Democrat*. Born at a time of heated controversy in a changing city of the early 1850's, the paper was launched by the Free-Soil Democrats and later became the chief organ of the emerging state Republican party. As its first editor, the energetic, militant, and controversial Frank Blair made the paper an influential one.

Missouri offered a splendid opportunity for artists who wanted to capture the natural grandeur of the country through landscape painting, to sketch the original inhabitants of America, or to portray on canvas the life and society of a frontier people. Unfortunately, most budding artists made Missouri only a temporary base of operations. No less than forty graphic artists had worked in St. Louis before 1840.

Probably the two most famous artists of the American Indian who worked in Missouri were Charles Bodmer, who traveled with Prince Maximilian of Wied on his western tour in 1832–1834, and George C. Catlin, who remained in St. Louis briefly. Chester Harding, a portrait artist, came to Missouri in 1820 to capture the famed Daniel Boone on canvas. While in the state Harding found additional subjects of interest, as did other portrait painters who followed him. The Frenchman Charles Alexandre Lesueur sketched village and frontier scenes in 1826; painting in the 1840's, Rudolph Friedrich Kurz of Switzerland used old buildings in St. Louis and Indian groups near St. Joseph as his subjects. Charles Deas came to the Mississippi River valley from Philadelphia in the early 1840's and settled in St. Louis, which he described as providing all that a painter could desire in patronage and appreciation. Deas painted such characters as "Long Jake," a mountain hunter, "The Indian "Guide," "The Voyageur," and "The Trapper." For the last five years of his life, Peter Rindisbacher lived in St. Louis where he produced his Indian genre and miniature specialties. Two other artists of significance were Manuel Joachim De Franca of Portugal, a fashionable artist in St. Louis, and Sara M. Peale, whose reputation is based primarily on her portraits.

The German-born Carl Ferdinand Wimar—probably Missouri's second-ranking pre–Civil War painter—came to St. Louis in 1843; although he returned to Europe for study in the 1850's, he made Missouri his home. Wimar's fame rests primarily on his western frontier scenes, especially his work on Indians and their habitat for which he traveled to Indian reservations for the scenes he recorded on his canvas. Wimar did four elliptical paintings of historical significance for the St. Louis Courthouse, which were completed during the early years of the Civil War.

George Caleb Bingham was clearly Missouri's outstanding early artist. Coming to Franklin in 1819 at the age of eight, Bingham spent his boyhood in Howard, Cooper, and Saline counties observing the new state in its formative years. A dynamic and restless mind and a determined and outspoken character aided Bingham in his role in the political controversies of his day. As a Whig he became a long-time friend of James S. Rollins, the prominent central Missouri political figure. A fine conversationalist, as well as a versatile, talented man, Bingham was more than an artist and he combated in an untiring and fearless manner anything he felt was wrong.

Bingham excelled in at least five areas of artistic achievement: portraiture, landscape, historical painting, figure sketching, and genre. In all of these he successfully captured the world he knew so well. Bingham painted not for other painters, but for a living world. His subjects varied greatly, but all received the keen understanding and sympathy of the artist. It has been said that he was not "a satirist, a reformer, or a moralist," but an artist of contemporary observations. To him an ordinary experience or an everyday occurrence offered the artist a creative challenge. Whether painting farmers, politicians, boatmen, or town drunks, Bingham displayed humor and warmth.

From Bingham's art, masterpieces of naturalness and simplicity, the viewer receives lasting impressions of Missouri scenes of the artist's time. "Raftmen Playing Cards" and "The Jolly Flatboatmen" depict river life, while "The Verdict of the People," "Stump Speaking," and "County Election" portray frontier politics. Several of his important works were done after the

Civil War; his famed "Order No. 11," created in 1865 but not exhibited until 1868, was perhaps his most controversial work and the creation of a man with strong convictions. Eastern critics often disapproved of Bingham's subject matter and found fault with his use of color, but Missourians appreciated his work and found it to be reflective of the life they knew firsthand.

A unique art form for mass entertainment was the panorama, and the Mississippi River valley was a favorite subject for this type of painting. An audience would watch a panorama, which was painted on long strips of canvas, being unrolled as they listened to a commentary describing the scenes. Of six known Mississippi panoramas, five of them were painted by Missourians.

From the beginning of statehood, most leading Missouri families had a few pieces of good art, and within two decades some individuals had assembled impressive art collections. Over twenty-five St. Louis citizens loaned valuable paintings for a benefit exhibition for orphans in 1838. One collector, Joseph Philipson, left more than 400 prints at the time of his death in 1844.

Commercial shows of art works had started as early as 1819 and progressed extensively during the following years. As national transportation improved, more art exhibitions came to Missouri, although mostly to St. Louis. Works of America's most important early school of painters—artists who painted Hudson River landscapes—were popular in Missouri. The St. Louis Mercantile Library Association began to assemble a permanent collection of art, which it offered first for public exhibit in 1846. Beginning in 1857 painting exhibitions became a regular part of the popular annual St. Louis Agricultural and Mechanical Association Fair. Early in the 1850's a St. Louis group began to advocate the establishment of a museum of art. The Western Academy of Art, established in 1860, had its work disrupted by the outbreak of the Civil War.

During the early decades of the nineteenth century American settlers coming to Missouri brought with them the old ballads that had crossed the Atlantic with them. Americans added to the old ballad form new subjects of their own experiences such as the glorification of the Fourth of July, political campaigns,

and frontier experiences. This musical literature, rather unsophisticated and covering a wide range of human emotions
including tragedy, love, honor, glory, and humor, were nevertheless an important part of the state's early musical history.
Although there is claim that the popular ballad of "Joe Bowers
from Pike," which was related to the decade of the gold rush,
was originated by Pike countians, Missourians and the Missouri
scene of the pre-Civil War period do not appear to have contributed substantially to this form of music.

There were many amateur musicians among Missouri's early
settlers. The most popular instrument was the fiddle, and "fid-
dling" was an important entertainment form, supportive of
many social activities. When dance time came, such tunes as
"Old Dan Tucker," "Zip Coon," and "Fisher's Hornpipe" were
favorites for the jig and the four-handed and three-handed reel.

Other Missourians brought with them a love and appreciation
for the more sophisticated and developed musical forms. The
decade of the 1830's was marked by a great increase in the general interest and appreciation of music. German migration
contributed substantially to the growth of musical interest and
involvement in the state. Fond of good music, German communities throughout the state organized choral and instrumental groups to offer entertainment and to provide a form of
recreation and enjoyment for their members. Churches, schools,
and special musical associations often sponsored these groups.

No later than 1839 there were at least three local instrumental
groups performing in St. Louis. The most important of the
early organizations was the St. Louis Musical Society Polyhymnia, established in the mid-1840's under the direction of
William Robyn. Private musicians and teachers throughout the
state organized smaller less-sophisticated groups of musicians
that frequently presented concerts and recitals. Band concerts
were popular, and many towns took great joy and pride in their
bands. "Opera of a sort" came to St. Louis in 1837, and ballet
arrived in 1839. Opera and musical comedy also appear to have
been popular as a form of entertainment to prewar Missouri.
Traveling singers presented both popular and operatic programs.
Jenny Lind's appearance in St. Louis in 1851 created so much
excitement that the house was sold out, and hundreds of tickets,

regularly priced at $5, were sold at a premium. A single concert of Miss Lind's netted $9,600, with an average price per seat of $9.

Among Missouri's important musical personalities, Johann Weber contributed much to the musical life of St. Louis. A court councilor of Coblenz in Germany and a scholar and musician of "superior attainment," he came to St. Louis in 1834, bringing with him a library that included works of such masters as Bach, Beethoven, Gluck, Handel, Haydn, and Mozart. Weber opened a music academy, taught music at St. Louis University, and organized the St. Louis Sacred Music Society. William Robyn, another German, came to St. Louis in 1837. As a teacher at St. Louis University he was the first to use a fine collection of instruments that had been brought from Belgium. Weber and Robyn did some limited composing, but Charles Balmer was a more prolific composer than either of them. Balmer wrote several hundred piano pieces and numerous songs and also founded and conducted the Oratorio Society. In 1849 Balmer, in partnership with C. Henry Weber, opened a music store and publishing house in St. Louis. August Waldauer, coming to St. Louis in 1844, produced a variety of compositions including schottisches, marches, polkas, and waltzes, and he was also a sentimental dittyist, writing such tunes as "I Love But Thee" and "Two Hearts That Beat As One."

Literature and the various arts all provided recreation for Missourians, but in their pursuit of pleasure the people took part in many other social activities. The first settlers in a new area had to be willing to undergo a period of loneliness, but few of them were antisocial beings, and they eagerly sought associations to bring pleasure into their lives. Most regions would have to wait several years for much formal organization for leisure time pursuits or for commercially sponsored opportunities to be brought to them.

The so-called "bee," where people got together to perform some necessary work and then turn the occasion into one of pleasure and recreation, continued to be a common Missouri institution. There were all kinds of bees—house-raising, barn-raising, corn-shucking, sewing, sap-collecting—for work and play.

Many other occasions justified a community gathering and

related recreation including weddings, church meetings, political speakings, militia musters, and even funerals. The recreational activities for all such occasions continued to reflect the characteristics of skill, strength, and speed needed and prided on the frontier. There was competition in running, jumping, riding, shooting, wrestling, and fisticuffs. Participants in the latter were seeking a championship, but this also afforded an acceptable way to settle personal quarrels. The most popular part of any gathering that included both men and women was the dance, which usually was the last event of the day, and whiskey never seemed to be in short supply.

Horse racing was very much a part of Missouri life, and nearly every community had a race track. The Jockey Club at Franklin had been holding three-day racing meets since before statehood. Very probably the good horses were owned by the more wealthy people, but racing events regularly attracted large crowds from all classes, and most participated in various degrees of wagering. Cockfighting had some popularity in the state, but it never gained the widespread public acceptance afforded to horse racing.

Fairs were an increasingly popular institution, and there were at least thirty of them lasting from two to six days in 1858. Practically all were agricultural fairs sponsored by a local agriculture society to exhibit items for improved farming and award prizes to the best farm produce, but they were also major social and recreational events.

The Fourth of July was the event of the year. The day featured parades, bands, sporting events of all kinds, orations, dramatic readings, and an abundance of food and drink, while calling forth special oratory damning England and King George III and praising America and American patriots.

Inns or taverns—although operated primarily to earn a profit for the owner—were an institution that served many purposes. Located in cities, towns, and along the routes of travel, they offered food, bed, and hospitality to new settlers and travelers. Frequently one of the earliest buildings in an area, the tavern became a center of activity. Missouri taverns provided a place to welcome newcomers, hold religious services, draw up dueling rules, discuss politics, lay out new towns, pass along information, and served as a social center for members of the community.

In the urban communities the pursuit of pleasure took a somewhat more sophisticated form than in the rural areas, because the greater number of people offered increased organizational and financial support. Elegant balls contrasted sharply with the frontier dances. In St. Louis balls had been common in the territorial period, and they developed into increasingly elaborate events of that society. All towns were "ball" towns, even if not in the league with St. Louis. *The Boon's Lick Times* in 1841 carried an article about such a ball in Boonville, which the paper's correspondent described as a glorious affair with more beauty and fashion than he had ever seen at any one such affair.

Great banquets, a prominent part of the more urban life, usually were held to honor a historic event, person, or special achievement, or to promote such things as a public improvement or a political campaign. The banquet offered food, fellowship, drink, and the opportunity for a wide range of speech and toast making.

The Mississippi River was a special recreational source available to St. Louisans. People could take excursions on the riverboats in the midst of beautiful scenery or attend dancing parties and theatre performances. Steamboat races created great excitement, and a favorite winter sport was ice skating.

Many of these various activities were, for some, not recreation but sin and debauchery, and they did not go unchallenged. For religious reasons some persons opposed all dancing. Missouri ministers and social reformers attacked gambling, card playing, drinking, and any recreational activity on Sunday, all of which fell afoul of the rules of most churches. Many of the newspapers supported the development of cultural activities for their community while at the same time condemning drinking, fighting, and cockfighting. Such actions of opposition may have put some restrictions on the more extravagant forms of recreation, but Missourians continued to enjoy themselves in their accustomed manner.

# CHAPTER VII

# THE SEARCH FOR
# SOCIAL IMPROVEMENT

While Missourians enriched the cultural and recreational opportunities of the state, they were also working toward improvements in the areas of education, religion, medicine, and social
reform.

Territorial Missouri had done little to promote public education, but the Constitution of 1820 mandated:

> Schools, and the means of education, shall forever be encouraged
> in this state, and the general assembly shall take measures to pre-
> serve, from waste or damage, such lands as have been, or may
> hereafter be, granted by the United States for the use of schools
> within each township in this state, and shall apply the funds,
> which may arise from such lands, in strict conformity to the
> object of that grant, and one school, or more, shall be established
> in each township as soon as practicable and necessary, where the
> poor shall be taught gratis.

Thus, although the constitution assigned the General Assembly
a responsibility in establishing a system of free public schools,
it implied that the township was to be the basic administrative
unit, while failing to require taxation or the appropriation of
other public revenue for school support.

Prior to the Civil War, the General Assembly enacted much
legislation setting forth purposes, programs, administrative procedures, and methods of financing a state system of public
schools. This legislation provided for a continuous, if irregular,
growth in centralized planning as major school leaders pushed
for greater state-wide standardization and coordination. Missouri's schools nonetheless remained largely under local control
—a reflection of both the New England township system and
the strong, contemporary Jacksonian emphasis upon local popular participation in public affairs. At the state level the General
Assembly continued to hold the reins. Chief executives made

recommendations, but the school laws were largely the work of the legislatures. In creating a state board and state superintendent of schools, the various assemblies assigned them the minimum supervisory or discretionary authority to shape the educational system.

Several early Missouri governors suggested the need for greater action in the field of education, but the first significant state effort to launch an organized system of public schools did not begin until Gov. Daniel Dunklin's term (1832–1836). The extensive recommendations made by the Dunklin-appointed Hertich Commission were not accepted, but the General Assembly enacted a much improved school code in 1835, which established a State Board of Commissioners for literary purposes, set the school term at six months, and designated a curriculum including reading, writing, arithmetic, geography, English grammar, and other subjects as funds might justify. Theology was not to be taught.

The 1835 code had not yet been implemented when the General Assembly replaced it with the Geyer Act in 1839. Providing for a comprehensive system of public schools at the elementary, secondary, college, and university levels, this measure reflected Thomas Jefferson's views on education, and the university received authority to oversee the entire structure. Despite its merits, the over-all plan was too complex, too standardized, and too costly to be realistic in frontier Missouri. Many Missourians objected to the highly centralized system, and even though it remained as the basic school law until 1853 state officials never attempted to implement its provisions.

Prior to mid-century, Missourians tried to finance their public schools primarily from endowments created from national grants and fees. The slow development of tax-supported schools was a reflection of the attitudes of the numerous settlers coming from the South, where education was traditionally viewed as a private concern, as well as of frontier Missouri's inadequate tax base. Since federal land grants made only limited amounts of money immediately available, other means of support would be necessary to the establishment of the first public schools. Community efforts, with families agreeing to share the costs, created most of the earliest schools, or teachers sometimes took the

initiative in organizing a subscription school with the fees paid
to them. With voter approval in 1825 the General Assembly
authorized districts to establish a school and to bill the parents at
a rate in accordance with the number of children attending. The
plan did not fire many people's imagination, however, and few
schools were established under this law. An 1835 state law giving counties authority to vote a small property tax represented
a small step toward public support for schools, but it was repealed in 1839. The General Assembly continued until 1853 to
reject all other proposals for appropriating public revenue or
authorizing taxation either at the state or local level to support
education. The proposed new constitution of 1845 included a
mandate that the General Assembly create a public school system
and that it levy taxes for educational purposes—a mandate that
ultimately contributed to the defeat of that document by the
voters.

The General Assembly did enact important legislation establishing more effective management of the several national
grants for educational purposes in the late 1830's. It established
a Common School Fund with Missouri's share (approximately
$382,000) of the 1837 distribution of the national surplus, along
with other monies received from the sale of saline lands granted
to the state at the time of Missouri's admission into the Union.
The Common School Fund was set up as a permanent endowment, with the interest earned from it to be used to support
public schools, although the legislation stipulated that no distribution could be made until the principal reached $500,000.
The first distribution totaling about $2,000 went to counties with
organized school districts on the basis of sixty cents per child in
1842. New legislation enacted in 1839 provided for a more
orderly and permanent system of handling the revenue earned
from the original national grant of the sixteenth section in every
township—a total of over 1,200,000 acres. The law authorized
the sale of these sections whenever three-fourths of a township's
voters approved, with the money raised going into a Township
Fund to be managed by the respective county courts. The township lands were sold for an average of slightly over $2.00 per
acre. The County School Fund, the origins of which are clouded,
was formed as early as 1825, when the General Assembly pro-

vided that fines, forfeitures, and penalties should be set aside for the use of schools in the county. An 1839 act continued this arrangement, and additional sums from the sale of swamp lands granted to the state by the national government contributed to the fund.

With these limited funds supplied primarily by the federal government, Missouri first attempted to establish and finance its public schools, but the amount was totally inadequate. The General Assembly defeated a bill in 1853 requiring each county court to levy an annual tax for schools. In the legislative debates, opponents of the measure stressed the unconstitutionality of delegating a legislative power more than they openly opposed a tax to support public schools.

In subsequent action that same year the General Assembly adopted the Kelly Act, which required that 25 per cent of the state's general revenue be apportioned among the counties to support public schools. Some political and educational leaders had long been stressing the importance of providing equal educational opportunities for all citizens in a democracy; these traditional values in American education now had a greater popular support, and the Kelly Act received strong support from members of both political parties. It substantially boosted the total amount of state financial aid, with the state distribution increasing from $27,751 in 1850 to over $262,000 a decade later, but a rapid increase in the number of school age children greatly reduced the impact of this increased state assistance. The Kelly Act also designated the county, with a county commissioner of common schools, to replace the township trustees as the principal educational administrative unit.

The General Assembly failed to grant authority to local governmental units to levy taxes for educational purposes, but it did enact special legislation in 1849 authorizing the city of St. Louis to levy a small tax on personal property if approved by a majority of resident property holders. Ten years later special legislation authorizing the city school board to levy a limited tax without a vote of the people was passed.

Unfortunately, the school funds were often subject to willful mismanagement, which the General Assembly frequently sanctioned by special legislation. Authorities most commonly misused the school funds by loaning them to finance internal improvements without securing adequate collateral. While no outright corruption was involved, the failure to complete the projects often led to default on the loans made from the school funds.

Initially the General Assembly apportioned state money only to organized school districts, thereby depriving needy counties of financial aid to implement the creation of new schools. However, in 1855 the legislature approved a statute allocating funds to all school townships organized or unorganized. Supporters of equalization also defeated a proposal in the mid-1850's to limit state distributions to not more than one-fourth of the amount of state revenue collected in the county, on the grounds that the proposal would have increased state aid to the more wealthy counties and decreased it to the poorer areas. Throughout the period, the state limited its consideration of public schools to the elementary level. A high school organized in St. Louis in 1852–1853 was Missouri's first public secondary school, with a second in St. Joseph not opening until the eve of the Civil War.

Churches, various organizations, and some individuals operated private elementary schools. These appealed to many Missourians, including some of the state's more prominent residents, who liked a church-related education or the status connected with private schools. Secondary education was almost exclusively a function of private schools commonly called academies. Only seven academies had been chartered by 1830, but the General Assembly granted charters to over ninety academies in the next three decades. Although private institutions, the chartered academies, exempt from taxation, operated under regulations imposed by the state in their charters. Charters usually required the academy to be coeducational, although few girls ever attended, and to admit children of the poor free of charge—for which the institution frequently received a share of the state's distribution of school money. Approximately 100 additional private academies operated before 1860 without charters from the state. Private school organizers frequently sold stock to secure capital to launch their institutions, and they then depended upon tuition and donations from interested persons or organizations to support regular operations. Some individuals organized academies to make a profit, but few succeeded. In addition to the regular schools, churches operated Sunday schools that often provided instruction in reading and writing along with the regular religious lessons.

State school authorities made efforts to set a standard school curriculum and operating practice. After the initial 1835 law to establish a curriculum, the state superintendent in 1855 issued a curriculum outlining a uniform elementary course of study based on a graded system and suggesting specific textbooks. This curriculum emphasized arithmetic, declamation, English composition, geography, grammar, music, orthography, reading, and writing, with graded offerings in algebra, astronomy, chemistry, geology, geometry, history, juvenile natural philosophy, logic, mineralogy, philosophy, rhetoric, and surveying. In spite of the high hopes and ambitions of the planners, in actual practice the schools were poorly organized and rarely had either teachers or the equipment necessary to carry out the provisions of the prescribed curriculum. Most private academies offered instruction in two departments: the junior branch curriculum, which included arithmetic, geography, history, literature, reading, and writing; and the senior branch curriculum, which included algebra, astronomy, botany, chemistry, composition, declamation, English language, French, geometry, Greek, history, Latin, logic, natural philosophy, rhetoric, surveying, and trigonometry.

While there were variations among individual schools, there was a common pattern in school operations during the pre–Civil War years. In Johnson County, for example, residents started a school in 1833 only six years after the first permanent settlement had been established. The parents paid the teacher, and students met in farm homes and a smokehouse until a log schoolhouse was constructed. Just as soon as the community was able it replaced the log building with a frame structure. These Johnson County residents, like their counterparts elsewhere, actively sought to provide educational opportunities for their children under adverse frontier conditions, even though this first school was sadly lacking in equipment and textbooks. After its formal organization in 1834, the residents presented a request for the formation of a school district as the first regular petition to come before the Johnson County court. The court honored the request, but, since no public funds were available, the school started as a subscription school. Subjects taught were reading, writing, arithmetic, spelling, history, penmanship, and music, with the teaching technique primarily rote memorization, reciting lessons in a singing rhythm—a practice common throughout the state. The state superintendent's 1855 curriculum attempted to end this method of instruction, but the impact of his order remains unclear. Finances were a constant problem, illustrated by the fact that a third Johnson County school operating a six-month term in 1849 received $53.60 public money and $5.00 per student from the parents.

Missouri school statutes made no special reference to race until legislation in the late forties prohibited the teaching of any slave to read or write. Traditionally, however, both slaves and free blacks had been denied any regular educational opportunities in Missouri. Free blacks regularly paid taxes to the city of St. Louis on property assessed at hundreds of thousands of dollars, but their children could not attend the city's schools.

Despite these barriers, a number of blacks achieved substantial levels of educational attainment. A few masters taught their slaves to read and write, while others permitted them to receive such instruction elsewhere. The slaves who learned some basic skills frequently instructed others. Henry Clay Bruce, once a slave in Missouri, recorded that his mother had each of her children educate a younger one; Bruce read well enough to understand the political situation and in fact favored Frémont in 1856—no doubt in a very quiet way.

Outside of the school system some whites, usually ministers, helped blacks secure at least a rudimentary education. John Mason Peck, a well-known Baptist minister, encouraged all blacks to attend his Sunday school in St. Louis, where several of them received limited instruction. Peck's work typified similar activities by other ministers. A group of St. Louis nuns operated a regular school for black children. The schools established, financed, and operated by the free black residents of St. Louis undoubtedly offered the best opportunity in the state for Negro children to secure an education; unfortunately little is known about these schools.

As a group, Missouri's early teachers varied greatly in ability and preparation. Many came into a district to teach and then moved quickly on to another school or out of the profession, but others remained. Some came from the best families in the community, some were drifting misfits, but most of them were as well trained as were members of other professions. Some of Missouri's teachers had received their education outside of the state, but Missouri's private schools and academies, lacking a teacher-training curriculum, nonetheless staffed most of the state's elementary schools. Regardless of the extent of training, the teacher's task was not an easy one. Limited facilities as well as student bodies composed of all grades and ages were serious handicaps to the teachers. The frequent financial dependence upon subscription payments and the practice of boarding with the parents must have discouraged many from even entering the profession.

School officials and educational leaders continued to advocate professional teacher training and normal schools, but Missouri failed to take steps to initiate any programs in this area prior to 1860. The city of St. Louis did, however, establish a training program for its teachers. Following eastern examples, Supt. Charles A. Putnam first organized normal training classes in 1854, for which the students were required to spend time as observers in the city's best elementary schools. Following its opening in the early fifties, the city's new high school included a normal instruction department. The organization of the Missouri State Teachers Association in 1856 reflected a growing professionalism among teachers themselves. The association added to the existing agitation for teacher training programs.

The extent of literacy is some measure of an area's educational facilities. According to the national census, even though interstate movement of people affected literacy rates, of Missouri's white population twenty years of age and over in 1840, 14.8 per cent could not read or write; twenty years later the figure had dropped to 12.3 per cent. For the same years, the Illinois percentage dropped from 13.9 to 6.7, while the national figure remained almost constant at approximately 8.5 per cent.

Numerous colleges sprang up throughout Missouri in the prewar years; some were short-lived, but others remain in existence today. Churches supplied the leadership, organizational effort, and financial support for most higher education. Established to train ministers, many of these church-related colleges soon expanded their programs into other fields.

The Right Reverend Louis William DuBourg, Bishop of Louisiana, laid the foundation for the first university west of the Mississippi River in 1818 when he helped organize a Latin school known as the St. Louis Academy. Renamed the St. Louis College after an enlargement of its curriculum, the institution encountered difficulties in the late twenties that apparently forced a temporary suspension of classes. The Society of Jesus assumed control of the lagging institution in 1829, bringing to it much added support. Three years later the General Assembly approved a charter for the Jesuit-sponsored institution to be known as St. Louis University. The university initiated a graduate program in theology in 1834, added postgraduate medical study in 1836, and a law department in 1843.

Maj. George C. Sibley and his wife, two pioneers in the education of women in Missouri, launched Lindenwood College as a finishing school for young ladies in 1829. Prior to moving to their nearby farm where they located the new college, Mrs. Sibley had taught a few girls in their St. Charles home.

Missouri Baptists were expressing the need for a church-related college to train young men for the ministry as early as 1834. The idea gained substance in 1843 when Dr. William Jewell of Columbia offered to give the General Baptist Association lands valued at $10,000 for a church college. After intense effort an endowment of almost $60,000 was raised, and the decision was made in 1849 to establish a Baptist college at Liberty and to name it William Jewell. The institution opened in 1850 with 137 students. Dependent upon tuition (from which candidates for the ministry were exempt), the school quickly encountered financial difficulties that forced it to close in 1855. A drive among Clay County residents and Missouri Baptists to increase the school's endowment enabled William Jewell to reopen in 1857.

Fulton College began operation in that town in 1851 to provide young men of the Presbyterian church with higher education. When it received a state charter and synod support in 1853, the school changed its name to Westminster College. Central

Methodist College, chartered as Central College in 1855, opened its doors to students in Fayette in 1857. Christian College for women, now Columbia College, supported by the Disciples of Christ, was founded in Columbia in 1851; the same denomination sponsored Christian University, now Culver-Stockton College, which began operations at Canton in 1853. Columbia Baptist Female College, now Stephens College, was incorporated in Columbia in 1857. In 1853 the General Assembly chartered the Eliot Seminary in St. Louis. When namesake Dr. William G. Eliot, a distinguished minister of St. Louis, requested that it not retain his name, the board redesignated the school as Washington Institute and finally as Washington University in 1857. The General Assembly granted the school a liberal, perpetual charter giving the governing board wide latitude in operating the school, although it prohibited instruction that was sectarian in religion or partisan in politics. The charter also precluded any sectarian or party test for the selection of the staff of the university and exempted all property held by the institution from taxation.

St. Mary's Seminary, organized at Perryville in 1818, continued to train Roman Catholic priests after statehood. Concordia Theological Seminary, set up in 1839 at Dresden, moved first to Altenburg and then to St. Louis in 1849; the school trained clergymen for the Lutheran Church Missouri Synod. The German Evangelical Church's Eden Theological Seminary began operation near Marthasville in 1850 as Marthasville Seminary.

Of the several short-lived colleges, Marion College near Palmyra was probably unique. Dr. David Nelson, a Presbyterian minister, came from Kentucky to found this institution of higher learning in a relatively rural area of the state. Granted a charter by the General Assembly in 1831, the college operated a program of student manual labor on college farm land to enable young men without adequate financial means to secure an education. Nelson, although originally a slaveholder, had become an aggressive antislavery advocate whose agitation against the peculiar institution made him *persona non grata* in slaveholding Marion County, so much so that heavy local pressure forced him to give up the college presidency and leave the state in the mid-1830's. In 1835 a Presbyterian theological seminary opened in conjunction with the college. Marion College could boast a program of considerable merit, several eastern professors on its staff, and some eastern financial support, but growth continued to be slow. The college closed during the depression, and the Masonic Grand Lodge of Missouri purchased its property in 1842 to open the Masonic College of Missouri to provide a college education for orphaned children of deceased members. Somewhat later the Masonic Grand Council moved the college to Lexington.

The University of Missouri in Columbia was the state's only public institution of higher learning before 1860, and because the General Assembly had failed to provide it with any public financial support it was not a large or flourishing institution. Confusion initially surrounded the university's structure, programs, and purposes. The Geyer Act, which authorized creation of the institution in 1839, contained a complicated educational plan providing for a university board of curators and a president having general administrative supervision and control over all other public colleges, seminaries, and academies in the state. The measure made no provision for a university faculty, and each college was to be self-governing and grant its own degrees. State action in establishing the university was not a party issue, although the Whigs probably favored higher education more than the Democrats.

The General Assembly passed the university bill only after agreeing that the proposed institution was to be located in whichever of the six central Missouri counties—Boone, Callaway, Cole, Cooper, Howard, and Saline—offered the greatest inducement for the university site. Boone, Callaway, and Howard counties actively competed for the university, but Boone County's offer to provide a cash subscription of over $82,000, along with land valued at over $35,000, made it the winner.[1] An unselfish devotion to the cause of higher education did not fully explain the generous bidding. Many leaders did have a sincere interest in the university, but the potential funds that the

1. When it learned that Howard County had purchased 200 acres of land at $30 per acre and valued it at $80 per acre in that county's offer for the university site, the Boone County committee bought 222 acres for $25 per acre and included that land in their bid at a value of $75 per acre.

university would bring into the community helped win support from merchants, real estate owners, and other special interest groups. Moreover, the opportunity to provide education for the youth of the community at considerable savings, along with the prestige of being the seat of a university, generated considerable backing for the campaign.

Boone County's offer provided land along with some immediate funds for the construction of buildings, but for its operations the university had to depend on student fees and on the income from the seminary fund, which the state had created with receipts derived from the sale of federal lands set aside to support such an institution. Following legislative provisions made by the General Assembly in the early thirties, all but about 3,000 acres of the land had been sold by 1839; the revenue was invested in the seminary fund, the interest from which—after the principal reached $100,000—was to be used to operate the university. State authorities invested the monies in stock of the Bank of the State of Missouri, from which the university received its first return with a $1662.30 dividend in 1842. Income from the fund was totally inadequate for operating and developing the school, but the General Assembly repeatedly refused to appropriate monies from the general revenue to supplement the university's limited income.

The governing body of the university was a board of curators composed of fifteen free white males elected biennially by a joint ballot of the General Assembly. The board named John Hiram Lathrop, who held a professorship of law, civil polity, and political economy at Hamilton College in New York, head of the new university. Without buildings or staff, President Lathrop utilized the facilities of Columbia College, which the city leaders had organized in 1833 hoping it might attract the university, until the completion of the first university building in 1843.

The newly formed university, enjoying the distinction of being the oldest state university west of the Mississippi and the third oldest west of the Allegheny Mountains, initially offered the traditional four-year liberal arts course. Despite its limited offerings during the prewar years, a substantial percentage of its graduates went on to professional careers. Nearly 40 per cent of the graduates during Lathrop's administration (1841–1849) became lawyers. In 1846 the university established a nominal connection with the Missouri Medical College in St. Louis, which would serve as its department of medicine. Dr. Joseph N. McDowell, a brilliant if sometimes erratic medical pioneer, had established a medical school as a department of Kemper College, started in St. Louis in 1836. The school continued as the Missouri Medical College after the demise of Kemper. The university added a program of civil engineering in 1849.

President Lathrop and Governors John C. Edwards (1844–1848) and Austin A. King (1848–1852) recommended the creation of a normal school in connection with the university to no avail. Early efforts of Sen. James S. Rollins to establish a professorship in the theory and practice of teaching at the university likewise failed. The General Assembly did approve legislation authorizing a limited number of students to attend the university tuition free, providing they agreed to teach in the state at least two years, and other students attended the university taking those regular courses that might aid them as future teachers.

Despite Lathrop's able and dedicated leadership the university grew slowly in its early years. In 1853 the school reached its peak prewar enrollment with 180 students. A substantial portion of those who did attend the university during its first decade were from central Missouri, especially Boone County, and the student body was strongly aristocratic and Whiggish in tone.

At mid-century bitter partisan politics involving slavery and the struggle for control of the Democratic party racked the university. The anti-Benton wing of the party managed to reorganize the Board of Curators in 1849. The new board openly criticized Lathrop's administration, treated him contemptuously, and forced him to resign. Charges made against Lathrop for being an antislavery advocate were not justified, but he was not sufficiently proslavery and was too closely associated with Boone County's Whig leadership to please the anti-Benton Democrats. After a short period with an acting president, the curators selected James Shannon, president of Bacon College in Harrodsburg, Kentucky, to head the university. Although relatively unknown to the curators, Shannon's active support of slavery must have pleased even the most partisan of the anti-Benton Democrats. Having been instructed by the board to speak throughout the state in behalf of the university, Shannon, who was also a minister, frequently discussed religion more than education in his many public appearances. A dramatic platform performer, he fashioned an elaborate and emotional biblical defense of slavery, which he often delivered. When the Shannon administration added some new tutors to the university's staff, the opposition charged that the institution was running a "speakers bureau" for the anti-Benton, proslavery forces of the state.

Understandably, President Shannon's actions pleased members of one political group, while alienating many other influential Missourians. Men like William F. Switzler and James S. Rollins found themselves completely cut off from the institution they had done so much to help establish. The more extreme B. Gratz Brown, editor of the *Missouri Democrat* and member of the General Assembly, denounced the "scoundrel" occupying that "sacred" desk inculcating youthful minds with "such treasonable and outrageous sentiments." Charges that Shannon had transformed the university into a school to train "Campbellite" ministers added to the growing discontent.

The Whigs and Benton Democrats joined forces against the Shannon administration in the 1852–1853 session of the General Assembly, creating a committee to investigate the teaching of party politics or sectarian doctrines at the university. Resentment from the university community concerning the action made it impossible for the committee to conduct a full and accurate investigation, but it did file a "not proven" report. The Whig-Benton coalition then struck at Shannon in an indirect way when it pushed through legislation in the General Assembly in 1855 disallowing any member of the university staff to preach or to practice any other profession. The board stuck by Shannon, but he declined reappointment because he could not have continued to preach. The law also eliminated the connection between the university and the medical school in St. Louis because that school depended on practicing doctors for its staff rather than on academics.

Injection of politics into operations hampered the university's internal effectiveness. The General Assembly reorganized the board to suit political motives and interjected itself, as did the board, into routine operational and academic matters unrelated to the broad policy and financial questions normally considered by such bodies. Despite its economic and political difficulties, however, the university broadened its scope considerably by the 1850's. In 1855 the General Assembly required the board to establish a primary school at the university to aid in the training of teachers, and a normal professorship, although short-lived, was established in 1856. The university lost much of its early provincial and elitist image as it began to attract a growing number of students from throughout the state representing a wider cross section of Missouri's population. Critics of this trend charged that the university had lowered its standards, while actually it was taking on a greater role in serving the interests of the entire state.

Social life was as yet limited; the university did little to promote or to provide extracurricular activities. It operated no dormitories, food services, or union facilities, leaving these up to the town, and did not allow students to spend time after classes in university buildings. The opening of the two colleges for girls in Columbia increased opportunities for sociability. Debating and literary societies, although considered quite academic, did provide for some socializing and student competition. Freedom was far from unrestricted, as illustrated by a rule requiring all students to pass through President Lathrop's lecture room going to and from classes so that he could keep them under his watchful eye. In addition, the faculty set policies governing off-campus conduct, but enforcement appears to have been lax.

Missouri's organizations for the advancement of knowledge and the dissemination of information were not limited to the schools and colleges. Libraries and museums were a part of the state's educational and cultural scene. The Western Academy of Natural Sciences in St. Louis was of special significance. The academy, founded in the 1830's to further altruistic aims, to explore the West, and to discover natural resources, reorganized as the Academy of Science of St. Louis in 1856. Dr. George Engelmann, a scientist, Dr. Frederick Adolph Wislizenus, a natural historian, and Karl Andreas Geyer, a naturalist, took active roles in the organization and helped give it a strong German influence. Through the publication of articles and the support of a museum and a library the organizations served as vital focal points for the exchange of information and ideas while advancing scientific knowledge and making the public aware of more sophisticated intellectual activities.

As on other frontiers, Missouri offered endless opportunities to ministers and organized churches. The Catholic Church had enjoyed official sponsorship during the Spanish period, but many cultured, nominally Catholic French families, influenced by such liberal writers as Rousseau, Voltaire, and Thomas Paine, openly criticized religion and the church. Freethinkers could also be found among the better-educated, upper-class American inhabitants. On the other hand, many rank-and-file Missourians preoccupied with their daily routines remained largely indifferent to formal religion. Ministers and other intensely religious-minded people viewed Missouri's early society as being overrun with drunkenness, gambling, fighting, general disorder, Sabbathbreaking, and upper-class freethinking. John Mason Peck, a prominent early Baptist missionary, described the Anglo-American population in 1817 as a low and indecent grade of infidels. Some twenty years later a New York visitor depicted St. Louis as a wicked city containing an excessive number of deists and infidels. In 1857 a strongly religious young lady from the East traveled through eleven Missouri counties and found widespread evidence of irreligion and the lack of churches. When seen through such eyes, Missourians had made limited religious progress by the time of the Civil War, when, in reality, the vast majority of early Missourians were strongly religious individuals anxious to have ministers and the church come into their communities.

St. Louis served as a center for Catholicism for Missouri and a wide western area. With the arrival of Bishop DuBourg in 1818, the Catholic church underwent a revitalization and resumed its active role in the religious life of St. Louis. In the early statehood years, however, the Baptist and Methodist churches, just starting to work in the urban communities, challenged the long-established Catholic dominance. St. Louis, as the urban center, attracted other religious groups as well; the first Protestant Episcopal church in Missouri was founded there in 1819. Because of its formalized nature the Episcopal church attracted few members in frontier and rural Missouri, but after the mid-thirties it experienced new growth. Unitarianism appealed less to Missourians; a congregation was formed in St. Louis in 1834, but there were only three Unitarian churches in 1850, one of which was out of existence by 1860. A few Jews entered the Missouri territory, and the state's first synagogue opened in St. Louis in 1839. Following the organization of Missouri's first Presbyterian church in 1816, that denomination grew rapidly and appealed predominantly to town people.

During the pre–Civil War period most Missourians resided in rural communities. At the time of statehood, the Methodists and the Baptists were the two most active denominations in rural Missouri. Soon thereafter the Cumberland Presbyterians and the followers of Alexander Campbell began to work actively in Missouri's rural areas. Like the more numerous Methodists and Baptists, they offered a philosophy and followed a technique that won special favor with most Missourians. Missourians joined these churches in great numbers because of their less formalized creed and ritual, greater democratic organization, willingness to emotionalize the personal experience with God, and offer of quick salvation and immediate membership in the church.

Given the sparse and scattered population, the traveling preacher was a central figure in the religious life of the young state. The Methodists are generally credited with developing the most effective use of the circuit rider, but traveling ministers from several denominations worked against the elements, fear of ambush, and numerous other inconveniences in their efforts to carry religion to isolated people. The people welcomed them and freely offered lodging in their homes. These ministers frequently organized new congregations or classes that met regularly to hear lay preachers or to study between visits of the preachers. As soon as a community gained an adequate population to support a regular church, they constructed permanent buildings and hired a resident minister.

The camp meeting, a frontier institution that predated statehood, had a place in Missouri throughout the pre–Civil War period. While the Methodist church made the most extensive use of the camp meeting, other denominations held such meetings, and some of them were interdenominational. As on the national level, Missourians gathered in large numbers at the meetings, which usually lasted for several days, in a highly charged emotional atmosphere. Many came expecting to be converted or to encounter new personal religious experiences, and the camp meeting ministry generally accommodated their expectations. Ministers frequently and with little difficulty worked the hopeful listeners into a near frenzy by placing great stress on the universal sin of all men and on the personal responsibility for salvation through a complete change of character. The physical manifestations of a religious change evidenced by the jerking of the body, rolling, barking, dancing, and the holy laugh were common, and too often people gauged the success of a meeting by the level of emotional fervor it generated. The camp meeting also offered the advantage of socialization to the isolated, which undoubtedly contributed to the attendance.

The excessive emotionalism of camp meetings caused some to question their effectiveness and desirability. John Mason Peck accepted the camp meeting only if properly regulated, but he disapproved of any induced excitement to produce conversions. Many sophisticated people remained skeptical and sometimes hostile toward the camp meeting, which they considered to be assemblies of the more ignorant and illiterate part of the population. Yet, even with its apparent faults, the camp meeting provided a religious experience and an opportunity for worship otherwise unavailable to many people on the frontier.

Techniques employed in the camp meetings reflected practices commonly used by most frontier preachers. In their efforts to guide their flocks, ministers emphasized the fear of eternal punishment more than the glories of virtuous living and eternal bliss, and they repeatedly attacked sinful living. Sin was not a vague abstraction, but a condition ever present and easy to specify —dancing, card playing, horse racing, gambling, swearing, drinking, fighting, and the quest for material goods—many of the things most enjoyed by the typical frontiersmen. Because most ministers believed the day of judgment was real and that it was at hand, there was a great urgency in their messages: "Repent now or face eternal darkness," was a constant theme.

A tendency to overemphasize the emotional aspects of the

frontier ministry has created a distorted image of an uneducated, illiterate, almost crude ministry, when in fact, the ministers differed little in the extent or nature of their training from that of other professionals and businessmen. The Catholic, Presbyterian, and Congregational churches, for example, established educational qualifications for entering the ministry. Although other denominations, like the Methodists and Baptists, granted a license to preach after a satisfactory trial sermon, few of the ministers were totally unprepared or unqualified. Most of the ministers of the "democratic" churches had at least a grade school education, and many had additional preparation. The worst offenders in the excessive play on emotions were most often the reformed drunkards, gamblers, and like characters who had turned to the ministry to save others from a similar fate.

During the decades of the 1830's and 1840's Missouri's religious practices and patterns underwent considerable transformation. Regular churches with full-time ministers gradually replaced the circuit riders and camp meetings. Most Missourians for a variety of reasons gave active support to bringing a permanent, fully organized church facility into their community. Individual desires for religious fulfillment, a commonly accepted assurance that religion with its traditional manifestations improved the community, and the promotional value in attracting new settlers all contributed to community efforts to found churches. Many relatively small towns had more than one church; a two-church town was most frequently Methodist and Baptist; the three- or four-church town had usually added a Presbyterian or Christian church or both.

Like the other social institutions, church organization and administration became more structured and centralized as Missouri outgrew the pioneer stage. The Methodist Episcopal church organized annual conferences of representatives from local churches in the region, who collectively served as the governing agency. Each conference was divided into districts, which in turn had a presiding elder. The national governing body of Methodism was the General Conference, with delegates from all over the nation, which appointed a bishop to preside over each annual conference.

The Baptists did not establish such a centralized structure because one of their most basic principles was congregational autonomy. They did form voluntary associations of local churches for denominational cooperation, but they lacked any governing authority. Several Baptist associations had already formed in Missouri when the denomination organized the Baptist Central Convention to cover the entire state in 1834; this became the Missouri Baptist General Association in 1838. The Disciples of Christ (the Christian church) held regular annual state meetings after the mid-1830's. Preaching dominated the early meetings, but after mid-century the state meetings became planning sessions for cooperation among the individual congregations.

The other denominations had a more structured organization carried over from the East. The Presbyterian and the Congregational churches worked out a "Plan of Union" under which individuals of the two denominations joined to form a single church congregation. The plan seems to have operated especially well in the sparsely populated areas where neither group could sustain a church organization. By 1840 the Plan of Union had created considerable controversy and was discarded, although the subject continued to generate debate within the Presbyterian church.

With the advent of a more structured church organization, early frontier cooperation diminished and denominational rivalry increased, with greater emphasis being given to special doctrinal beliefs and creeds. The differences between Methodists and Baptists over such questions as man's free will and the necessity of baptism by immersion intensified after 1840. The increasing number of Christian ministers called with great zeal upon all to unite in one creedless, nonhierarchical, nonpresbyterial fellowship based on the Bible and simplicity of the early church of the Apostles. Other denominational ministers in turn proclaimed more vigorously their own creeds to offset the work of those they labeled "Campbellite preachers."

The religious diversity of migrating Germans influenced greatly the state's religious nature. Some of the German immigrants were Catholics, and they held strictly to that faith after their arrival in Missouri; those whose backgrounds were in the Reformed and Evangelical churches were representative of a liberal Lutheranism, while a conservative Lutheran group of approximately 600 came from Saxony in the late 1830's. This Saxon group, strongly evangelistic in advancing their conservative doctrinal purity, had a rather cool reception in the state from other German immigrants with different religious views, but these Saxons joined in forming the Lutheran Church Missouri Synod, organized in Chicago in 1847. Those Germans who came to Missouri with less fixed denominational loyalty most frequently joined the Methodist church.

Church membership statistics for this period are lacking or totally unreliable, and even the accuracy of the number of churches of various denominations is questionable. The census figures reporting an increase from 880 churches in 1850 to almost 1,600 in 1860, however, do reflect significant religious growth within the state.[2]

In addition to its role in winning converts, providing a religious experience for its members, and making available educational opportunities, the church also influenced the more general character of Missouri society. The majority of Missourians strongly opposed any connection between church and state, but organized churches supported various attempts by the state government to regulate personal conduct and to fix moral standards. Missouri statutes, for example, made laboring on Sunday a serious civil offense. Although many ministers and church groups participated in the temperance movement, Missourians failed to respond with legislation to advance this cause.

Most of the churches tried to regulate the moral conduct of their members in accordance with a church-made code. Domestic affairs, drinking, gambling, swearing, Sabbathbreaking, fighting, and general moral behavior came under review of the church. The Methodists added the wearing of costly apparel,

---

2. The census tabulation of 1860 provides an indication of the relative strength of the various denominations:

| Methodist | 526 | Presbyterian | | Episcopal | 18 |
|---|---|---|---|---|---|
| Baptist | 458 | (Cumberland) | 98 | Jewish | 2 |
| Christian | 150 | Roman Catholic | 88 | Unitarian | 2 |
| Presbyterian | | Lutheran | 55 | Mormon | 1 |
| (Regular) | 127 | Union | 54 | | |

singing songs or reading books that did not contribute to the love of God, or laying up earthly treasures to the list of forbidden fruits. The moral codes and trial procedure for those accused of violating them were similar for all denominations. The accused, after being charged by either a member of the church or the minister, was tried before the congregation or a committee thereof, with the local minister presiding. If the church had higher governing bodies, findings of guilt could be appealed. Jacob Lanius, a Methodist minister, recorded in 1836 the necessity of expelling a member for "getting beastly drunk." The Bear Creek Christian Church ousted a member for intoxication and for beating a slave girl to death, while another member received the same penalty for gambling. The Zoar Baptist Church of Saline County found one of its members guilty of gross immoral conduct for obtaining money under false pretense. The accused left the area before the trial, but the church went ahead with the proceedings and struck his name from its rolls. Satisfactory evidence of repentance normally resulted in relief from the penalty imposed by the churches. After a member admitted to a charge of making sugar on Sunday and stated his intention to continue doing so, the Mt. Prairie Presbyterian Church ousted him from the congregation; but, when a few months later he demonstrated adequate evidence of repentance, they reinstated him. Local circumstances often affected the proceedings, and wide discrepancies sometimes existed in both practices and punishment, even within a single congregation.

Obviously, the churches exercised little influence upon the conduct of the numerous individuals who maintained no formal church affiliation, although a large segment of the community considered a proper relationship with a church to be important either from an honest concern for personal salvation or from a concern for community acceptance.

Some of the opposition to the moral crusading of the churches came from lawyers, who especially criticized the churches for getting involved in affairs more properly left to civil authorities. In disciplining its members for actions that are generally defined as civil offenses the church probably contributed to establishing a higher degree of order and morality on the Missouri frontier than otherwise might have been, but it is doubtful that the church codes and courts served in lieu of the civil institutions in the early years.

Missourians objected to any participation of the organized church or of individual ministers in politics. A minister seeking public office or using his pulpit for political purposes lost influence with the congregation and often his job. There were many kinds of ticks, Jacob Lanius commented, but "Polly Ticks" were the most injurious for Methodist preachers.

In all sections of the state there were churches in pre–Civil War Missouri with both white and black members, and rules for church membership do not appear to have distinguished between the races. According to Missouri law, a slave needed his owner's permission to attend a religious service, but the churches rarely required any specific consent, even for membership, since most slaves attended their master's church. There is little evidence that the churches practiced a segregation of the races in the actual services. Some informal seating division undoubtedly existed, but attempts to segregate the races were probably less rigid than in the postwar years. Churches did generally exclude blacks from social affairs and any role in church administration. The church program and the nature of services were also primarily designed to serve whites, and some churches scheduled separate meetings designed to appeal more to black members. Negro ministers licensed by some of the denominations and some preachers without license often spoke at such meetings, but these were far from independent congregations. Henry Clay Bruce recounts the story that a black minister's wistful comment about being "free from death, free from hell, free from work, free from white folks, free from everything," brought a threat from the white master present to revoke the minister's license. Clergymen appear to have been free to minister to the religious needs of the blacks so long as they did not take any action, by word or deed, to disrupt the institution of slavery or create slave discontent.

There had been a few Negro churches in the state before the Civil War, but state law and public opposition made their existence difficult. The statutes forbade slaves from holding religious services and required the presence of white officials at any religious gathering of blacks presided over by a black minister. In 1822 the First Methodist Church in St. Louis reported ninety-five white and thirty-two black members. A few years later the church segregated the congregation, although for some time the same minister served both. The Methodist Church Missouri Conference reported a total membership of 22,408 white and 2,329 blacks in 1846. The black Baptists of St. Louis organized a congregation in the early 1830's, which they designated the First Baptist Church. The pastor was Berry Meacham, a former slave who had managed to purchase his freedom and was also a rather well-to-do St. Louis businessman. Other black churches were operating in St. Louis before the Civil War, including at least two designated as the First and Second African Church and an African Methodist Episcopal Church. Richard Anderson, a highly respected black minister, presided over a church congregation of a reported 1,000 members about equally divided between whites and blacks.

The intensification nationally of the controversy over slavery produced a North-South split in major church denominations. While it was at a national level and unrelated to any specific conditions in the state that the break first came, Missourians and their churches had to consider their own positions and their relationship to national bodies. In border-state Missouri most churches supported slavery without commitment to the "positive good" theory, and they also opposed abolition.

In most ways the split that occurred in Methodism is indicative of the problem with which all of the nationally organized churches were confronted. Most Methodists sought to avoid an absolute choice or a direct confrontation, but a growing radical group in the North demanded that the slaveholders either give up their slaves or the church, and they attempted to use the national governing body to force the issue. A major confrontation occurred over the status of Bishop James O. Andrew of Georgia. Bishop Andrew had acquired slave property by marriage and by inheritance. The fact that Georgia law prohibited an owner from freeing his slaves in that state, and that one of the slaves refused to accept his offers to send her to the Liberian settlement of former American slaves or to a free state in the North, left the bishop with limited alternatives. Northerners condemned him for accepting the services of slaves and for never having spoken out on the evils of the institution. He could have, his critics said, moved North and then freed them. The General Conference held in New York in 1844 in effect suspended Bishop Andrew from office, with the four Missouri delegates voting against the suspension. The General Conference appointed a committee to draft plans for an amicable settlement of the slavery problems, or, if this proved to be impossible, to draft and recommend plans for a friendly division of the church. The committee reported a plan for division that included the right of the southern churches to form a new conference and to retain within that conference ownership and full control of their property. Delegates from the southern churches convened in Louisville in 1845 and decided upon separation. They organized the Methodist Episcopal Church, South and called a meeting of the first General Conference for the following year.

Missouri Methodism, which was heavily southern in its position on slavery, considered the national plan of division at the annual state conference in 1844. The conference approved separation and sent delegates to the conference of the southern churches. Delegates from the churches with heavy German membership were the sources of the limited votes opposing this action. A minority in many Missouri churches opposed separation, but this group most generally followed the action of a clear majority in joining with the Methodist Church, South. A few Methodists did leave their church voicing angry charges against the action of the local churches as well as against that of the state conference, which voted 86 to 14 to join the Methodist Episcopal Church, South in 1845. The Methodist Church of the North was left without an organization in Missouri until a dozen Methodist ministers meeting in St. Louis organized a new Missouri Conference, which affiliated with the Methodist Church, North in 1849. By 1859 this church claimed about 6,000 members, but it represented only a fraction of Missouri's Methodists, since the Southern Conference claimed almost 44,000 members in the state. Unfortunately, the desired friendly separation failed to materialize in Missouri. In the decade of the 1850's both groups launched evangelistic and competitive efforts for new converts. With some ministers of the northern church becoming involved in the limited abolitionist activity, any past love or tolerance gave way to increasingly bitter and hostile confrontations.

The major national connection for the Baptist churches in the 1840's was the joint Triennial Convention of the General Convention of the Baptist Denominations in the United States for Foreign Missions and the Baptist Home Missionary Society. The denomination's common unity was strained when some southern associations sent protests to the 1841 Triennial Convention against the antislavery activities of northern Baptists. A group of northern churchmen meeting in Boston in 1843 projected a new Baptist Association if the forthcoming Triennial Convention did not take action to end any association with slaveholders. Moderates managed to table the slavery question at the 1844 convention, but it was only a temporary respite. Southern associations appear to have forced the national association into making a decision that, regardless of how it was made, would disrupt the national connections by bringing before the foreign mission board nominations of slaveholders for appointment as missionaries, and they demanded a statement of policy on the eligibility of slaveholders for such positions. When the board declared slaveholders disqualified, the associations of the slaveholding states withdrew from the existing national groups and formed the Southern Baptist Convention in 1845. The following year the Missouri Baptist General Association formally joined the Southern Baptist Convention.

The Presbyterian church division over slavery came much later than the Methodist or Baptist breaks. Starting in the late 1830's other internal questions had caused Presbyterians to group themselves into an Old School and a New School. Antislavery partisans in the New School wing forced the issue in the 1857 General Assembly of the church, causing all Presbyterian synods in the slaveholding states to sever connections with the national organization. Within Missouri the Old School policy of ignoring the slavery question remained popular, and attempts by members of the as yet small New School to raise the issue caused many Presbyterians to switch their affiliation from the New to the Old School churches.

Persons migrating to Missouri in pre–Civil War years did

not find a healthful situation. Illness was frequent and the threat of disease constant. Malaria and cholera posed the greatest health danger, but other ailments that threatened Missourians included ague, a malarial fever, scarlet fever, measles, mumps, smallpox, whooping cough, and dysentery. Like their counterparts elsewhere, Missourians knew little about the prevention or cure of illness.

Most Missouri doctors practiced medicine on the basis of the late eighteenth-century theories, which explained diseases as resulting from irritation or excitement. Consequently physicians commonly attempted to depress or to calm the patient by means of bleeding, physicking, sweating, diuretics, and emetics designed to purge the body of all irritations. After depression the patient received tonics and stimulants to rebuild the body. In their training and treatments, Missouri's medical practitioners were in step with nationwide prevailing practices. The best qualified had attended a medical college; others without such opportunity studied with an established doctor. Men with such backgrounds were considered "legitimate" doctors. Physicians varied greatly in their efforts to continue formal medical study, to keep abreast of recent medical knowledge, and to conduct research of their own, but most of them had at least a modest collection of the most used and approved texts of the day dealing with general medical practice, anatomy, surgery, specific diseases, pharmacology, and midwifery.

Missouri doctors occasionally differed with nationally accepted standards. Some of them questioned the commonly held theories of disease and related treatments, and, by practicing medicine on a basis of the observation of actual results from the application of cures and treatments, they contributed to an important transition in medicine. An important example of a new practice was the use of quinine to treat fever generally and malaria specifically, pioneered by Missouri's Dr. John Sappington.

Sappington earned a diploma from a one-year medical course at the University of Pennsylvania in 1815. Even the great Dr. Benjamin Rush could not dissuade Sappington from questioning the current theories for the treatment of disease. Setting up a practice in territorial Missouri near Arrow Rock, Dr. Sappington launched a nonconforming practice in which he soon began to attack bloodletting, purging, and other related treatments. He experimented with quinine, which he found to be an effective treatment for fever. Other doctors had tried quinine to combat fever, but they had used it as a stimulant after depressing the patient; Sappington used it immediately. In the early thirties he began to devote much of his time to the manufacture and wholesale marketing of "Dr. Sappington's Anti-Fever Pills," one of the best-known patent medicines of the century. People desperate for relief from malaria and related fevers bought the pills by the millions. Sappington's use of quinine represented an important advance that soon became standard practice. Sappington also authored *The Theory and Treatment of Fever*. Published in 1844 for the general public as well as for doctors, it was written in nontechnical language and sold at a low price.

To many of his peers the seller of quinine pills was no medical hero. Some members of the medical society in St. Louis charged him with being a vender of quack pills, and they denied him membership in the society. Very probably most of the St. Louis doctors objected to Sappington's society membership primarily because he secured a patent for his pill and then acted as manufacturer and wholesaler.

Missouri had other physicians of national stature. Dr. William Beaumont of St. Louis probably had the widest reputation of Missouri's doctors in research and writing. The army transferred Dr. Beaumont, a military surgeon, to Jefferson Barracks in 1834. Well received in the city, he soon established an extensive practice in St. Louis in addition to his duties as an army surgeon. For several years Beaumont had conducted gastric experiments by observing the digestive processes through a fistulous opening in the upper abdomen of a French Canadian voyageur. Dr. Beaumont published the results of his experiments in *Experiments and Observations on the Gastric Juice and the Physiology of Digestion* in 1833. The book won wide attention, was translated into foreign languages, and was credited with launching modern gastric research.

Efforts to advance medical knowledge and to bring a higher degree of professionalism into the practice of medicine centered largely in St. Louis. The first medical journal west of the Mississippi River, the bimonthly *St. Louis Medical and Surgical Journal*, began publication in 1843, and the *Missouri Medical and Surgical Journal* was launched two years later. St. Louis also claimed the state's only two medical schools.

A license to practice medicine was so easily secured that outright medical quackery was a growing problem. Sharp practitioners and clever advertisers, these quacks dispensed their services, drugs, and sure cures for every known health problem to a gullible, uninformed, and unprotected public. Reflecting a concern for their own interest and for the public welfare the St. Louis doctors moved against the quacks by organizing the Medical Society of Missouri in 1837. This group of doctors agreed to conduct their practice under rules set by the society, and they established requirements for the admission of new members. One major purpose of the society was to identify properly trained, professional practitioners from the irregulars or quacks. The society acted quickly to stop doctors from advertising and from dispensing drugs, and it established a rule that a member could not hold a patent for the manufacture of secret cures. Physicians in other parts of the state formed similar medical societies, and by 1850 these local groups had joined together to form the Missouri State Medical Association.

Most of the state's doctors were general practitioners who procured their own drugs, mixed them, and dispensed the medicine. This combination of services decreased as the medical societies sought to disassociate medical practice from the dispensing of medicine, but they were continued longer in some areas because even the legitimate doctor had no other choice.

Missouri's doctors often found time to engage in various other activities. Many of them owned large farms, raised fine stock, and speculated in land; others owned stores, mills, or newspapers. They actively participated in most civic enterprises and appear to have been respected and influential community leaders. Politics attracted many doctors, sometimes to the point that it overshadowed or replaced the practice of medicine. Dr. William Carr Lane served as mayor of St. Louis; the prominent Dr. John J. Lowry of Howard County appeared at times to be more politician than physician; Dr. Lewis F. Linn, Senate colleague of Thomas H. Benton, is remembered more as the father of Oregon than for his contribution to medicine.

The lack of knowledge concerning the cause or prevention of infectious diseases made control almost impossible once a communicable disease entered a community. The proximity of St. Louis to the river subjected that city to constant exposure to diseases carried by immigrants and crews from literally all over the world; once introduced into St. Louis these diseases were carried into the state's interior regions.

Asiatic cholera apparently was the greatest killer of the time. The danger from cholera was constant, but three major outbreaks occurred in 1832, 1848, and 1853, with the most severe one starting in late 1848 and cresting the following spring. By the spring of 1849 many of the business houses and city agencies had ceased to function in the panic-stricken city. A disastrous fire that destroyed some twenty-eight boats and 418 buildings located near the docks added to the city's troubles. In June alone approximately 1,900 persons died, while an estimated 20,000 people, including the city council and other officials, fled the city. The disease produced a political crisis that prompted a public meeting in late June, the result of which was a committee of safety with near dictatorial power over the city. With quick and energetic action the committee conducted a massive city cleanup, established temporary hospitals, quarantined the ill, and took such less-effective measures as the burning of tar, coal, and sulfur to clean the air. Since the bacterial cause of cholera was not found until 1883, no one knew to attack the germ that was the real enemy. The disease finally began to loosen its grip on the city, and the committee declared the cholera epidemic over in August. There were several additional victims in the next two months, and the true death figure was probably higher than the over 4,200 reported. The idea that cholera was related to personal filth and intemperance was so strongly fixed that many people tried to hide the fact that it had victimized members of their family.

Once cholera hit St. Louis, the city's unpurified water and its inadequate sewage disposal system had caused it to spread rapidly. The use of natural limestone sinkholes and caves as sewers had been a cheap but dangerous means of sewage disposal. Heavy rains had clogged entrances and produced a great open sewage lake as a bacteria breeding ground. In 1850 the city started construction of a better system.

Other river towns had their victims, although St. Louis was hardest hit. More than half of the nearly 300 Belgian immigrants who arrived in Kansas City's East Bottoms in 1849 died, and as the disease spread to the city proper it caused approximately 400 additional deaths. Few statistics for other portions of the state are available, but the disease undoubtedly took its toll in most river counties.

Along with the economic and political equalitarian aspirations of the Jacksonian period, humanitarian impulses in Missouri produced a campaign to eliminate social evils and to aid those with personal inadequacies. Missourians followed the American tradition of public responsibility for the honest indigent, and in line with common practice most of them considered public care a function of local government. State legislation was necessary, however, to authorize local political units to carry out certain social welfare activities, and it appears that the General Assembly may have exerted some legislative pressure upon the local units to act.

Early state statutes continued territorial laws making each county responsible for providing care for the lame, blind, sick, and any other persons unable to support themselves due to age or infirmity, and authorizing county courts to levy taxes for such poor relief. The legislation failed, however, to establish an organized program or to suggest methods for handling relief needs. County judges had to devise methods in their individual counties—a potentially costly responsibility. When a resident of Cooper County without relatives or other means of support became paralyzed in 1821, he became a public charge at a cost of two dollars a day. With the total county revenue for 1822 less than the cost of supporting its one-patient welfare program, county officials petitioned the state for help unsuccessfully. The county court then levied a special tax. Although such situations must have been the exception, Governor McNair called the General Assembly's attention to the inadequacies of existing law in providing care for the unfortunate who could reasonably expect aid from their government. The legislature failed to respond to the Governor's message, and the burden of caring for the poor remained with the counties.

In the early years local officials commonly provided some form of outdoor relief by farming out or boarding out public charges to residents who could then use them as workers. In cases of the incapacitated poor, the county paid a family to take care of them. Other forms of outdoor relief included small county pensions, medical services, and the assumption of burial costs.

State law also made each county court responsible for the care of every orphan or minor child without proper parental support. In these cases the counties usually employed the apprenticeship system until the individual reached a given age, with the master obligated to teach the apprentice to read and write in addition to his trade or business. In the case of a black or mulatto child, the master was not required to fulfill the educational obligation. Undoubtedly some masters exploited the system, but it appeared to most Missourians as satisfactory and required little support from the public purse. Few communities had enough orphans to consider institutional care.

As the need increased, counties organized an almshouse or county farm where the poor lived at county expense. The county normally contracted with an individual to take care of the county poor, as certified and assigned by the court, authorizing the contractor to use the labor of those able to work. In 1843 the General Assembly authorized county courts to buy 160 acres of land on which to build and operate a home for the poor. The county courts admitted individuals classified as paupers to the almshouses—commonly known as poor farms or poor houses. These county institutions housed a varied clientele including both black and white, men, women, and children; some were mentally deficient, some were physically handicapped, others aged. All were poor, and the adults forfeited their right to vote by accepting almshouse residency. The almshouse personnel were untrained, and the facilities totally inadequate to provide proper care for such a diversified group as their residents. If they were able, almshouse residents worked on the county farm or were hired out to neighbors who paid the county a small sum for the labor performed. Although Missourians provided at least minimum care for the "honest" poor, standards were strict and the stigma of pauperism impressed upon those who became public charges. Especially in rural areas men were expected to support self and dependents, and failure to do so was considered a sign of moral or personal deficiency. It followed that the unemployed or vagrants were dealt with very harshly. Authorities frequently hired these men out for a period of time to work for the highest bidder or lashed them if no bids were received. One objective of such practices, as with other public assistance programs, was to keep the costs as low as possible.

With some apparent change in attitude toward the less fortunate, aided by a general resurgence in the economy, the decade of the 1840's brought several social reforms and alterations in the welfare system. The urban areas, particularly St. Louis, devised the more progressive welfare innovations and humanitarian projects. In rural areas the problems understandably seemed to be less serious, as opportunities for self-maintenance were more plentiful there than in the cities. Moreover, small-town and rural residents, preoccupied with their own efforts to make a living, remained largely unaware of the social needs that plagued the urban communities.

In contrast with the countryside, urban areas presented a different situation. Crowded with immigrants and transients, the cities also provided fewer opportunities of caring adequately for a large family. The excessive numbers of these less-fortunate inhabitants sometimes created serious problems for the local community. Consequently, programs for social reform and public welfare services generally received greater support in the city. Long before the state's rural areas had moved to deal with the problem, St. Louis had, after receiving special permission from the state, constructed an almshouse in 1827 on property that had been donated to the city.

Care of the mentally ill and retarded was a problem common to all areas. Since people normally attributed mental illness to some moral deficiency, relatives often attempted to keep the disturbed member of the family hidden from society. The actual number of afflicted persons remains unknown. The census of 1840 listed less than 300 insane persons in the state, but a legislative committee report classified almost 1,300 persons as insane or as idiots, including ninety-two public charges. Confronted with this serious problem authorities seldom considered the needs of the afflicted. In the first decades of statehood officials classified these unfortunate individuals as criminals or paupers before confining them in jails, garrets, cellars, and even log pens. Following their establishment the county almshouses often received these persons.

As Missourians became more social reform conscious, they moved toward assigning the state an increased responsibility for the care of the mentally ill. In 1847 the General Assembly established a state asylum, which opened four years later in Fulton. The law provided that the asylum accept those who sought admission and could pay the regular costs. In the cases of public charges the county authorities were required to pay $2.50 per day and certain miscellaneous expenses for each inmate they sent. The asylum, which offered a minimal standard of institutional care, generally failed to provide programs of training or rehabilitation. Overcrowded from the outset, the facilities proved wholly inadequate to meet the needs of the state, and the General Assembly had to provide $130,000 for expansion in the late 1850's.

On a philanthropic basis, institutional care for orphans also came into existence. Five orphanages were operating in 1840, and the number more than doubled in the next two decades. St. Louis had the most serious problem; in 1854 that city had nine orphanages, seven of which the Catholic church operated.

Increased public concern also resulted in state efforts to provide greater aid to the blind and the deaf and dumb. The state occasionally had approved special appropriations to individual indigent families to send an afflicted child to an out-of-state institution, but it had failed to establish any over-all program to care for these handicapped. When the Sisters of St. Joseph opened an institution for the deaf and dumb at Carondelet in 1838, the state paid the school to accept public charges. In the late forties the General Assembly adopted a more direct role with the passage of legislation creating a state school for the deaf and dumb. Opened in Fulton in 1851, the school enrolled eighteen persons the first year and increasing numbers after that, but served only a small part of the residents of the state with speech and hearing problems. Students were enrolled only if between the ages of ten and thirty; the term was for three years, with special attention devoted to instruction in rudimentary skills. Those who were able to do so paid eighty dollars per year; if the county court certified the individual as a public ward, there was no charge. At the same time the General Assembly approved the creation of this special state school, it authorized the payment of eighty dollars per year, later reduced to sixty, to a parent or guardian for the education of a deaf and dumb or blind person between eight and twenty years of age.

Institutional aid for the blind in Missouri developed almost directly from the work of a blind man, Eli Whelan. A graduate of the Pennsylvania Institute for the Blind, Whelan came to St. Louis as a teacher in 1850. With support from St. Louis philanthropists he opened a school for the blind in his home in 1851. In the same year the General Assembly agreed to appropriate $3,000 per year for five years to aid the school, providing that St. Louis supporters would contribute $2,000 annually, that all blind persons who applied would be allowed to enroll, and that no charge would be made for the indigent. The school began operating under this arrangement with the students learning a trade, some basic academic subjects, and, at their option, studying music. In 1853 the state provided the funds to purchase a site and construct a new building; ten years later the school for the blind formally became a public institution.

For the indigent ill, the state provided little institutional care. Missouri's first governor pointed out that many individuals in transit on the rivers and among each new group of settlers became ill before becoming acclimated and did not have the means to pay for medical care; consequently he recommended that the state operate a hospital at some point on the Missouri River. The General Assembly failed to act until 1831, when it authorized the establishment of a public hospital in St. Louis. The relief of the poor in cases of illness continued to be handled largely by county charity.

The criminal code of early Missouri was harsh, with corporal punishment prescribed upon conviction of a large number of relatively minor offenses. Local officials used the pillory and the lash extensively to support law and order, but juries became increasingly reluctant to apply the stringent penalties prescribed by the law. Those working for social improvement advocated confinement, with some chance to reform the individual, as morally and socially superior to corporal punishment. In 1835 the state outlawed whipping and the pillory as forms of punishment except in cases involving certain crimes committed by slaves.

A newly established state penitentiary, built in Jefferson City, received its first prisoner in 1836. In an attempt to reduce the costs of maintaining a prison, officials often contracted the prison inmates as laborers to private parties. Contractors frequently exploited the prisoners, and the practice lessened the authorities' control over the inmates as well as their opportunity to conduct programs of rehabilitation. Moreover, to the more socially-minded reformers, prison conditions were intolerable. Minor offenders and hardened lawbreakers were thrown together in cramped quarters. Since separate facilities were unavailable, authorities isolated women inmates from the men by strict confinement in small cells. Poor food and inadequate sanitation facilities added to the problems of prison life. In fact, prison officials made no real effort to rehabilitate the prisoners or to prepare them to return to society as more productive citizens. The prison was operating on the lowest cost system possible. While there continued to be a growing public concern for more positive efforts to carry out a rehabilitation program, no significant changes were forthcoming.

Capital punishment and public executions also came under attack by reformers. The *Missouri Statesman* condemned capital punishment as a remnant of barbarism that taught disregard for the human race and corrupted the moral sense of all who witnessed its execution. Despite the growing opposition to the practice, some 5,000 or 6,000 persons, including women, observed a public execution in Jefferson City at mid-century, and the *Glasgow Times* reported a public hanging in 1858. In response to increasing popular pressures, however, the practice rapidly moved toward extinction in Missouri. Opposition to capital punishment seems to have been less widespread and its influence unimportant.

With large numbers of idle young people, many of whom

were orphans or lacked parental supervision, St. Louis faced a serious problem involving juvenile delinquency. In early decades, authorities sent the young offenders to a workhouse or to prison, but in 1851 concerned citizens succeeded in securing the establishment of a reform school designed to gainfully employ young people and to provide some directed study and recreation. Boys under eighteen and girls under sixteen were sent to the reform school for violation of a criminal law and were admitted upon complaint of parent or guardian, or because of incapacity or moral depravity of parent or guardian. Overcrowded facilities at the reform school led the city to organize a House of Refuge in 1853 to receive younger offenders, boys under sixteen and girls under fourteen, who might be placed there at the discretion of a judge rather than in a workhouse, jail, or penitentiary.

In the field of social improvements much remained to be done, but during the decades of the 1840's and 1850's, public attention was increasingly focused upon more dramatic developments as Missourians found themselves embroiled in the controversies involving economic change and the problems of slavery.

# CHAPTER VIII

# POLITICS AND STATE
# ECONOMIC POLICY

If there had existed political columnists and professional prophets of the time, they could have had a field day projecting the two decades following the elections of 1840. As the decade of the 1840's opened, it was obvious that the problems of currency and banking would continue to be bitter and divisive issues in Missouri political and economic life. A greater agreement over internal improvements, land policy, and even on the tariff might have been part of the forecast, but so would explosive new issues involving western expansion and the question of the extension of slavery into the territories. More strictly related to internal political behavior were problems relating to congressional redistricting, reapportionment of the General Assembly, and the tenure and selection of public officials. All of the above factors would have been made more complex by the struggle for political power within the state, which, in part, reflected major national trends. The names of new young and ambitious politicians who would soon challenge "Old Bullion" Benton would probably have arisen. Missouri interests had long been tied with the South in common policy against the Northeast, but there were indications, a sharp prognosticator would have pointed out, that the next few years would see the intensification of the sectional issues dividing the North and South, and that changes in Missouri would end the unanimity that previously existed as to the state's proper sectional ties. More effective party organization was sure to come, but it should have not been too difficult to predict a future division within the political parties, especially the Democratic. Some writers would have, undoubtedly, informed their readers that it would be almost impossible for the diverging forces within the two parties to come together to form a third party, although the most daring of the prophets might have suggested that an abortive effort would be made to form a new Southern party or a new Union party as the nation passed into the second half of the century. One thing was sure—an exciting and dramatic period of Missouri history lay ahead.

Disagreement over currency and banking policies produced the first issue of the new decade that seriously disrupted the internal harmony of the Democratic party and created strong opposition to Thomas H. Benton. The banking controversy had carried over from the previous decade, but the increasing importance of the money question built up the steam in the political boiler. Those who wanted to suppress paper notes, make gold and silver the only currency, and rigidly limit banking institutions were termed "Hards." The other group, favoring liberal bank charters and bank notes for currency, were termed "Softs." The two labels applied to diverse groups in the 1840's that were difficult to identify by any other single criterion. Although the Whigs were most commonly soft and the Democrats more commonly hard, party alignments were not firmly fixed on the question. Perhaps the most solid identifiable front was the frontier agrarian attachment to Benton.

Determined to protect itself and to further the cause of conservative banking, the state bank's continued refusal to extend its own circulation or to accept the notes of any non-specie-paying bank brought forth great criticism from commercial interests. The Softs continued to use paper notes of out-of-state banks, but, since it was quite inconvenient to do so, they exerted pressure and sought political means to force the state bank to handle this paper and to liberalize its own note issues. Commercial groups also developed illegal banking services through corporations that had been chartered under special legislation for other purposes. By the end of 1840 over fifteen companies were issuing scrip, handling out-of-state bank notes, and conducting a general banking business. Believing firmly in the principle of hard money and fearing that the action of the Softs prevented a true test of their doctrine, the Hards were determined to uphold the Missouri bank, to drive out of the state all nonstate bank-issued paper currency, and to close the "illegal" banking operations.

Between 1838 and 1843 the Hards sought legislation to outlaw the circulation of any paper currency in Missouri except that of the state bank. Gov. Thomas Reynolds advocated such legislation in his November, 1840, inaugural address and he urged an inquiry into the activities of corporations issuing notes. Two years later, Reynolds charged that the illegal banking that had come into existence would have disastrous financial results if not stopped.

When the national depression hit the state in 1842, Missourians again experienced a period of intensely hard times. Prices declined drastically—in some places bacon dropped to 1¢ per pound, hogs to $1.25 each, cows to $5.00 a head, wheat to 25¢ per bushel, and oats to 12½¢ per bushel. The circulating scrip and out-of-state bank notes depreciated or became worthless, and foreclosures and bankruptcies were common. The Hards blamed the Softs and their paper currency for the troubles, as Democratic party lines were also being strained. The *Jefferson Inquirer* of Jefferson City, championing the cause of the Hards, damned all paper issues and accused St. Louis of trying to dictate to the whole state. In January of 1843 the *Inquirer*'s editor announced that: "War has been declared by the press of St. Louis, both Whig and Democratic, and it is a war in favor of small notes against hard money." As an organ for the Softs, the *Missouri Reporter* of St. Louis aimed its guns at the central clique, while all Softs aimed at Benton to knock this political kingpin from his agrarian-based throne.

The Hard-Soft struggle overshadowed all else in the 1842–1843 session of the General Assembly. Under the leadership of Thomas B. Hudson of St. Louis, the Democratic Softs managed to elect, with Whig support, Ferdinand Kennett as president of the state bank. The Hards were not defeated in their major goal, however. In February of 1843, after making each bill since 1838 a bit less severe than the previous ones, two laws to regulate currency circulation were passed. Introduced by Claiborne F. Jackson, a central Missouri Hard, the Jackson bills were labeled by Softs as the bills of "Pains and Penalties." The laws made it illegal for any public or private corporation, moneylender, or exchange broker to pass any bank notes or paper currency less than ten dollars; to receive or pass any suspended or non-specie-paying bank notes, or for any corporation to exercise any banking functions. The bills did not, how-

ever, make it unlawful for individual citizens to pass or receive
such currency. C. F. Jackson and Benton were not always to be
in such close agreement.

In his November, 1840, inaugural address Governor Reynolds
not only criticized corporations for issuing currency, but he also
charged the recent and extensive issuance of charters with creating privileges and economic inequalities dangerous to republican institutions. The Governor's position represented a reaction
against corporations and a temporary return to a reduced role
for the state in the economy. The failure of most of the earlier
chartered companies to even begin operations, the disastrous
results of public-supported railroad corporations in other states,
hostility toward those chartered companies that engaged in a
banking business, and the influence of the central Missouri politicians all contributed to this changed attitude. Thus, the General Assembly issued only a limited number of charters during
the first half of the decade.

The Democratic party leadership apparently believed that the
state had no direct responsibility to provide relief or to aid in
economic recovery. Both Governor Reynolds and his elected
successor John C. Edwards (1844–1848) indicated there was
little, if anything, the government could do. Reynolds considered retrenchment a proper policy, and he made it quite clear
that he would not initiate governmental action beyond a traditional republican role of an earlier day. When former Governor Boggs proposed that the Bank of the State of Missouri
issue $5 million in notes on the credit of the state, his suggestion
won no substantial support. The *Jefferson Inquirer* termed it
the "wildest thing of the kind ever offered," and Reynolds denounced those who contended that currency issues were a good
way to solve the state's economic problems; there would be no
more loan office experiences for the state.

Congressional districting became an issue of the early 1840's.
Since statehood, Missouri had elected her representatives to
Congress by a general ticket, that is, every voter in the state
voted for as many candidates as the state had seats in the House.
Congress passed a law in 1842 requiring each state legislature
to establish a number of districts equal to its number of congressmen, with the people of each district electing one con-

gressman. Under the operation of the general ticket system, central Missouri, a Hard stronghold, had furnished all of Missouri's Democratic representatives for a decade. Pure power politics dictated that this Hard wing of the Democratic party would oppose congressional districting, while Soft urban interests supported it. Proponents of districting stressed compliance with the national law, and the right of all sections to representation. Hards charged that the districting legislation was unconstitutional and appealed to state pride not to yield to such a usurpation of power by Congress. Benton opposed the district bill in the Senate debate, but within the state he seemingly tried to avoid the issue. The old Jacksonian must have recognized that his forces had been caught in a political trap. Congressional districting was in keeping with his traditional appeal for more effective popular democracy, but in this specific instance it would increase the power of the opposition, which he considered as committed to a program dangerous to the best interests of the whole people. Governor Reynolds failed to call the General Assembly into special session to take the necessary steps to implement the district system for the 1842 election, and in the 1842–1843 session the legislature passed a law continuing the general ticket system for the 1844 election.

A similar issue was the continued problem of legislative apportionment. The General Assembly of 1840–1841 increased the number of counties from 60 to 77, but the total number of representatives was raised only from 98 to the constitutional limit of 100. Since the constitution guaranteed each county at least one representative, the more heavily populated counties lost votes in the House, while the overrepresentation of the smaller counties was increased. The Softs opened a drive for a constitutional convention as a means to achieve a balance more favorable to their areas and interests in the General Assembly. Here again many old-line Jacksonians were caught in the pinch between the possible loss of political power and an old political principle voiced to gain that power. The Democratic party organization, dominated by the Hards of central Missouri, opposed a redistribution of the General Assembly and a constitutional convention. Democratic Softs of the urban areas were, to say the least, restless under such party leadership, while the

Whigs were highly disapproving of the existing system of representation. Reapportionment and a constitutional convention were perhaps too much tied to the issues of money and banking to stand on their own right. The Hards believed, with a basis of truth, that the Softs wanted the convention primarily to alter the constitutional limitations on banking and currency, and they voiced their opposition on those grounds.

Although it did not appear to be such a prominent issue as the previous questions, the agitation for popular election and limited tenure of judges and administrative officers continued to affect Missouri politics in the early 1840's.

With all major offices at stake and the preceding issues heating the political bloodstream in Missouri, the 1844 elections were sure to call forth the best of the political gladiators, and to add greater dimensions to the contests, major national issues forced their way into the arena. John Tyler's ascendancy to the presidency after the death of Harrison in 1841 produced fundamental changes in both national and state politics. To avoid the loss of any of the diverse groups within the party, the Whig national convention had not framed a platform in 1840, preferring to let Harrison stand on a cider barrel placed outside a log cabin. Given the Whig principle of legislative leadership and the presence of the elderly Harrison in the White House, Whig leaders envisioned the final culmination of the American System under the direction of Henry Clay playing the role of a prime minister. When Harrison died on April 4, 1841, Clay and his associates had to deal with Tyler, a Virginian, whom they had placed on the 1840 Whig ticket to appeal to Southern Democrats. Tyler favored neither Clay's program nor the Whig system; after he vetoed two Whig-sponsored bank bills, the Harrison cabinet, with the exception of Daniel Webster, resigned in protest in September of 1841. Webster stayed on as secretary of state until May of 1843, at which time Tyler moved his secretary of the navy, Abel P. Upshur of Virginia, into that spot. Shortly after his appointment, an explosion accidentally killed Upshur and Tyler replaced him with John C. Calhoun. Acting as the Democrat he had always been, Tyler moved to reshape that party along southern lines with Calhoun as the chief architect. Calhoun, the leading advocate of nullification and slavery extension, represented views with an explosive potential. Tyler's actions stunned Missouri Whigs along with many, but certainly not all, Missouri Democrats. In Missouri, Whiggery gained very little from the national victory in 1840 except that Tyler's action widened the split within the Democratic party.

In 1844 Missouri politics got caught up in the attempt to annex Texas—especially in relation to Benton's re-election. As Tyler's secretary of state, Calhoun negotiated a treaty with Texas for its admission into the Union. With Benton voting against it, the Senate killed the treaty in June of 1844. Benton did not oppose the annexation of Texas, but he objected to the timing, procedure, and alleged motives of the promoters. He charged that Calhoun was pressing for annexation to advance the interests of slaveholders and to disrupt the Union over the slavery issue, and that lesser interests were promoting annexation hoping to profit from speculation in Texas land and scrip. Since Mexico had not recognized the independence of Texas, Benton argued that annexation without an agreement with Mexico would result in an unnecessary and unjustified war. Benton was also concerned that a war would cut off the flow of silver from the Southwest so important to his hard-money policy. In time and with negotiation, Benton tried to assure the voters, annexation could be honorably carried out. The annexation of Texas was highly popular in Missouri. Many Missourians cared little about Mexican reaction if indeed such a problem entered their minds, and the opposition effectively charged Benton with failing to support the best interests of Missouri and the South. Standing in the wings and ready to take on a leadership role in politics was David R. Atchison, who expressed the view that annexation was the only way to prevent constant trouble with Mexico.

When Sen. Lewis F. Linn died unexpectedly in October of 1843, Governor Reynolds appointed Atchison, a resident of Platte County, to Linn's Senate seat. Atchison had passed the major test of Democratic party loyalty in the late 1830's by supporting the Jacksonian antibank position. As a member of the General Assembly and as a circuit judge, Atchison's popularity soon revealed him to be a man with political potential. As a resident of the northwestern part of the state, he was untainted by association with the Central Clique. He had avoided the latest banking and currency fight, but he supported a constitutional convention to reapportion the General Assembly and congressional districting. Some Softs looked upon Atchison as an ally against the Hards of the Boonslick country. Preparatory to the 1844 campaign, a group of Democrats held a convention in Clinton County in March, 1843, at which they nominated Atchison for governor and announced support for Tyler's reelection. James Birch, the politically inconsistent leader of the Clinton County convention, also sought the support of Whigs for the Atchison candidacy. There was one little slip: neither Birch nor any of his associates had conferred with Atchison, who refused to accept and actually repudiated the nomination of the Clinton meeting.

It is not fully clear just where Atchison stood politically in 1843–1844, but Reynolds and Atchison had been carrying on a personal correspondence in which the Governor frequently sought Atchison's advice and received considerable sympathy concerning his problems in dealing with the intraparty factionalism. Atchison assured Reynolds that he did not seek the governorship or any other office. Nonetheless, Reynolds was under great personal strain in the last months of his term,[1] and his appointment of Atchison may have been influenced by their pleasant personal association. Undoubtedly the Governor hoped the selection would help to unify the party and avoid the outburst that was sure to follow the appointment of a Central Clique man. In appointing Atchison, Reynolds rejected the advice of central Missouri's Hard leaders who favored John Miller. The Atchison appointment did win, however, the public approval of both factions of the party, and, for the moment, contributed to party unity.

Thus, as the Hards and the Softs squared away for the elections of 1844, the money question, although still primary, was interwoven with other questions that related to state economic policy, to popular democracy, and to the Texas issue. An anti-

1. Governor Reynolds shot himself on February 9, 1844, and left a note saying that the slander and abuse leveled at him while he was in office had made his life a burden.

Benton movement in the pre-election period further strained the still formative party structure.

There had been a significant growth in political party organization following the Whig convention of 1839 and the Democratic convention of 1840, but a permanent party organization continued to face opposition from those who considered themselves Independents or who did not believe in or perhaps even feared that political organization would give too much power to party managers. Benton held such fears. The growth of party organization after 1840 was, however, more popular and successful among the Democrats generally than among the Whigs. Most Democrats realized that unless some organizational unity was created the Whigs would be winning elections with only a plurality.

In 1841 the *Jefferson Inquirer* presented a plan for establishing a permanent organization for the Democratic party, with emphasis on the *permanent*. It proposed the convening of annual county conventions to nominate candidates for offices, send delegates to a state convention, and appoint a standing party committee. Many politicians and editors supported the proposal, and sentiment for such grass-roots organization appears to have been strong. By the winter of 1843–1844 many counties had formed some kind of a permanent Democratic organization, but they differed in structure, and they lacked a common understanding of the functions of the conventions and the committees. It was generally agreed that the county conventions should nominate candidates for the General Assembly, but there was disagreement on other county officials. Factions sought to secure control of the county conventions and committees, with the Central Clique Hards the most successful in such efforts. Most political leaders continued to depend primarily upon the press to promote candidates and party campaigns.

The county meetings and the controversies between newspapers foretold the struggle for party control that came in the 1844 state convention. The battle lines were drawn between the Hards and the Softs—the Benton and anti-Benton forces. In a resolution of instructions to the secretary, the convention ruled that only the resolutions, motions, or proposals receiving a majority vote were to be mentioned in its records, thus the relative strength of the two factions has been difficult to determine. The Benton Hards won the first victory with the election of Sterling Price as chairman. The convention then tabled all resolutions pertaining to congressional districting, a constitutional convention, and currency and banking. The Softs supported A. A. King, a favorite of the northwestern part of the state and an open opponent of the Central Clique, for governor. Col. M. M. Marmaduke, lieutenant governor and acting governor following the death of Reynolds, was the leading Hard contender in the preconvention period. A Benton supporter, Marmaduke was a member of the Central Clique and a committed Hard; he opposed congressional districting and a constitutional convention. There had to be compromises, but they were shaped primarily by the Hards of central Missouri. Rather than force an absolute factional showdown, the Hards decided not to present Marmaduke's name to the convention and instead supported John C. Edwards, who won the gubernatorial nomination. Edwards, a close friend and strong supporter of Benton from central Missouri, was a moderate on the money question who favored congressional districting and a constitutional convention. The convention nominated Benton for re-election and endorsed Atchison to fill out Linn's unexpired term. The Hards pushed resolutions through the convention to enforce party discipline. One resolution pledged all members of the convention to support the convention candidates in the general election; a second recommended that all Democrats vote only for candidates for the General Assembly who would pledge, if elected, to vote for the election of Thomas H. Benton and David R. Atchison as United States senators. The Hards came out of the convention in control of the party name, but far from unified.

Atchison, who had support in both factions, wrote to Marmaduke that he was resolved to sustain the nominees of the convention. On the other hand, Claiborne F. Jackson, central Missouri Hard and a candidate for the General Assembly, announced that if elected he would not vote for Benton or any other man who opposed the annexation of Texas. The split between Benton and the Central Clique over slavery was in the making. The strong anti-Benton Democratic Softs refused to abide by the convention's action. Even before the convention,

Charles H. Allen, a lawyer from northwest Missouri and a life-long Democrat, had announced his intention to run for governor. Without convening a convention, Soft leaders put a full slate of Independent candidates in the field with Allen at the head of the ticket. The Whigs supported the Allen ticket, and although they did have some local candidates for the General Assembly, they concentrated generally on the election of anti-Benton people.

The Democratic party's moderate gubernatorial candidate reduced internal party differences. In the campaign the Hards had the advantage of the regular party name, and they exercised great influence through the county organizations that had been developed. Atchison, without serious opposition from any quarter, made no major speeches during the 1844 campaign and through his friends worked for Benton's re-election. Benton conducted a vigorous campaign in defense of his stand on Texas to counter the opposition's widespread attack on him over that issue. John C. Edwards won the race for governor over Allen by well over 5,000 votes out of better than 80,000 cast. The Hards won four of the five congressional seats by substantial majorities, losing the one race because their candidate died just prior to the election. In the General Assembly, Atchison was easily elected to the Senate with 101 of a total of 130 votes cast. Benton's election was not, however, so easy. There were 52 Whigs in the General Assembly and 80 Democrats, but it was unknown how many of the latter were Benton or anti-Benton men. With 67 votes necessary for election, a combination of unified Whigs and only 15 dissatisfied Democrats could defeat Benton's re-election. At least 15 anti-Benton votes were available, but no coalition could be worked out and the opposition failed to even offer a strong, positive contender. Thomas B. English, a Soft Democrat from Cape Girardeau County, was placed in nomination against his own announced reluctance to run in opposition to Benton. The Whigs could not come up with a candidate, and the General Assembly cast 74 votes for Benton, 32 for English, and 25 for twelve different men.

A series of compromises and some political horse trading in the 1844–1845 session of the General Assembly led to Jackson's election as speaker of the House and to an agreement by the

Benton forces to support a resolution instructing the state's senators to vote for the annexation of Texas. Jackson and his supporters could vote for Benton after all. When the resolution actually came up the Jackson men insisted it should include the words "immediate annexation"; the Benton men fought for and secured the wording for annexation "at the earliest practical moment." The Hards agreed to accept congressional districting as in keeping with popular demand, but with a bit of face saving they refused to acknowledge national authority to order such an action. The General Assembly established congressional districts in 1845. After the state elections of 1844, the newspaper war subsided, and a degree of surface harmony was restored among Missouri's Democratic party factions.

The Texas issue was so intense and potentially divisive that Martin Van Buren, who appeared an almost certain choice for the Democratic nomination, and the expected Whig candidate Henry Clay published letters of mutual agreement in April of 1844 to oppose the immediate annexation of Texas in an effort to keep the issue out of the national campaign. The Democrats, pushed by the South, rejected Van Buren, and James K. Polk, riding into the Democratic convention on an expansionist dark horse, carried off the prize. More than 41,000 Missourians voted for the Democratic national ticket in November as Polk carried the state easily over the Whig ticket headed by Clay. Missouri Whigs, happy with the national convention's selection, worked hard in Missouri, but could produce only a little over 31,000 votes for the man who had once been the most popular national figure in the state. The national election had a significant impact on the future of the Democratic party in Missouri, for it marked a second major step in turning the national Democracy away from the old Jacksonians and toward a party led by Southerners who sought to direct its policy in the interest of slavery and territorial expansion.

When President Tyler, just prior to Polk's inauguration, took steps to initiate the entry of Texas into the Union under the terms of a joint resolution of Congress, Benton opposed Tyler's action despite strong sentiment in Missouri favoring the President's course. Benton, who had been active in Congress on the annexation resolutions, argued that the intent of Congress had been to authorize negotiations with Mexico—not to deal directly with Texas as Tyler had done. The Oregon boundary dispute with England became a companion issue with Texas annexation. Most Democratic newspapers in the state favored the 54° 40′ line, and 54° 40′ resolutions were popular with Democratic meetings across the state. Benton recommended to Polk a settlement at the more defensible forty-ninth parallel, the line that was finally accepted. Although these latest Texas and Oregon questions had produced controversy within the state, the final settlement of both was generally accepted by Missourians as satisfactory and left limited scars on the party skin. When war did come with Mexico, Benton gave it his full support, and Missourians united behind the flag. The problem of slavery in territory acquired from Mexico would, however, be far more difficult to resolve.

Probably the most important state political action during the administration of Governor Edwards (1844–1848) was the effort to adopt a new constitution. The creation of nineteen new counties by the Hard-controlled 1844–1845 session of the General Assembly intensified demands for a constitutional convention to equalize representation in the legislature. With the constitutional limit on the total number of representatives already reached, more heavily populated counties lost representatives to the new counties. It seemed obvious the General Assembly was not going to correct its own malapportionment.

The call for a constitutional convention cut across party lines. Whigs strongly favored a convention, but the Democrats were divided on the issue. In the older, more populous areas, Democrats, most of whom were Softs, experienced the same loss of voting power as did the Whigs. Opposition to the convention on the grounds that it might sweep away existing constitutional restrictions on banking and note issues had to give way to the rising popular demands for a convention that were based on such democratic principles. Moreover, some old-line Jacksonians might even have believed that a convention could be used to tighten control over charter issue and corporations. The General Assembly submitted the proposal to the people, who approved by a large majority.

The convention convened in November of 1845 and wrote a

new constitution, which the people narrowly rejected in a referendum held in August, 1846. Although the proposed constitution failed to win approval, the document reveals much about state policy developments, political divisions, and constitutional trends. It would have restricted the power of the General Assembly to incur debts, to create banks, to authorize lotteries, to charter corporations, and to enact local and private bills. In general, the document reflected a growing lack of confidence in the legislative branch, but some of the changes did reveal an understanding of the need to transfer responsibility for conducting many routine functions from the legislative branch to an administrative agency.

The constitution of 1845 included a new basis for representation in the House of Representatives. Attempts to continue a guarantee of one representative to every county produced opposition from the population centers of the state. The final article allowed each county one representative regardless of its population, but it also established a ratio system for additional representatives according to population. Some equalization would have resulted, but the less-populated rural counties were most favored in the apportionment. The constitution also would have limited the regular session of the General Assembly to sixty days.

The proposed document continued the governor's power to appoint supreme court judges, but it made circuit judges elective. Judicial terms would have been fixed for supreme court judges at twelve years and at six years for circuit court judges.

Delegates from frontier counties, where the sentiment against corporations and banks remained strong, pushed through the convention a series of constitutional limitations upon those institutions. The proposed document prohibited the creation, renewal, or extension of any corporate body with authority to issue paper money. Charters to municipal, charitable, or educational institutions were to be subject to repeal by a majority vote of the General Assembly, and other charters were limited to a period of twenty years. In dealing with widespread criticism of limited liability, all stockholders were to be responsible in their individual capacities for all debts and liabilities of the corporation. The state was not to own stock in a corporation, deposit money in one, or make loans to one. Every Whig in the convention voted against the constitutional provisions on corporations, and those provisions had much to do with the defeat of the constitution at the polls. The reapportionment change probably produced little offsetting support among Whigs, for it was not really satisfactory to the more populous areas, nor did it create many votes for the document in the smaller counties, which were better off under the existing constitution.

The article on education made it mandatory that the General Assembly establish and finance free public schools. Some people wanted schools, but many voters apparently did not want to pay the taxes to support them. The proposed constitution would have broadened popular participation in the amending process by requiring a referendum on all constitutional amendments, which were to be proposed by the General Assembly every four years by an absolute majority of each house.

After the rejection of the proposed constitution, the General Assembly made a number of constitutional changes proposed therein through the amending process, but it failed to approve the extreme limitation upon corporations. Amendments ratified in 1849 set the term of office for circuit judges at eight years and that of supreme court judges at twelve years, and the 1850–1851 session produced amendments establishing six-year terms for both sets of judges and providing for their popular election. At the same time, a constitutional change made the secretary of state, attorney general, auditor, treasurer, and registrar of lands elective for four-year terms. Use of the long ballot came to Missouri through the continued impulse of the Jacksonian movement.

In 1849 the General Assembly finally ratified an amendment for legislative reapportionment. Similar to that proposed in 1845, the new system gave each county one representative regardless of population, but the ratio schedule, which increased the number of representatives for the more populous counties, still favored the more rural, sparsely populated areas. One practical effect of the new apportionment was to increase anti-Benton county power in the Geueral Assembly.

The 1848–1849 session of the General Assembly passed 131 public acts and 580 private acts, including a large number providing for the relief of individuals (commonly to increase time for debt payment), granting special charters of incorporation, relating to individual roads, mills, ferries, and dealing with petty details of court administration. In order for the General Assembly to serve its fundamental purpose of legislating on major policy matters, most of the subjects of special legislation should have been handled by administrative or judicial officers under general law. Although the proposed constitution of 1845 contained limitations on special legislation, this problem was not alleviated until after the Civil War.

As the 1846 off-year elections approached, the depression had passed and Missouri's economy was again moving forward. With the questions of expansion and slavery extension temporarily quiet, only the issue of currency, and Benton personally, threatened Democratic party unity. The return of good times had partially mitigated differences on the currency question, but enough division remained to produce Hard and Soft as well as Benton and anti-Benton tickets in all five of the newly created congressional districts. With the two Democratic tickets developing, the minority Whigs saw a chance for victory. Leaders decided not to hold a state convention fearing that a Democratic consolidation might come from a show of organized Whig strength; instead they agreed upon candidates by private correspondence and announced the ticket in the Whig press. When the results were in, the regular (Hards) Democrats had won a solid victory in all five districts. In central Missouri's Third District the Whig candidate did run a strong race, but he still lost to James S. Green, a Benton supporter who subsequently switched to become one of Old Bullion's foes.

The Democratic party appeared to be in good condition to enter the 1848 campaign. Advancement made in party organization had contributed to the party showing in 1846. The Democratic title had come to be recognized as important, and neither faction wanted to break from it. Hards had made important compromises since 1844 on all but the central issue of currency, making it easier for all but the most extreme Softs to remain within the party.

In the mid-1840's the Whig party also represented important political values to those who worked under its label. A combination of diverse forces nationally, Whiggery had greater unity in Missouri. Although some individual rivalry existed, the Missouri Whigs were well enough united in 1848 to support any Whig for governor who had a solid record of adherence to traditional Whig principles—primarily support of a national bank and aggressive governmental aid to advance business, financial, and general economic development. The plague of nativism that had hit the party had also been arrested. Anti-foreign, anti-Catholic sentiment in St. Louis, organized as the Missouri Native American Association in the early 1840's, attracted some Whigs and weakened Whig party unity. However, when Luther M. Kennett, a former Whig running for mayor, was defeated in 1848, the movement became dormant until 1854. Edward Bates, returning to the political front, took an active role in reshaping the Whig central committee into a more effective instrument for promoting the causes of Whiggery. The Whig nomination for governor went to the well-known James S. Rollins from the Whig enclave of Boone County in central Missouri. Primarily because they believed he had the best chance of any of the aspirants to be elected, Missouri Whigs backed Gen. Zachary Taylor for the presidential nomination.

The slavery question still posed an ominous threat to the unity of both parties, and the Wilmot Proviso demonstrated the seriousness of the danger. In August of 1846, while Congress considered the Administration's request for funds to facilitate negotiations with Mexico, David Wilmot, a representative from Pennsylvania, proposed an amendment to establish the condition that neither slavery nor involuntary servitude should ever exist in any part of any territory that might be acquired from Mexico.[2] The House approved the Wilmot Proviso, but the bill did not get through the Senate prior to adjournment that same month. Early in 1847, attempts to attach the Wilmot Proviso to another request for funds produced one of the most politi-

2. Wilmot was not attacking the slave system out of his concern for the blacks. He was motivated more by his concern for the welfare of the free white laborers and opposed slavery extension because he believed it brought disgrace to free white workers. Wilmot told Congress that he wished to preserve the fair country in question to the sons of toil of his own race and color.

cally divisive debates in congressional history. The controversy reached from Congress to the Missouri General Assembly, which, in the 1846–1847 session, passed a resolution instructing the Missouri senators and requesting the Missouri representatives to abide by the terms of the Missouri Compromise. Four days after the Missouri resolution was passed, John C. Calhoun enlarged the area of conflict by presenting a series of resolutions to Congress (February 19, 1847) setting forth the southern demands for the right of persons to carry slaves into all territories. There was no constitutional power, the resolutions stated, for Congress to limit the movement of citizens and their slave property into the territories or for Congress to place any restriction whatsoever on the rights or institutions of an incoming state, other than that its government must be republican in nature. Benton had voted against the Wilmot Proviso every time that it came up, but he was provoked that it had come up at all. Benton wanted to quiet any debate over a question he thought nugatory, since he believed the areas in question were unsuited to slavery, but he took up the debate publicly against the Calhoun resolutions. Congress, Benton insisted, did have the power to regulate slavery in the territories, and he charged that Calhoun was pressing a highly charged "principle" to dissolve the Union. Such a position got Benton in much trouble with an important group of his supporters—the Central Clique.

In a major address in Jefferson City in May, 1847, Benton reviewed the slavery question and stated his warning that it could break parties along sectional lines and finally bring about the destruction of the Union. Even though Missouri was a slaveholding state, she should not, he demanded, follow the lead of John C. Calhoun and his propagandist resolutions. As the state Democratic convention approached, factional disputes developed in the counties over control of convention delegations. The old Hard and Soft labels were used, but the chief division was now "for Benton" or "against Benton"—against the extension of slavery or for it. The older Hard-Soft alignments did not correspond with the newer alignment on slavery. In the preconvention activity, there were four leading candidates for nomination of governor. M. M. Marmaduke, a Hard and Benton's firm friend, had Frank P. Blair, Jr., as a manager. Blair had come to St. Louis in 1842 and joined his brother Montgomery in a law partnership. Fearless and driving, Blair was emerging as a power in Missouri politics. C. F. Jackson, Central Clique leader and a keen politician with prosouthern leanings, was making his bid for the post. A. A. King, a Soft candidate in the 1844 convention who had avoided the ensuing factional fight, and James M. Hughes, the choice of the St. Louis Softs, rounded out the field. The convention agreed to compromise with the nomination of King and the adoption of a set of strong pro-Benton resolutions drawn up by his supporter, Frank Blair. There was no major defection from the state party ticket in the August elections. King won by almost 15,000 votes in a total cast of just over 82,000 even though Rollins, varying from most past Whig candidates, conducted a vigorous campaign throughout the state. The Democrats swept all five congressional seats.

On the eve of its convention, the national Democratic party was split three ways. A free-soil wing wanted to restrict slavery to its present boundaries; a southern wing wanted to force it into all territories; and a third wing expressed a willingness to do whatever was necessary to win. The convention nominated Lewis Cass, a Michigan conservative and expansionist, who had indicated his acceptance of popular sovereignty to determine the status of slavery in the territories. The party platform evaded any commitment on the crucial slavery problem. Benton, and men like him, had a difficult decision to make. He had done much to establish party loyalty and regularity; now the party position was not acceptable to him on a question that he believed endangered the Union.

When the national convention failed to seat the New York delegation of Barnburners (the Van Buren radical Democrats) a group seceded from the convention and nominated Van Buren for the presidency. The following August, delegates from eighteen states gathered at a free-soil convention in Buffalo, New York. The Buffalo meeting included men from the Liberty party determined to stamp out slavery, antislavery Democrats who favored Van Buren, and northeastern "Conscience Whigs" who also opposed slavery. Opposition to the extension of slavery and the failure of the existing parties to take an acceptable stand against slavery brought these diverse groups together. Adopting a platform that included free homesteads, the newly created party coined a rhythmic slogan of "Free soil, free speech, free labor, and free men." The convention nominated Van Buren to be the standard-bearer for the new Free-Soil party.

Benton could agree with many of the free-soil goals, and Van Buren was a close political friend, but the Missouri senator realized that the new party had little chance to win, and he feared that the increased agitation might further advance a disruption of the Union. Moreover, neither Van Buren nor the free-soil doctrine was popular in Missouri. Benton consequently chose to avoid active involvement in the campaign. He officially endorsed the Democratic party ticket, yet his opponents severely criticized him for not taking a more active part in the campaign. The editor of the *St. Louis Union* damned him for not stopping the Van Buren free-soil movement. Blair established his short-lived newspaper the *Barnburner* in St. Louis and launched a free-soil campaign. Benton stood aloof from Blair's action, but this won him no sympathy from any quarter. If Benton had difficulty making a candidate commitment, he acted clearly to block the extension of slavery into new areas. In August, 1848, the same month the Free-Soil party was formed, he moved that the Senate accept a House bill establishing a territorial government for Oregon that prohibited slavery in that territory. Atchison voted "no" along with every other southern senator except Benton and Sam Houston of Texas.

When Congress adjourned in August of 1848, Atchison returned to Missouri to campaign for Cass. He especially stumped the western part of the state, along with men like C. F. Jackson, Willard P. Hall, and James Birch, all of whom equally denounced Van Buren and free-soilism. The Free-Soil party failed completely in Missouri. Cass carried the state, but Taylor won the presidency by a narrow margin.

Following the election, Missouri Whigs scrambled for federal patronage, but the spoils were limited primarily to local post offices and land offices. Missouri Whigs promoted Bates and Leonard for a cabinet post, but apparently neither received serious consideration in Washington. The patronage drive produced some internal discord, because the group that pushed Leonard and Bates ignored James S. Rollins, the man who had devoted much time and energy to the party.

In the General Assembly, the anti-Benton forces initiated an all-out campaign against the Senator's re-election. On January 15, 1849, Claiborne F. Jackson introduced a set of resolutions before the General Assembly declaring that Congress had no constitutional power to legislate on the subject of slavery in the territories except on the question of fugitive slaves, that any right to prohibit slavery in any territory belonged exclusively to the people there and could only be exercised by them at the time of the framing of a constitution for statehood, and that the conduct of the northern states on the subject of slavery had released the slaveholding states from adherence to the Missouri Compromise line, even if such act ever did impose any obligation upon the slaveholding states. The resolutions sanctioned the application of the principle of the Missouri Compromise to the newly acquired territory for the sake of harmony and the preservation of the Union, but in the event of the passage of any act in conflict with the above principles they declared that Missouri would cooperate with the slaveholding states in such measures as might be necessary for their mutual protection against northern fanaticism. The resolutions further instructed Missouri's United States senators to act in conformity with their terms.

The Jackson resolutions were little debated and passed both houses with large majorities; Governor King signed them in March. The limited opposition in the General Assembly came from the Whigs led by the artist-politician George Caleb Bingham, who offered a moderate substitute resolution in the House stating that although Congress had power to legislate on the subject of slavery in the territories, it would be unwise to exercise that power.

Following the adoption of the Jackson Resolutions, Blair and Benton charged that there was a plot against Benton directed by Missouri "field marshals" for Calhoun. Since the Jackson Resolutions had attracted limited early attention, most Missourians initially failed to recognize their underlying political purpose. Although there is no evidence to support the existence of a carefully laid plot directed by Calhoun—as Benton and Blair charged—Benton's opponents did intend to hand the old Jacksonian, who had made the right of instruction a truism for "good" Jacksonians, a set of instructions that would leave him no out. If he obeyed the instructions, he would have to vote against his proclaimed "right" side of the issue and with the forces he said threatened the Union; if he failed to follow the instructions, he violated his own established political principle of the accountability of an elected representative to his constituency.

On the national scene the Southern Address, setting forth the extreme southern position on slavery, emerged from a congressional caucus the same month that the Jackson Resolutions were introduced in the Missouri General Assembly. While Senator Atchison actively participated in the preparation of the Southern Address, Benton had refused to attend the caucus. Only forty-eight of the 121 southern congressmen signed the address; of the seven-member Missouri delegation, Atchison alone signed; he was moving to the side of the southern "ultras." The two men obviously were to be focal points for the confrontation coming in Missouri.

Benton refused to accept the Jackson Resolutions, but he also declined to resign. Instead he chose to put the entire issue before the electorate. A letter addressed to "The People of Missouri," in May, 1849, launched his great appeal to overrule the commands of the General Assembly. Benton followed this with one of the most strenuous speaking tours in his long political career. The Jackson Resolutions and his appeal from them became major issues in the elections for the General Assembly in 1850. Atchison took up the challenge from Benton to fight for what he thought to be the right of the southern cause. The campaign was conducted largely in 1849 because both senators were too involved in Congress in 1850 to canvass the state.

Speaking in Jefferson City on May 26, Benton trained his heavy batteries on John C. Calhoun in a twenty-three-column speech. In Boonville for a major speech on June 9, he set forth the reasons for his appeal. His explanations were long, but in substance he charged that the resolutions did not come from the true will of the people, that they were unconstitutional and based on erroneous interpretations of facts and laws, that they promoted dissension in Missouri and national disunion, that they pledged Missouri to a combination of states to resist constitutional authority and to cooperate in the ultimate civil war, and that in reality they were nothing more than a contrivance to chain Missouri to Calhoun's doctrine of nullification. Moreover, Benton announced that if slavery did not exist in Missouri, he would oppose its introduction into the state just as he was opposing its extension into areas where it did not then exist. These were strong words for the southern power in Missouri, but Benton made it clear that in this respect he would not compromise the issue. "Between them and me," he declared, "henceforth and forever, *a high wall and a deep ditch!* and no communication, no compromise, no caucus with them." In the old, Hard, prosouthern center of Fayette, he labeled the idea that the North sought to abolish slavery as a falsehood launched by Calhoun and his followers in a wicked attempt to unite the South against the North. Times had changed, as Benton now portrayed the North as Missouri's best friend. He equated the Southern Address with the Jackson Resolutions as advocating nullification and treasonable doctrines. Working an old Jacksonian national theme, he sought to relate the interests of the rank-and-file Missourians with those of the northern workingmen.

As Benton traveled around the state, something he had not done in the peak of his power, his speeches became increasingly bitter and vindictive; he grew more arbitrary and egotistical, more aloof from those who might help or support him, and more personal in his attack upon Missouri leaders, many of whom had been strong earlier supporters. He gave his enemies no quarter, and they gave him no relief as they followed him everywhere he spoke, provoking occasional threats of violence and creating a constant air of intense hostility uncommon even in that day of rugged personal politics. In a letter to the editor of the *Platte Argus*, Atchison announced that, because Benton had betrayed the people of Missouri and was attempting to carry the state into the ranks of free-soilism and abolitionism, he was now "making open war upon him" and would do all possible to drive him from the Senate of the United States. The

Hards of central Missouri, who had been a most important source of his earlier support, became his most bitter enemies as the central issue moved from money and banking to the extension or nonextension of slavery. Benton had announced no compromise, and his opposition sought none. He returned to Washington after his speaking tour with confidence that the people would sustain him; Atchison remained equally convinced that Benton had no chance to survive politically.

The Congress that assembled in December of 1849 faced some of the most difficult sectional problems thus far in the nation's history. With California seeking admission to the Union, a growing national concern over fugitive slave laws, and the status of the southwestern territories unsettled, moderates feared that the rising tide of sectional extremism might lead to disaster. On January 29, 1850, Henry Clay introduced in Congress a series of resolutions to deal with those problems, launching a prolonged debate that lasted until the last of five bills—collectively known as the Compromise of 1850—was passed the following September. The committee to which Clay's propositions were referred reported out an omnibus bill covering the territories, a bill to prohibit the slave trade in the District of Columbia, and one for a more strict fugitive slave law. In the debate over the omnibus bill, Atchison worked with the moderates to support it, although he strongly opposed certain of its provisions, including the admission of California as a free state. Benton opposed the omnibus bill because he wanted California statehood considered on the merit of its own case, and because he opposed any payment to Texas in return for a settlement of the boundary question on the grounds that it benefited only those who held Texas securities. The omnibus bill did not pass, and it was broken down for trial by separate measures. After this action, Atchison joined the ultrasouthern Democrats to oppose those bills disliked by the slaveholding states. He voted only for the legislation that established New Mexico and Utah as territories without restriction on slavery and the Fugitive Slave Law. Benton voted for California admission without slavery, for the organization of New Mexico and Utah, for the suppression of the slave trade in the District of Columbia, against the Texas boundary provision, and he did not record a vote on the Fugitive Slave Law.

Missouri congressmen were not prominent in the debates in the House, but their votes reflected the division within the state and party. Only on the fugitive slave bill did all five Missouri congressmen vote together—for the bill. Only James Green voted consistently with the ultras of the South, and no representative stood consistently with the antislavery forces of the North.

Although moderates throughout the nation rejoiced following the adoption of the compromise in the belief that it had produced a final settlement of the slavery controversy, Missouri politics remained unsettled. The election of a senator brought the bitter controversy between state factions more than ever into the open arena.

Early in 1850 the *Jefferson Inquirer* divided Missouri voters into three groups, which it labeled Democratic, Whig, and disunionist. This classification reflected Benton's efforts to tie disunionism around the necks of his opposition and his determination to get a "clean ticket"—one without any taint of Calhounism's secession, disunion, or nullification. He believed that if the Calhoun faction was confined to their own ticket they would be defeated. When feelers were put out with regard to finding a new base for a united party, Benton refused to budge, announcing that he would rather sit in council with those who died of cholera in St. Louis than go into a convention with a gang of scamps.

Missouri Whig leadership was also split over the question of the right of Congress to legislate on slavery in the territories, but the leaders managed to keep their differences private. For the most part, they divided into two camps—the urban, business Whig nationalists and the central Missouri slaveholding States' rights Whigs.

The elections of 1850 resulted in a loss of strength for the Benton Democrats and in gains for the Whigs. In the congressional elections the Whigs captured three of the five districts, but only in one did the Whig candidate win by a majority. The total congressional vote in the state showed 31,786 for the Whigs, 25,307 for the anti-Benton candidates, and 20,176 for the Benton men. The lack of a Benton candidate in the Second District altered somewhat the meaning of the totals, but the division was, nevertheless, evident. The Whigs also won a plurality in the General Assembly with a total of 64 seats in the two houses; the Benton Democrats won 55 and the anti-Benton men 37. During the campaign the germ of a new States' rights party had been planted in central Missouri. John B. Clark, the Whig candidate for governor in 1840, although holding to his title as a Whig, joined with Jackson on a States' rights ticket to win a seat in the state House of Representatives from Howard County in 1850. Ambitious to be Benton's successor or perhaps to put himself at the head of a new southern States' rights party, Clark let it be known that he was tired of consulting Leonard.

When the General Assembly met to elect a senator for the seat currently occupied by Benton, some lines were firmly drawn, and others were still dangling. Whig leaders who opposed the Jackson Resolutions and the extension of slavery urged Leonard to run for the Senate. Leonard, however, declared that he would accept the office only if assigned to it, and then only with the understanding that he stood with Benton on the power of Congress in the territories. Prosouthern Whigs refused to agree to such a condition—which also eliminated Rollins, whom the press had revealed to be in essential agreement with Benton on the slavery question. Clark was certainly free from any taint of Bentonism, but St. Louis Whigs were unwilling to accept a central Missourian, and moderates declined to support the man they thought most apt to disrupt the party and the Union. St. Louis Whigs favored Henry S. Geyer, a prominent St. Louis lawyer recognized for his legal ability, but because of Geyer's generally known proslavery views many Whigs opposed him as the party's senatorial candidate. Following the appearance of an old letter in which Geyer had stated that Congress had no power over slavery in the territories, the anti-Benton papers in St. Louis declared him acceptable for the Senate. Meanwhile the *Missouri Republican* carried an article in which Geyer repudiated any sympathy for the Jackson Resolutions and stated his support for congressional power to legislate in the territories, thereby satisfying the moderate Whigs.

Although some confusion existed, neither Geyer nor any of his supporters rushed to clarify his position on the issue.

Voting on a senator started in the General Assembly on January 10, 1851, with the first ballot giving Geyer 64 votes, Benton 55, and the anti-Benton candidate James Green 37. The factional lines were drawn, and until some faction gave way no senator could be elected. Although approached by Rollins for a compromise, the Benton men would not give in on the slavery question or their candidate. Benton received the same 55 votes on the fortieth and last ballot that he had on the first. The majority of these votes were cast by legislators from the state's predominantly agrarian regions, and they represented the last legacy of the original Jacksonian movement in Missouri.

Moderate Whigs failed to exercise aggressive leadership even though they very much wanted the next senator to be a Whig, as long as it was not Clark. A bargain was finally struck. As the balloting continued, Geyer sent a letter to friends in Jefferson City stating that he opposed congressional interference with slavery in the territories, and some anti-Benton Democrats swung their support to him as a result. There was more dealing, as factional leaders also made some agreements over patronage. In return for an agreement from Whigs to support anti-Benton Democrats for all of the other important posts that the General Assembly could bestow, including the management of the state bank, the anti-Benton forces switched to Geyer, who was then elected. Benton's long and influential career in the Senate of the United States was ended.

Geyer's election displeased Whigs of the Leonard and Rollins posture. They would have preferred a combination with the Benton wing of the Democratic party, but they had gotten a Whig senator the only way they could. Edward Bates had advised that the Whigs stand firm and refuse to make any alliance with the southern Democrats, but he had little influence. The Whigs won the seat, but Geyer was soon more evident in the Senate as a southern Democrat than as a Whig. While the Whig action might have helped offset the formation of a more radical States' right party combination, the old-line, national, American System Whigs gained nothing.

Throughout the decade of the forties controversy over public economic policy, especially with relation to the role of the state in economic development and to the nature of corporate structure, continued to be a major political theme. Governor Edwards (1844–1848) differed little from his predecessor in his views regarding state action to relieve economic distress. His first message to the General Assembly reflected a philosophy of limited government. The well-being of the economy, he said, rested on the labor of the people alone; the government should execute all laws equally and exercise proper police power; it should pass no laws to force equality or to create inequalities, and laws by which members of corporations were exempted from individual responsibility should be repealed. The Governor did recognize the possibility of a state role in the construction of internal improvements, but only when finances were available. In spite of the Governor's early concern about corporate special privileges, the General Assembly turned down his request for a moderate extension of stockholder liability.

By the middle of the decade, although men had lost much in the depression that they could never recover, the serious dislocations caused by the depression had begun to subside. In his 1846 address, Governor Edwards found much to praise, but expressed concern about the want of prosperity in a state with such great resources. According to Edwards, Missouri needed to develop manufacturing in order to make its extractive products more attractive in the market and to place the state in a more favorable position in its eastern trade relations, to increase the variety of economic pursuits, and to improve the transportation system. By the time he left office, Edwards advocated a more active role for the state. In his 1848 message he expressed his belief that conditions then justified the launching of a system of internal improvements. He recommended that state charters, with proper safeguards for equality among all persons and without special exclusive privileges, be issued to encourage manufacturing, which would diversify the state's economy and provide improved markets for Missouri products. Specifically, he suggested that the General Assembly should enact a general incorporation law.

In the campaign for the governorship in 1848, the Whig candidate James S. Rollins made a major issue of Democratic failures to produce internal improvements and advocated the use of the credit of the state to aid private internal improvement companies. The Democratic candidate, Austin A. King, denied his party's indifference and slowness, but he showed more caution against the possibility of a large public debt being created for such purposes. Following his election, he expressed this caution in his inaugural address of 1848 by emphasizing the need to guard against any impairment of the credit of the state.

In his speech Governor King offered few guidelines for specific economic action, but the General Assembly embarked upon a new surge of corporate formation. The legislative session of 1846–1847 had issued only thirty-two charters, while the 1848–1849 session chartered 142 companies, thirty of which were transportation corporations. Missouri's Democratic-controlled state government appears to have finally accepted not only a more positive role in moving Missouri from its frontier, predominantly agrarian base to a more highly developed stage, but also in using the corporate device to help accomplish that change. Democratic leaders did not, however, repudiate their old Jacksonianism, since they believed that the right kind of incorporation laws would open new opportunities to all men on an equal footing in perfect agreement with economic democracy and its equality of economic opportunity. New manufacturers would produce markets for the Jacksonian-favored farmer and, perhaps, votes from a new business group.

The General Assembly enacted a general incorporation law in 1849, which contained a compromise on the crucial question of liability. Stockholders were made liable to creditors to an amount equal to their stock plus profits and dividends paid to them; directors were made liable for debts in excess of the capital stock. As important as such legislation might be, this first general law apparently had little influence on corporate development. Since the law did not prohibit the continued issue of special charters, it still left open the possibility of special-privilege grants. The destruction of official records by fire has prevented an accurate account of charter issue during the first few years under the law.

The General Assembly meeting in 1848–1849 moved to commit the state to a much more positive role in the state's economy. It approved small appropriations for river improvements and authorized over $5,000 to survey and mark the route for the Hannibal and St. Joseph Railroad in return for that amount of stock in the company, although the company never applied for or received the money. More importantly, the General Assembly authorized the counties along the route of the newly chartered Pacific Railroad Company to purchase stock in the company. In 1850 Governor King, in something of a reversal, proposed that state credit should be used to assist financing railroad construction. The legislature responded, and King signed the bill that same year that authorized state bonds to be issued in the amount of $3,500,000 to aid the Hannibal and St. Joseph Railroad Company and the Pacific Railroad Company in securing capital for construction. With this action a new era of state financial aid began.

The public nature of railroads was undoubtedly responsible, in a large part, for the willingness of Missourians to support state aid to companies that would construct and operate such a transportation system. It was evident that private capital in Missouri was not adequate to launch such expensive and risky ventures. The public interest involved in the railroads, plus the state's financial commitment, however, caused the legislature to put some control features in the company charters. All but one of the charters for the state-aided railroads allowed the state to purchase the railroad after from forty to fifty years at a price established by appraisers mutually agreed upon by the state and the companies. Some of the charters of the late 1840's contained regulatory provisions and limitations on dividends that were not included in the post-1850 charters.

State economic policy of pre–Civil War Missouri never fully departed from a concern for the farmers. Supporters of state aid repeatedly stressed the benefits to be derived by agrarians from such diverse programs as internal improvements and manufacturing. Throughout the decades most sessions of the General Assembly took some action designed more directly to aid the agrarian economy, although a large part of it was of limited significance. The legislature chartered many and various agriculture associations organized to promote improvement in agricultural production and marketing, and small appropriations were made to them in the 1850's. Tobacco probably more than any other single crop was singled out as a product for special state protection and aid. The First General Assembly had established a system of public warehouses and inspection for tobacco, and a new state tobacco warehouse was constructed in St. Louis in 1843. Tobacco being exported from the state was not legally required to pass through state inspection, but apparently most of it did. The state also gave attention to improvements in the production and marketing of hemp. In 1841 the General Assembly approved state inspection laws for Missouri beef and pork. The inspection legislation was designed primarily to assure a high quality and thereby improve the market for Missouri products, rather than as an exercise of police power to protect the Missouri buyer against misrepresentation or to protect the health of the consumer.

As the first half of the century closed amid economic change and political strife, Missourians moved into the crucial decade of the 1850's with a badly damaged Whig party and with the pro-Southern leadership of the state taking over the party of Andrew Jackson and Thomas H. Benton.

# CHAPTER IX

# SLAVERY AND THE TRANSITION
# OF THE DEMOCRATIC PARTY

The Missouri General Assembly had elected the proslavery, States' rights advocate Henry S. Geyer to the United States Senate over Unionist Benton, but the prosouthern party still had not gained full control of the state. Governor King, who opposed any form of nullification, called for adherence to congressional decisions regarding slavery in the territories. In February of 1851, just after Geyer's election, King laid before the General Assembly, at the request of the president of the ultra-Southern Convention held in Nashville, the set of resolutions passed by that body asserting the constitutional right of secession. Both houses responded with resolutions that contained a strong indictment of the Nashville action. When a Benton Democrat introduced a resolution to affirm the Jackson Resolutions and announced that a vote to table would be a repudiation of the resolutions, the resolution was tabled. It was something of a legislative maneuver, but the Benton men claimed a great victory.

In the early fifties Dred Scott's legal efforts to win freedom for himself, his wife, and their two children brought the slavery question and related internal party politics into the Missouri courts a decade before the United States Supreme Court handed down its controversial *Dred Scott* v. *Sandford* decision in 1857.[1] While the state case created no public interest, it did relate to the continuing struggle among Missouri's factional political leaders.

The facts upon which lawyers based the suit for Scott's freedom were neither unusual nor disputed. Dred Scott had been brought to Missouri as a slave by his owner Peter Blow. After Blow's death in 1832, the administrator of the estate sold Scott to Dr. John Emerson of St. Louis. On duty as an army surgeon,

1. John F. A. Sanford, whose name was misspelled in the official reports, was Scott's owner at the time and a party to the case.

Dr. Emerson took Scott to the free state of Illinois and then to Wisconsin Territory, which was free territory by virtue of the Northwest Ordinance. While in the latter area Emerson purchased a slave, Harriet, who later became Scott's wife. By 1838 Emerson and his two slaves were back in St. Louis. Dr. Emerson died in 1843, and the Scott family became the property of his widow. Offering a partial cash payment and a promise of full payment later, which would be secured by a prominent St. Louis citizen, Scott sought to purchase freedom for himself and his family. Mrs. Emerson refused the offer. With the help of white friends Dred and Harriet Scott instituted a case in the St. Louis County circuit court of Missouri asking for their freedom on the grounds that as residents of a free state and a free territory they had become free persons. That the Scotts would win their freedom seemed almost certain because the state supreme court had consistently ruled for the plantiff in similar previous cases; but the trial, which opened in June of 1847, ended with a jury verdict in favor of Mrs. Emerson. The decision hinged on the inadmissibility of hearsay evidence. To prove that Scott was actually held as a slave his lawyers depended on Samuel Russell's testimony that he had hired Scott and paid Mrs. Emerson for his services, but upon cross-examination Russell admitted that his wife had made the actual arrangements. Lawyers for the Scotts filed a motion for a new trial on the grounds that the verdict did not accord with the evidence in the case or with the law. Circuit Court Judge Alexander Hamilton granted the new trial, and the state supreme court upheld his action on an appeal. In the second trial, which took place in early 1850, the jury's verdict freed the Scotts. This time the court accepted a deposition from Mrs. Russell that she and her husband had hired the Scotts and paid Mrs. Emerson for their services. Mrs. Emerson then appealed the case to the state supreme court.

Up to this point the case had been a genuine legal controversy over the status of the two Negroes. The Emerson attorneys had based the defense upon the grounds that the civil laws of Illinois and of the Northwest Ordinance were subordinate to the military code governing Dr. Emerson; they had not raised any question concerning the power of Congress to legislate on slavery. As the case moved to the state supreme court, personal politics and the politics of slavery entered into it. When the court began to hear the case in 1850, two of the three judges, William B. Napton and James Birch, were prominent and rabid anti-Benton politicians who between them saw in the case a chance to strike a blow at Benton, to fuse Whigs and Soft Democrats, and to strengthen their faction by rendering a judicial opinion that Congress had no power to legislate on slavery in the territories and that specifically the slavery provisions of the Missouri Compromise were unconstitutional. The election of 1850 came before the case had been completed and, although it had not been an election issue, both Napton and Birch were defeated for re-election. Their defeat, however, did not remove all political considerations from the case. In a 2-to-1 decision, handed down in March, 1852, the new court overruled the clearly established precedent. State courts, the opinion held, were not required to give consideration to the laws of other states or to congressional legislation for a territory; rather, each state had the right to decide the degree of comity that should be extended. Reflecting political overtones, the majority opinion stated that changing times made the former decisions no longer applicable. Moreover, the decision contained a justification of slavery as the will of God. Judge William Scott, a Napton, anti-Benton cohort, wrote the majority decision with which Judge John F. Ryland concurred. Judge Hamilton R. Gamble's opinion held to precedent; times might have changed, Gamble wrote, but principles and the law had not. The supreme court's ruling voided the lower court's decision and remanded the case to the same court for retrial. Scott's attorneys next took the case to the federal district court in St. Louis in 1854 on the grounds that it was a suit between citizens of two different states. Mrs. Emerson had moved to Massachusetts, and the ownership of Scott appeared to have passed to John F. A. Sanford, a New York resident.

In spite of the politics involved in Missouri's high court, the case had aroused little public interest in the state. Not until it reached the United States Supreme Court on appeal by the Scotts did the case become a national *cause célèbre*. Even then the national press gave the case very limited coverage until just prior to the decision, which was handed down in 1857. A few months after the nation's high tribunal ruled that the Scotts were not entitled to their freedom, Taylor Blow acquired the Scotts and freed them through Missouri's prescribed legal action. Within two years Dred Scott died from tuberculosis.

In spite of internal differences, the Democratic party managed to establish an essential unity in its state convention of April, 1852. Gen. Sterling Price, supported by States' righters and moderates, won the party's nomination for governor over Thomas L. Price, favorite of the Benton faction. A popular Missourian, Sterling Price had served in the General Assembly and Congress and had resigned the latter post to command the Second Missouri Mounted Volunteers in the Mexican War. The convention named Wilson Brown, a minor Benton man, to the ticket as candidate for lieutenant governor, and the moderates secured a platform that avoided either extreme on the question of slavery.

Democratic unity hurt Whig chances for victory in 1852, especially in view of the growing strife within the minority party's ranks over the question of slavery. Geyer's election to the Senate had badly damaged moderate Whiggery, and the Geyer forces invited further dissent when they introduced a resolution in the Whig convention requiring all candidates to endorse the right of slaveholders to carry their property into the territories. Even though moderates defeated the resolution, the Whigs' need for unity suffered a serious blow. A practical question Whiggery had to answer was whether alignment with the Benton, free-soil Democrats or with the southern, States' rights faction least violated the "true Whig principles." James S. Rollins had been interested in the gubernatorial nomination, but the single Democratic ticket made him reluctant to run. Furthermore, southern Whigs thought him too much in tune with Benton. The convention first named Alexander Doniphan, who had gained fame in the Mexican War, for governor; when he refused to accept, it compromised on James Winston, a highly respected Springfield lawyer. Winston was a hardworking Whig, but many old-line party members considered him too provincial and unsophisticated to project the image of classic Whiggery. Again, the Whig party's leaders were unwilling to run for office. For the national ticket they endorsed

Millard Fillmore for President and Missouri's Edward Bates for vice-president, both the choice of the moderates. Bates denied that he was a free-soiler, and in standing by the twin compromises of 1820 and 1850 he probably represented the dominant Whig viewpoint.

When Missourians went to the polls in 1852, they elected Sterling Price governor by a majority of approximately 14,000 votes out of 79,000 cast. Without apparent enthusiasm on either side, Franklin Pierce, the Democratic presidential nominee, defeated the Whig candidate Gen. Winfield Scott by a substantial margin.

Benton, not one to be easily removed from politics, won election to the national House of Representatives from the First District, which included St. Louis and some twenty counties to the south. The other four seats went to two Whigs, one Benton Democrat, and one anti-Benton Democrat. Election to the House of Representatives was not Benton's highest goal; with Atchison's Senate term due to end in 1855, Benton announced early in 1853 that he was a candidate for that post.

A growing interest among northwestern Missourians in land just west of Missouri opened a political debate of great ramifications. Willard P. Hall of St. Joseph introduced a bill into the United States House in December, 1851, to organize the Territory of Platte, but the measure failed to pass. The following June a public meeting in Parkville adopted a set of resolutions petitioning Congress for immediate territorial organization of the area west of Missouri and for the right to settle there just as soon as the Indian titles could be extinguished. The residents of Atchison's home county sent their resolutions to the senator, who presented them to the Senate without comment. Even some Wyandot Indians provided additional support for the proposal when they sent Abelard Guthrie to Washington in the winter of 1852–1853 to lobby for territorial status. Indian leaders believed that territorial status would encourage settlement and help secure the route for a national railroad, with a resulting increase in land values. They would in time, Indian leaders reasoned, have to give up the area anyway. Guthrie found only Hall and John S. Phelps of the then current Missouri delegation willing to help. When Atchison told Guthrie that he opposed the proposal because the Missouri Compromise disallowed slavery there, and that he would never agree to the territory being organized as free soil, Missouri's pro-Benton papers gave wide coverage to Atchison's response.

Hall again introduced a territorial bill in December, 1852, with the name of the proposed territory changed to Nebraska. Hall's bill passed the House, but did not come before the Senate for consideration until the final day of the session. Leaving his chair as president pro tem to join in the debate, Atchison helped defeat consideration. He objected to Hall's bill on two counts: that only a very small portion of the area would be open to settlement, since the Indian titles in most of the region had not been extinguished; and that the Missouri Compromise gave the North an unfair advantage over the South in its settlement. Nevertheless, Atchison told the Senate he had come to the conclusion that the time had arrived to organize the area as a territory. This Atchison speech, on March 3, 1853, undoubtedly was a source of confusion for many Missourians. On the one hand, Atchison pledged himself to continued opposition to the organization or the settlement of Nebraska without the right of slaveholders to carry slaves thereto. On the other, he stated that the Missouri Compromise was irremediable, and that he was prepared to submit to it. Atchison seemed to pledge himself to abide by the Missouri Compromise and to secure southern equality with the North by guaranteeing the right to carry slaves into the area. Just how he would square this apparent inconsistency was not made clear. During the debate on the Kansas-Nebraska Bill, the Richmond *Enquirer* set forth the radical southern creed with the declaration that the Compromise of 1850 had abrogated all previous conditions of a conflicting character on slavery extension. Atchison had not announced an agreement with such a position, but subsequently in the Missouri campaign he indicated that the principle of popular sovereignty incorporated in the Compromise of 1850 supplanted the total restriction imposed by the Missouri Compromise.

Benton made his proposal for a central railroad to the Pacific Coast a central theme of his campaign for return to the Senate. Despite his earlier opposition to such projects, Benton found Jacksonian principles to support his stand. The railroad was national, and it was needed by all of the people. He advocated government construction to cancel the schemes of incompetent applicants who sought to turn the project into a great stock-jobbing business. To advance the railroad, Benton pushed territorial status for Nebraska, the region through which the road would run. Thus, soon after the Compromise of 1850, the attempt to organize the Nebraska Territory reopened the question of slavery extension. The resulting fight left the party of Andrew Jackson in Missouri in a state of complete disorder, as well as the Whigs. Benton charged that Atchison opposed territorial organization in an effort to kill the central railroad, and that he used a false argument about Indian titles. These charges temporarily put Atchison on the defensive, but he reacted by making it clear that, during a campaign tour in the state in the summer of 1853, he would support territorial organization so long as there were no restrictions on the introduction of slavery into the territory, and he was unwilling to accept the decision of those who settled there. He did not oppose a railroad to the Pacific, but he questioned the feasibility of the central route and called for a survey with final decision to be made by the President, who would be free from local pressures; he distributed evidence supporting his contention that very little if any land was legally open for white settlement in Nebraska, but he also indicated that he would support action to extinguish Indian titles.

Sen. Augustus C. Dodge of Iowa introduced in Congress the proposal that ultimately became the Kansas-Nebraska Act in December, 1853. Dodge's bill was referred to the committee on territories chaired by Stephen A. Douglas, who then guided the bill through the tortuous trails of the slavery bramble bushes before President Pierce finally signed it into law on May 30, 1854. Douglas first believed the difficult slavery question had been settled with the inclusion of the doctrine of popular sovereignty, which was at least one step short of an emotionally charged, outright repeal of the long-standing Missouri Compromise, but before the bill finally passed, the slavery forces had succeeded in making the specific repeal of the Missouri Compromise a part of the act. The original bill was also changed to provide for the establishment of the two territories of Kansas and Nebraska.

Atchison played a major role in the action to secure the repeal of the Missouri Compromise, but this was a job done primarily behind the scenes in Washington and was not directly a part of Missouri politics. With the exception of Benton, then serving his term in the House, the entire Missouri delegation voted for the final version of the Kansas-Nebraska Act.

Benton denounced the Kansas-Nebraska Act in a long and emotional speech that was printed and distributed to rally public action in opposition to the measure. The doctrine of popular sovereignty had no appeal to the old Jacksonian in this instance. It was, he argued, a "new-found" doctrine that ran counter to a constitutional right and to the historic practice under which Congress had guided the infant territories to adult statehood. It was the work of nullifiers that produced the repeal of the great Missouri Compromise—those who would push slavery into new areas and who threatened the destruction of the Union.

The Kansas-Nebraska measure was the major national question of its time, but probably in no state did it create greater public excitement than in Missouri. It came as the final round in the bitter fight between Benton and Atchison; the General Assembly would render the decision when it met to elect a senator. Benton, however, was now fighting before an unfriendly crowd. His popularity had declined, and a majority of Missourians seemed clearly to favor the Kansas-Nebraska Act and popular sovereignty.

Another ramification of the act was a contribution to the disruption of the Whig party in Missouri. The moderates, many of whom were slaveholders, were Union-minded men for whom the stability of the Union was of cardinal importance. A second major Whig group, with leaders like Geyer and John B. Clark, strongly defended States' rights and supported the South. Many of the States' rights Whigs joined forces with the anti-Benton Democrats. While some of the moderates agreed with Benton, there was inadequate cement to bind the diverse interests of these Whigs and old Democrats into an effective political union. The Whigs were too divided to join en masse either wing of the Democratic party.

The re-emergence of a national American nativist movement following the election of 1852 further undermined Missouri's weakened political party structure. By 1854 the American party, as the nativists called their organization, was an important force in national politics. Commonly known as the Know-Nothing party, the movement gained considerable strength in St. Louis by the late fall of 1854, primarily resultant from the hostility toward the city's large German, Irish, and Catholic elements.

In a strenuous race for the congressional seat from the First District, which had been reduced to the city and county of St. Louis, a coalition of Whigs and Know-Nothings supporting the wealthy manufacturer and Whig political leader, Luther M. Kennett, brother of Ferdinand Kennett whom the Softs had put in earlier as president of the state bank, defeated Benton for re-election to Congress. There was a major struggle to win the German vote in this election. Blair and Brown had carefully cultivated the German element, and the Benton Democrats had depended heavily on their support since the break in the Democratic party. With the state patronage being dispensed through Atchison, Thomas C. Reynolds was appointed United States district attorney in St. Louis and enlisted in the effort to defeat Benton by wooing the Germans from the Brown-Blair fold. Having been educated at the University of Heidelberg, Reynolds was able to make appealing speeches to the Germans in their native language. The strongly anti-Catholic Henry Boernstein, editor of the *Anzeiger des Westens*, was brought temporarily into the anti-Benton fight. With considerable maneuvering, Benton was made to appear as anti-Catholic to separate him from the Catholic voters, while Kennett, as a Whig, sought the German and Irish vote and as a Know-Nothing bid for nativist support. Trusten W. Polk, running as an open anti-Benton candidate, came in a poor third in the race because many of his cohorts cast their votes for Kennett in a frantic attempt to defeat Benton. The antagonisms created, especially the raising of the religious issue, resulted in considerable violence,[2] but the defection of the Germans was temporary. Brown worked especially hard to convince them that Reynolds and the anti-Benton group represented the very worst of Know-Nothingism, and by

2. A running controversy between Brown and Reynolds resulted in a duel between the two after the August, 1856, elections. Neither man was seriously wounded.

1856 the German element in St. Louis was back as a strong supporting force in the coalition being shaped by Brown and Blair.

When the results of the 1854 election for the General Assembly were in, the Whigs had a plurality, and the Democratic split assured that no one faction could secure the election of its candidate without drawing support from one of the other groups. In the combined membership of the two houses the Whigs had 60 members, the anti-Benton Democrats 57, and the Benton Democrats 43; the Know-Nothing party was not organized adequately to field a slate of candidates. Atchison and Benton had been for some time the senatorial candidates of their respective wings of the Democratic party, but the Whigs had their usual trouble coming up with an acceptable and aggressive candidate. A continued lack of agreement as to which brand of Democracy was least objectionable continued to plague the Whigs, and they could not win without some Democratic support. Southern Whigs refused to join with the Benton faction, and Rollins had lost their support for his favorable attitude toward Benton's position in the past. Abiel Leonard, leaning to the southern wing, was a moderate on the slavery question, but, after he secured assurance from the lawyers of the state that he could run unopposed for the state supreme court in January, 1855, he withdrew for all practical purposes without releasing his followers to work for the Union-minded, moderate Rollins. Actually, even with their plurality, the Whigs were hardly in the driver's seat. Atchison's advisers were determined to make no compromise; the Benton men were not going to desert their ancient leader. With the extreme States' rights Whigs threatening to support Atchison, the Whig caucus put up Doniphan, a friend of Atchison's and his former law partner, who was a States' righter with a rather inconsistent position on congressional power to legislate on slavery in the territories, although he did oppose the Missouri Compromise.

On the first ballot, Atchison received 56 votes, Benton 41, and Doniphan 57; the voting remained virtually unchanged through the forty-first ballot, which showed Atchison 58, Benton 38, and Doniphan 56. At this point the General Assembly accepted a stalemate, and a concurrent resolution was adopted postponing the election of a United States senator until the following November. The 1854–1855 joint session of the General Assembly was filled with angry verbal exchanges, which at times appeared to border on personal violence. When the session ended there was no clearly recognizable Whig party and, for practical purposes, Jacksonian Democracy died as the Benton Democrats lost significance as a political force. The seat remained vacant until 1857, when the General Assembly named James S. Green. In the meantime, Benton launched his candidacy for governor in the election of 1856, and Atchison turned his attention to making Kansas into a slave territory. In early January of 1856 Atchison withdrew as a candidate for the Senate.

With such disruptive forces denying harmony in either camp, many men from different backgrounds began to look to the nativist-based American party as a possible vehicle for carrying forward the common cause of national unity. If the nationalism based on ethnic origins of that party had been badly misplaced, perhaps its appeal could be redirected toward a more desirable end. An influx of new members—limited in the beginning almost exclusively to the St. Louis area—soon gave the party strength throughout the state. The American party expanded its organization, and in February, 1855, it created a grand council for the state. Before the end of the year local councils were operating in most of the counties. The movement threw off all of its secrecy and operated as an open political party as it expanded beyond its narrow nativist origins. Its future in Missouri politics was uncertain, but politicians had to reckon with the American party and decide their own reactions to it. Thomas L. Anderson of Palmyra saw the American party as the only party that promised the South preservation of her institutions and yet was broad enough to sustain the Union. A future governor of the state, Silas H. Woodson, wrote the Whig leader George R. Smith on February 23, 1856, that if the American party succeeded the Union would be safe and state domestic institutions would remain untouched. If the party failed, Woodson predicted disunion and internecine war. To Frank Blair, who was looking with favor upon the possibilities of the new Republican party taking shape nationally, Know-Nothingism was, at first, only an expression of disappointment with both old parties.

Some Democratic leaders described it as a Whig trick, while others charged it with being an ally of the newly formed Republican party and dangerous to the Union.

Rollins turned to the American party in early 1855. Others soon followed, especially Whigs, who were convinced that only through a new political organization could they hope to gain control of the state. These men turned to Know-Nothingism as the best of existing alternatives to check the controversy over slavery that threatened the very fabric of the nation. They were in no way bigots; they did not support ethnic and religious intolerance. It was in fact political expediency that created the merger of diverse forces that made up the American party in Missouri. It seems improbable that at any time could an ethnic and religious intolerance under a label of "Americanism" and a proper concern for the well-being of the nation blend into a sound base for action and, as events proved, the American party could not alter that probability.

The call, issued by almost 500 men, for a state-wide mass meeting to be held in January, 1856, in Boone County signaled the start of the movement of old-line political leadership into the American party. With more Whigs than Democrats among the men who signed the call, the former dominated the convention. The meeting adopted a set of resolutions that could also serve as an American party platform. These resolutions denied Congress the power to legislate on the question of slavery in the states where it existed or to exclude any state from admission into the Union because of any slavery provision, or lack thereof, in its constitution; they also called for enforcement of the Fugitive Slave Law and prevailed upon Congress to refrain from any further attempts to regulate the institution of slavery in the territories and to avoid all further agitation on the slavery question. The resolutions concluded that strict adherence to these principles and views was necessary to preserve the peace and perpetuity of the Union, and that no man or party should have Know-Nothing support unless publicly avowing the above principles. In March, 1856, the influential William F. Switzler, editor of the *Missouri Statesman* and leading Whig of the state, announced for the American party, and most of the state's Whig papers followed suit. Another Whig, George R. Smith, helped organize the American party's state convention, which met in St. Louis in April. The Know-Nothings, however, offered a weak compromise, more proslavery than antislavery, and failed to quiet the storm brewing between the Atchison and Benton forces.

"The slavery agitation," artist George Caleb Bingham wrote to Rollins in early 1854, "is too convenient an instrument in the hands of demagogues to be dispensed with." All of those who spoke out on the institution of slavery or its extension were certainly not demagogues, but enough politicians did use the issue in an attempt to further their political careers that it became the major agitator in the Missouri political kettle. The extent of antislavery sentiment within Missouri will probably never be known. Such sentiment appeared limited, but the state's powerful and aggressive proslavery forces undoubtedly inhibited some Missourians from openly expressing their antislavery sentiments. Missourians generally had always assumed blacks to be inferior, but racist arguments in support of slavery as well as the entire slavery issue became increasingly pronounced during the decade of the 1850's, permeating elections, campaigns, and public life.

After the passage of the Kansas-Nebraska Act in 1854 the question of slavery expansion passed from the realm of debate into the field of physical violence. Geographically Nebraska offered little attraction to slaveholders, and no problem developed there, but Kansas was a different situation. Attempts to implement a policy of popular sovereignty brought death, violence, and destruction to Kansas during its territorial years. As Missourians became involved in the turmoil of the neighboring territory a dramatic but generally sordid chapter of the state's pre–Civil War history began to unfold.

Western Missouri slaveholders, with some 50,000 slaves worth an estimated $25 million, were especially concerned about the status of Kansas. Already dissatisfied with the ineffectiveness of the Fugitive Slave Law, they believed that a free Kansas would provide a convenient haven for runaway slaves. Moreover, the logical area for expansion was to the west, and Missouri slaveowners who thought they might migrate to new land wanted to take their slaves with them. On a broader scale, Atchison and others looked upon Kansas as the key to the future of slavery in the United States, believing that its loss would lead to the end of slavery in the entire South. Atchison chose to take whatever action necessary to establish proslavery control of the Kansas territorial government, and, thus, to assure that the territory would develop into a slave state. There were others, not Missourians, who were determined to gain control of Kansas in the interest of free soil. Caught in the middle were the bona-fide settlers who would have, without the slavery agitation, settled Kansas in accordance with the traditional pattern of the western movement. When the first land-seekers moved across Missouri's western border in 1854 no land was legally open for settlement. Men simply selected a choice location and staked out a claim by right of pre-emption. This practice produced extensive claim rivalries that sometimes erupted into open violence, which was further intensified, or by some justified, as proslavery men tried to block antislavery claimants and vice versa. Organized efforts by both northern and southern elements to promote their respective interests in Kansas worsened the difficult situation. Eli Thayer received a charter for his Massachusetts Emigrant Aid Society in April of 1854, which he had organized for the stated purpose of making Kansas a free state. The company also planned to buy land in Kansas and to sell it to settlers at a "very handsome profit"; later reorganized as the New England Aid Company, it became the best known of several similar eastern groups. Missourians expressed great concern about the operation of the eastern companies or societies, but spokesmen also exaggerated the extent of their operations. They settled fewer than 500 persons in Kansas in 1854, and in 1855 they were involved in the settling of only about 1,250.

Proslavery Missourians soon responded to the alleged challenge from the North. In July of 1854 a meeting at Weston organized the Platte County Self-Defensive Association to block settlers sent out by the northeastern aid societies, to help proslavery settlers migrate to Kansas, and to send men into Kansas whenever necessary to defend the proslavery settlers or to drive out the abolitionists. Atchison had participated in calling the Weston meeting, but he did not return home from Washington in time to attend. Benjamin F. Stringfellow, who soon emerged as one of the most extreme of the proslavery advocates, took a leading role in the association's activities. Stringfellow vehemently denounced the North, asserted the superiority of southern civilization, declared the inferiority of the Negro race, glorified the superiority of white people, and alleged that having an inferior race to do the menial work enhanced and ennobled the white society. Similar views were expressed elsewhere, and the Reverend Leander Ker's *Slavery Consistent with Christianity*, published in Weston, sought to give them a religious sanction. No public figure, however, outdid the president of the state university, James Shannon. With the Bible as a source, Shannon proclaimed the positive good idea of slavery throughout the state. In bombastic, fiery oratory he demanded the "cure or kill" treatment of free-soil fanaticism.

Most northwestern Missourians were united in their hostility to abolitionists and to free Negroes, but dissension did develop within the association over the vigilante action used by extremist leaders to expel free Negroes and punish alleged abolitionists. Frederick Starr, a Presbyterian minister who came to Weston in 1850 as a representative of the American Home Missionary Society, became a prime target of extremists. A man with considerable missionary zeal, Starr's antislavery views soon became well known. He also broke some of the unwritten but fixed rules of the proslavery society in his ministerial association with the black people. He refused to join a proslavery organization, but he joined a nonslaveholding squatters' association organized to take up land in Kansas. Starr never publicly proclaimed abolition, but members of his congregation, led by members of the Platte County Self-Defensive Association, tried him for having taught a school for Negroes, for advising two slaveholders to free their slaves, and for having ridden with a Negro wench in a buggy. The minister was exonerated, but the pressure remained, and his church recalled him to the East.

At a meeting of the Platte County Association, Stringfellow sought the adoption of a set of resolutions proclaiming the positive good of slavery, but they failed to win approval. Such extremist action contributed to the association's quick decline, although a number of similar groups were organized in the northern and central western counties in the fall of 1854. These groups were most commonly known as Blue Lodges, and Atchison and Stringfellow helped organize many of them to achieve essentially the same goals as the earlier Platte County group. Atchison wrote to Jefferson Davis in September of 1854 that he expected trouble with the "Negro heroes" in Kansas, and that it would be necessary "to shoot, burn & hang, but the thing will soon be over; we intend to 'Mormanise' the Abolitionists." In reality, Atchison appears to have been milder than his words. He was, nonetheless, so completely involved in the Kansas struggle that he neglected all else. He attended only a part of the 1854–1855 session of Congress and in January, 1856, withdrew his name for consideration as a candidate for re-election to the Senate.

Missourians first went into action in Kansas when several hundred of them rode into the territory to cast votes to assure the election of a proslavery delegate to Congress in November, 1854. More than 6,300 persons cast ballots in the March, 1855, election for members of the territorial legislature, even though a February census had listed less than 3,000 persons as eligible to vote. A large number of Missourians had suddenly established a temporary residence in Kansas or, as leaders advocated, had decided that they were going to settle in Kansas. Unfortunately, the Kansas-Nebraska Act had not set forth any residency requirements for voting. The Missourians, moving in such force and with a display of arms, undoubtedly discouraged any official from challenging their vote. The voter invasions were generally popular in Missouri, especially in the border counties, and Senator Atchison's open support added prestige and validity to such a course of action. The *Industrial Luminary* of Parkville criticized Missourians for interfering in the Kansas elections and was rewarded when a mob dumped its press and type into the river. Iowans similarly participated in Nebraska's first territorial election, but slavery was not an issue.

Kansas's internal troubles became increasingly complex. The proslavery territorial legislature elected in March, 1855, wrote the slave code necessary to establish slavery there. Antislavery settlers in turn reacted by convening a free-state convention, which drafted a state constitution that was approved by their voters in December, 1855; the free-state forces proceeded to elect a set of state officials in Januray, 1856. Only antislavery people had participated in both elections, but Kansas had two opposing governments. The national administration recognized the proslavery territorial government and maintained a territorial governor in Kansas.

Winter temperatures had not reduced the heat generated among the slavery antagonists. In December, 1855, a not too uncommon frontier dispute generated a major confrontation. Franklin N. Coleman, a proslavery man, shot free-stater Charles Dow in a land dispute. Sheriff Samuel J. Jones then arrested Jacob Branson, a friend of Dow's, on a peace warrant charging that he had participated in a meeting of free-state men to consider action in connection with the killing, and that he allegedly threatened retaliation. Free-soilers rescued Branson from the sheriff and took him to Lawrence, where they organized a defense to protect him from rearrest. When Sheriff Jones called for help, many Missourians responded under Atchison's leadership and joined the force drawn up outside of Lawrence to assure execution of the law by the proslavery officials. Open conflict seemed certain. Atchison, fearing that an attack on Lawrence might trigger a dangerous public reaction to the proslavery cause, helped avoid an immediate clash. Moreover, the proslavery forces recognized that the free-state men were prepared to offer strong resistance to any possible attack.

Early in 1856 Atchison issued a call for young men from the South to come to Missouri and Kansas well armed and with enough cash to last them one year. To the father of one such young man Atchison wrote that the boy had become a good "border ruffian," and that, although he accepted the term, Atchison wanted to clarify any misleading interpretation: the border ruffians were, he wrote, men of property, and men of education; they were the best kind of men who would not stand by and see wrong done.

The proslavery raid on Lawrence in May of 1856 provoked widespread criticism. During the month previous, Sheriff Jones had been shot while in Lawrence seeking to arrest some free-state leaders. Early erroneous reports indicated that Jones had been killed, and angry extremists called for the destruction of "abolitionist" Lawrence. While public emotions were high a

Douglas County grand jury, without any real evidence, issued bills of indictment against several free-state leaders and recommended the closing of the Free State Hotel, a political headquarters, and of Lawrence's two free-state newspapers. When United States Marshal Israel B. Donaldson attempted to serve the indictments, he encountered resistance in Lawrence. He then issued a call for citizens to assemble to assist him in the execution of his duty. Atchison and a group of Missourians were among those who answered the call. The free-state leaders, seeking to avoid open conflict, permitted Donaldson, Atchison, and some others to enter the town and even assisted them in making two arrests. Donaldson then dismissed the men. Sheriff Jones was also with the force before Lawrence that day. Not to be stifled again, Jones assumed command of a group of the men that raided Lawrence, destroying the two newspaper offices and their equipment and burning the Free State Hotel, along with several homes; according to some reports the raiders committed two murders. Apparently Atchison did not participate in the raid into Lawrence, but instead attempted unsuccessfully to dissuade those more bent on violence.

The Lawrence raid triggered the fury of the fanatical John Brown, who had come to Kansas to strike his blow for freedom. In late May, Brown and a handful of followers murdered five unarmed men in the vicinity of Dutch Henry's Crossing at Pottawatomie Creek, not far from the town of Osawatomie. Brown's attack intensified both fear and hatred, and the Missourians responded by destroying Osawatomie. In June of 1856 Atchison and his followers closed the Missouri River to any traffic that might aid the free-state forces of Kansas, including immigrants with antislavery views.

The conflict between the two groups did not abate. In August Daniel Woodson, acting territorial governor, called upon all law-abiding citizens to assist in putting down open rebellion in Kansas. Again Atchison responded. He entered Kansas with about 500 men and took command of a force of over 1,000; a part of this group destroyed John Brown's camp, but they did not capture Brown. This was Atchison's last military intervention in Kansas. Early in 1857 he moved to the family farm in Clinton County, which occupied his major attention during the next several years, and dropped completely from the Kansas and Missouri political scenes.

Federal troops entered Kansas in late 1856 and managed to establish temporary order. Election contests continued, but Missouri voter intervention also ceased. The elections held in 1857 placed the antislavery forces in control—the almost inevitable result of the increasing number of free farmers from the middle west who had taken up residence in Kansas.

Violence on the border was renewed, however; after 1857, bands of Kansas Jayhawkers repeatedly raided Missouri's western counties. These groups most usually degenerated into expeditions of robbery and destruction. Some of the raiders had a twisted image of a moral crusade, some desired revenge, others sought a sense of excitement, and still others were merely after the loot to be taken. In the spring of 1858 James Montgomery launched a series of vicious raids into western Missouri, making him among the most hated and feared of the Jayhawkers. Western Missourians organized to oppose the invaders, but finally in the fall of 1858 Missouri's Gov. Robert Stewart assigned state troops to patrol the border. The governor of Kansas cooperated by establishing a similar patrol. With the exception of a raid by John Brown in December, 1858, to free eleven slaves, the border remained relatively quiet until the elections of 1860. The last months of that year brought a revival of the border conflicts that forced many to flee their homes. From this point on the border conflict would merge with the Civil War.

Benjamin F. Stringfellow, with more extreme rhetoric and emotion than Atchison, had urged Missourians to create a proslavery Kansas, but when Kansas was lost for slavery he accepted the decision and moved to Atchison, Kansas. One of his primary interests became railroad promotion; when the war came, Stringfellow stayed with Kansas and the Union.

In the meantime, Missouri's Gov. Sterling Price had done little to cool the intense passions. At his inaugural in January, 1853, Price praised the Compromise of 1850 and the prominent place it held in both parties. After the conflict in Kansas erupted Price leveled an emotional charge that the enemies of constitutional liberty in Europe had sent agents into the United States who were rallying a party of desperate and unprincipled men to crusade against the institution of slavery. Misleading the ignorant, he proclaimed, they were avowing themselves enemies of the Constitution and the Union, and with treasonable designs the abolition party, the Governor added, was attracting corrupt politicians in the northern states as a way to obtain votes. Price failed to make clear just how or why opposition to slavery was treasonous or a danger to constitutional liberties.

Actually, few Missourians and no major political leaders had come out for abolition, but they did oppose the extension of slavery. Such later antislavery men as Blair and B. Gratz Brown were still supporting slavery where it already existed in the early fifties, and they expressed no moral criticism of the institution. Brown even stated that he believed the Negro to be inferior to the whites. Blair and Brown were satisfied to make their stand against the extension of slavery on the economic grounds that a slave labor force detracted from immigration and held back the progress of new areas. In 1855 Brown, through his *Missouri Democrat*, continued to attack both abolitionists and disunionists. As both men, but especially Blair, looked more and more toward the Republican party, they began to appear to *status quo* Missourians as extremists even though the Republican platform was limited to nonextension. It was not until 1857 that slavery really came under any attack in Missouri. Missourians, nevertheless, entered the elections of 1856 with great internal tensions and divisions over slavery extension, over attempts to equate antiextension with abolition, and over national policies.

A Whig convention had been projected for April, 1856, but it failed to convene, since the party had virtually ceased to exist in Missouri. Many of its Union-minded members had moved into the Know-Nothing party and were actively organizing that party for the coming campaign.

Before any state conventions were held, Blair, Brown, and other Benton Democrats met with moderate Know-Nothing leaders in an effort to effect a coalition opposed to the southern Democrats and to offset what they considered to be the threat of nullification and possible disunion. At the Know-Nothing state convention, Rollins tried unsuccessfully to secure an agreement for the party to join with the Benton people; under such circumstances he wanted to head the state ticket. Other leaders preferred a candidate from the anti-Benton wing of the Democratic party. The choice fell upon Robert C. Ewing, a former Benton Democrat, with the rest of the ticket divided between old-line Benton men and Whigs.

Both Democratic factions had members on the party's state central committee, and each committee faction issued a call for a state convention to meet in Jefferson City on April 21. After some effort to bring the two groups together, ex-Governor King reported to the Benton men that reunion could not be accomplished under honorable terms. For all practical purposes, the two groups proceeded to prepare for the 1856 campaign as opposition parties. Brown's nomination of Benton for governor surprised many because it appeared to be a reversal of the coalition policy that Blair and Brown had helped formulate. The reasons for the switch were complex. A recent city election in St. Louis had shown such strong German opposition to the Know-Nothings that Benton men feared a possible loss of support from this important group for any ticket bearing the Know-Nothing label. But there were probably deeper motives involved. Benton had refused to have anything to do with the new Republican party that had been organized in opposition to the Kansas-Nebraska Act, but Blair was increasingly attracted to its strong antislavery stand. He did not attend the Republican national convention, presided over by his father, in February, 1856, but he was named as a member of the Republican National Executive Committee. Blair, denying the authority of the convention to make such an assignment, pledged to Missourians that he would not abandon the old Andrew Jackson-Benton wing of the Democratic party. It appears fairly clear, however, that Brown, who found the switching of party affiliations no problem, and Blair were planning, without advance publicity, to form a Republican party in the state. This would not be easy, since the epithet "Black Republican" had already come into common usage in Missouri. Looking to the possibility that the Benton wing of the Democratic party might be turned into charter members of a future Republican organization, the planners, by flattering Benton with the nomination for governor—although Blair doubted that he could win—sought to secure his support for a Republican national ticket headed by John C. Frémont or, at least, to get Benton's acquiescence to such a movement. The Benton party's platform closely approximated the one later adopted by the Republican party in its national convention, and the dominant personalities behind the Benton group later became early members of the Republican party when it was organized in the state. Blair must have realized that as a party the Benton Democrats were very weak, and that the effort to run Benton without other support and with an antisouthern coalition already in the field would bring its sure *coup de grâce.*

The convention of anti-Benton Democrats at Jefferson City nominated Trusten Polk for governor. A member of the state constitutional convention in 1845, Polk's first try for elective office was as an anti-Benton candidate for Congress in Missouri's First Congressional District in 1854. He was badly defeated by Benton, but he secured the gubernatorial nomination as a strong anti-Benton, States' rights, proslavery man. This group emerged from the state conventions in control of the regular party name and organization; in Missouri the party of Jackson had been captured by southern, proslavery forces.

The campaign debates raged over States' rights, nullification, and the status of slavery in the territories. Benton's call to avoid agitation on the slavery question proved impossible, and his concern for the Union brought him into direct conflict with the southern extensionists, whom he blamed for the tensions. Ewing and his Know-Nothing supporters, stressing the American party's position of moderation on slavery and of devotion to the Union, claimed their party could save the Union from disruption and preserve the domestic institutions of the states. Polk won the governorship with a plurality of less than 41 per cent. Ewing had polled 35 per cent and Benton got the remaining 24 per cent. Had Benton not been in the field, the more moderate party and candidate might have won. Blair managed to win a seat in the national House of Representatives with his St. Louis-based political support.

Missourians had a choice of three of the four presidential tickets in 1856. The candidate of the national Democratic party, James Buchanan of Pennsylvania, represented an attempt to secure a sectional compromise; the party's platform endorsed the Compromise of 1850, the Kansas-Nebraska Act, and popular sovereignty. The Benton wing of the party had no chance to shape the party platform or to take part in the selection of its candidate, since the national convention rejected its delegation and admitted the delegation from the anti-Benton group. The Benton men knocked down a doorkeeper and forced their way into the hall, but they withdrew after a rebuke from the presiding officer. The convention's action left the Benton forces in Missouri without any national party affiliation.

The American party nominated Millard Fillmore and adopted a nativist platform that reflected the origins of the party; the candidate was not, however, a strong nativist. The platform stressed national unity, but the unity of the party itself was destroyed at the convention. When a northern resolution that no candidates should be named who would not support an extension of the Missouri Compromise line failed to pass, the Northerners bolted while the southerners stayed to nominate Fillmore. The northern wing would later declare for Frémont. When Missouri's American party stayed with the convention and Fillmore, organized Know-Nothingism in the state found itself attached to a proslavery position.

Missouri's Edward Bates presided over the final Whig national convention—a "collection of fossils" according to the *New York Tribune*. The convention rather weakly nominated Fillmore, as the American party had already done, called for preservation of the Union, and issued a warning against the dangers of sectionalism.

The newly formed Republican party, which stood squarely against the extension of slavery and stressed the constitutional right and moral obligation of Congress to prohibit its extension into the territories, fielded the fourth national ticket. The convention found a glamorous candidate in the western explorer John C. Frémont—Benton's son-in-law. An effort to get a Republican party electoral ticket in Missouri failed because of vigorous opposition from Benton and the press. Blair had suggested that such a ticket would be injudicious, although he favored Frémont and was disappointed that Benton not only refused to support his son-in-law but announced for Buchanan. Missourians gave Buchanan a solid victory.

Missouri's traditional party labels and organizations had practically disappeared or lost their earlier identifying characteristics by 1856, but the basic issues remained unresolved. There was great political activity in the last part of the decade involving the efforts of individuals and factions to make new alignments to support their positions on slavery and on the nature of the Union. Secret and public caucuses were plentiful, and new political groupings were formed and then dissolved as leaders changed their party and factional affiliations. The labels "conservative" and "radical" are frequently used in discussions of the politics of the period, but they are difficult designations to define clearly. Only in a limited sense could they, in their full context, be applied to the formation or attempted formation of political parties. There was, broadly speaking, a conservative position represented by those who sought to avoid a sectional conflict and to quiet the dispute over the extension of slavery. These men or groups were Union-minded, but they were not necessarily antislavery and they proposed no change in that institution where it existed. Any effort to link the conservatives with earlier parties has limitations, although most of them had political backgrounds in the Whig party or in the Benton wing of the Democratic party. Not all persons with such prior political connections, however, took this conservative stance. There were two radical positions reflecting a more positive commitment to a course of action on slavery and a greater willingness to risk disunion in an effort to force into being their special views. One group of radicals stood absolutely opposed to any extension of slavery and exhibited hostility to the institution itself. Most adherents to this radicalism were Union-minded men who also favored the exercise of national power to advance their interest in railroads, and business and commercial development. The second radical position sought to guarantee the absolute right of slaveholders to carry slaves into the territories. Leaders of this persuasion were the slaveholders who had long been a power in the Democratic party, and since the mid-forties many of them had been anti-Benton Democrats. The strong and positive assertion of the doctrine of States' rights, with its challenge to national power, gave the latter position, in a different political sense, a conservative hue as it stood against change.

In January, 1857, the General Assembly met in joint session to select two United States senators. James S. Green of Louisiana, one of Benton's old supporters and then a member of the ultra-southern party, was easily elected to fill Atchison's seat, which had been vacant since 1855. Benton's followers, still loyal to their man, cast thirty-three votes for him, but he ran a poor second. In the contest to replace Geyer, who did not seek re-election, the legislators chose Governor Polk by a large majority. The proslavery Democrats clearly controlled the Missouri legislature.

As the southern radicals appeared to be consolidating their control of state politics, the radicals oriented toward the North opened a frontal assault upon slavery. In February of 1857 B. Gratz Brown made a major speech in the Missouri House calling for the emancipation of all slaves in the state. The speech contained no emotional appeal for a moral crusade. Brown did not speak as a humanitarian; instead he offered economic reasons to support his call. He stressed that emancipation would attract an increased immigration, stimulate trade and commerce, and cause the value of Missouri land to increase. Brown agreed with the criticism being voiced that Missouri's economic growth had been too slow, and he argued that slavery had been the cause. If not fully clarified or actually realized, Brown was appealing to Missourians to abandon an outmoded system of agrarianism based on slave labor. He proposed gradual emancipation with compensation, but Missouri's proslavery party considered Brown's proposal nothing short of fanatical abolitionism. The General Assembly made its position clear when it adopted by an overwhelming majority a resolution stating that emancipation was inexpedient, impolitic, and unwise.

Early that same year the Brown and Blair *Missouri Democrat* came out with a bold, open call for emancipation. The paper then took up the campaign for a free white labor movement and by the summer had earned a national reputation as an advocate of that cause.

The first chance to challenge the new southern party came in

August, 1857, with the special election for governor necessitated by Polk's resignation to accept the Senate seat. Leaders with diverse political backgrounds, including old-line Whigs, Benton Democrats, Know-Nothings and Frank Blair's semisecret Republicans, worked out an agreement to support James S. Rollins for governor. In announcing his candidacy by letter to the *Missouri Statesman*, Rollins emphasized that he was responding to the invitation from various groups, and that he was running as an Independent. As the campaign progressed, the word "Opposition" came into common usage in regard to the Rollins candidacy. The controlling Democrats, taking the name of National Democrats, put up Robert M. Stewart of St. Joseph, whose campaign was managed by Claiborne F. Jackson. Stewart had the advantage of a traditional party name and an existing organization. He also had the support of most of the county papers that strongly criticized Rollins on grounds that his position on slavery verged dangerously close to emancipation; a few even went so far as to charge abolition. Rollins conducted a vigorous campaign. He had a wide range of support from such leaders as the old Whig George R. Smith, the 1856 American candidate for governor, Robert C. Ewing, and Frank Blair. Despite the efforts of Rollins toward moderation, another prominent supporter B. Gratz Brown continued to preach the radical antislavery cause.

The vote was close, with Stewart the winner by slightly more than 300 votes in a total of over 95,000 cast. The former Whig strongholds, the larger towns and more thickly populated, economically advanced areas, gave a majority vote to Rollins. Stewart carried the traditionally Democratic controlled rural, less developed agrarian counties. Ironically, Rollins won in 19 of the 27 largest slaveholding counties and had a majority of the combined vote of all of them. Stewart was victorious in 21 of the 27 counties with the smallest slaveholdings. Slaveholding, as such, therefore, would not appear to have been a decisive factor in the election's outcome. Rollins's conservatism on the slavery question, especially well known in the old Whig areas, made him acceptable to most slaveholders. The charges of the county papers against his alleged radicalism apparently had greater influence on voters in the more rural, traditionally

Democratic areas. Men in the state's predominantly agrarian areas may have left Benton, or he may have left them in the changing times of the fifties, but it is impossible to discount the idea that these rural voters still looked upon the Democratic label as most representative of their traditional values and as opposed to national power and commercial interests.

After his defeat, Rollins continued to advocate the formation of an entirely new Unionist party to oppose the National Democrats. He, and others like him, wanted the new party to avoid the nativism of the Know-Nothings, the radical emancipation sentiment of the abolitionists, and the free-soil position of the growing northern-based Republican party, but the chances for creating such a coalition rapidly diminished as moderation lost its appeal amidst the resurgence of extremism on both sides.

In spite of the continued plea by Rollins for moderation, Brown intensified his push to advance the Free White Labor Movement. William F. Switzler claimed in 1858 that less than 15,000 persons in Missouri favored emancipation, but Missouri's antislavery forces were determined to prove Switzler wrong and to enlarge their following whatever its size.

After the apparent proslavery southern takeover of the party in 1857, Brown declared that he would cooperate with any party, anybody, or anything to defeat the then existing Democratic party leadership. Brown seemingly chose to key an opposition offense to the advocacy of the Free White Labor Movement. Undoubtedly the depression of 1857 had made laborers more responsive to political appeals offering to improve the conditions of the workingmen. Speaking at a Jackson Day meeting at St. Louis in January, 1858, Brown made the cause of free white labor his primary subject. Free labor and slave labor were, he stated, incompatible institutions; one or the other was sure to dominate or banish its rival. The picture being drawn was indeed a bleak one: black slave labor not only degraded the white worker, but also threatened the very existence of free labor.

Even the strongest opponents of slavery, however, continued to consider Negroes inferior. Moreover, some feared the competition from free black labor, and nearly all considered the problems of social adjustment in a biracial society too great to be resolved. The great percentage of Missourians strongly opposed free blacks living in their midst.

Proposals to resettle Negroes in Africa had been offered quite early in the state, but they had gained little support. After 1850 colonization seems to have attracted a growing number of adherents in Missouri, especially among church leaders. An increasing number of Missourians who had come to consider slavery as immoral but refused to accept free blacks in their society began to view colonization as a way out of their dilemma. One Presbyterian minister attempted to demonstrate that colonization would complete a divine plan and show God's power of making good out of evil. Using a tortured form of reasoning, he contended that geography had literally blocked European entry into Africa. Thus, he believed, the Americans had brought the Africans to the United States where they were converted, educated, and more generally civilized; now, through colonization, they would be returned to Africa as improved persons to in turn improve that land and its people.

It remained for Frank Blair, among the politicians, to announce a colonization plan for use by the free white labor leaders. He presented an elaborately drawn plan in a major address in the national House of Representatives in January of 1858, just after Brown's Jackson Day speech in St. Louis. Blair frankly acknowledged that the widespread fear of the free Negro in white society made any emancipation of the slaves impossible without assurances of their removal. Although some believed that colonization might be the best thing for the blacks, Blair's proposal made it clear that the major concern was to benefit white laborers, white land seekers, and the whole of white society by removing blacks because they were "found to be fatal to the interest of our race." Brown praised the plan of his friend and cousin.

Newly elected Gov. Robert M. Stewart strongly condemned the antislavery movement. It was his party, Stewart proclaimed in his inaugural address, that offered the only hope to defeat the traitorous, seditious, and revolutionary faction that had recently been organized to overthrow the Constitution and destroy the Union. The vile slander, as Stewart termed it, being circulated by the enemies of the social system that white labor was degraded by the existence of African slavery must be repelled.

The Opposition suffered a severe defeat in the off-year election of 1858. The Democrats won 74 seats in the Missouri House, the Opposition 58; in the Senate they had 24 to the Opposition's 9. The make-up of the General Assembly was not, however, clearly indicative of the popular will, because the apportionment for representation was still working for the agrarian Democrats. The sections carried by the Opposition held approximately 50 per cent of the population and, interestingly enough, some 54 per cent of the slaves and 77 per cent of the foreign-born inhabitants. The congressional races revealed considerable party confusion, but the Democratic party was certainly the strongest single force. Blair failed to win a majority vote in his bid for re-election to Congress, but after filing a long list of charges including bribery and fraud the United States House seated him in 1860 by a straight party vote.

After the 1858 election Blair and his lieutenant Brown turned their attention to the task of making the Republican party a viable party for 1860; at the same juncture the increasing control of the National Democrats by the proslavery faction was moving that party toward a more extreme position. As Governor Price had done before him, Governor Stewart charged in his annual message in December, 1858, that the recent discord was the work of agents introduced into this country by European enemies of free government. In justifying slavery and white supremacy the Governor damned the abolitionists. They did not, he said, want really to elevate the Negro, but to degrade white labor to the level of the blacks. Sounding a class conflict theme, Stewart accused the abolitionists of planning to establish "the English system of slavery—the dependence of labor upon capital—of all forms of slavery the one which is best calculated to engender sentiments of hostility to the social system, and render the laboring classes helpless, dependent and wretched." Stewart directed his comments less against action taking place in Missouri than against that on the national stage, but the General Assembly had plans afoot to reduce the problem, as its leaders saw it, within the state. The legislature in 1859–1860 passed an act that would force all free Negroes to leave the state or be sold into slavery. Despite his rhetoric and strong proslavery stance, Governor Stewart was unwilling to commit Missouri to such an extreme course of action, and he vetoed the bill. More moderate on the question of the Union than some other leaders of his party, Stewart would soon advise against secession in a time of still greater crisis.

Thus, as the decade closed, Missouri was torn internally by the same issues that hardened the nation's sectional alignments and ultimately provoked the war between the states. This dramatic switch from the unity that had prevailed in 1820, when Missourians had united in their demands for statehood without restriction on slavery, revealed the intensification of the slavery problem and the changing nature of Missouri society that had occurred in the ensuing four decades. As a new state, Missouri was the nation's westernmost outpost. Sparsely populated, its frontier agrarian economy and social institutions strongly reflected the southern heritage of the majority of its residents. New immigrants from free states and from abroad, especially those arriving after 1840, contributed to a diversification of the state's economy as commerce and business developed important connections with the North. These years also witnessed the growth of a culture that increasingly mirrored the nation's diverse make-up.

The political parties that had come to represent significant values to most Missourians by 1840, and that had served as important instruments in shaping compromise and public policy, broke down in the decade of the 1850's. With the proslavery forces taking over the party of Andrew Jackson and Thomas H. Benton, and the Whig party disintegrating, men and groups sought to form new coalitions and parties. Amid the high emotionalism a growing number of extremists on both sides of the slavery and Union questions challenged and threatened to overwhelm those who favored a course of moderation.

Missouri could properly and proudly claim a rich and diverse culture and a well-developed and varied economy, but such diversity, unfortunately, made unanimity on the problems of the day probably more difficult for Missourians to achieve than for the people of any other state in the Union. As the nation stood on the brink of disunion, Missourians faced not only their internal problems, but also the still larger question of the state's future alignment, should a division of the Union actually occur.

# ESSAY ON SOURCES

The purpose of this essay is twofold. First it is designed to indicate the sources consulted in the preparation of this study, and secondly it is offered as a guide for further reading. The list is necessarily selective, but an attempt has been made to include the most pertinent material dealing with Missouri's history from 1820 to 1860.

List of Abbreviations Used

*The Bulletin* for *Bulletin of the Missouri Historical Society*
*MHR* for *Missouri Historical Review*

General Histories and Reference Works

David D. March's excellent four-volume work *The History of Missouri* (New York and West Palm Beach, 1967) is the best general history of Missouri, while the most recent one-volume treatment is Duane Meyer, *The Heritage of Missouri: A History* (St. Louis, 1970). Other single-volume general histories include Edwin C. McReynolds, *Missouri: A History of the Crossroads State* (Norman, Oklahoma, 1962); Frederic A. Culmer, *A New History of Missouri* (Mexico, Missouri, 1938), and Eugene Morrow Violette, *A History of Missouri* (reprint ed., Cape Girardeau, Missouri, 1957). The latter, first published in 1918, is still of value especially for the pre-1900 period.

Floyd C. Shoemaker's *Missouri and Missourians: Land of Contrasts and People of Achievements*, 5 vols. (Chicago, 1943) continues to be an important source of information on the state. An older study still useful as a general reference is *Missouri: Mother of the West*, 5 vols. (Chicago and New York, 1930) by Walter Williams and Floyd C. Shoemaker. *Missouri: A Guide to the "Show Me" State*, rev. ed. (New York, 1954) compiled by workers of the Writers' Program of the Work Projects Administration in the State of Missouri contains a great deal of general history and Missouriana. Two early reference works of value are John T. Scharf's *History of St.*

*Louis City and County from the Earliest Period to the Present Day*, 2 vols. (Philadelphia, 1883) and Walter B. Stevens, *St. Louis, The Fourth City, 1764–1909*, 2 vols. (St. Louis, 1911). Ernest Kirschten's *Catfish and Crystal* (Garden City, New York, 1960) is a more recent popularly written history of St. Louis. The published county histories are too numerous to include here, but many of them contain useful information relative to local and state history.

MANUSCRIPT COLLECTIONS

Important manuscript collections related to the 1820–1860 period in the holdings of the Missouri Historical Society in St. Louis include the Lewis F. Linn Papers, the George R. Smith Papers, the Samuel Treat Papers, and the Hamilton R. Gamble Papers, the latter of which are disappointing in their mention of politics prior to 1860. The William P. Napton Diary, starting in 1825, spans several years of Napton's career.

The State Historical Society of Missouri in Columbia holds the valuable Abiel Leonard Collection, the Thomas A. Smith Manuscript Collection, and the lengthy Charles Daniel Drake Autobiography, which is informative but contains little on political affairs. In addition, the David Rice Atchison Papers, the Daniel Dunklin Collection, and the Abiel Leonard Papers are in the Western Manuscripts Collection at the University of Missouri.

Only a small number of Thomas H. Benton's papers were preserved, consequently both the Missouri Historical Society and the State Historical Society of Missouri have only a few Benton documents.

OFFICIAL DOCUMENTS

The congressional debates and proceedings on questions concerning Missouri are found in the *Annals of the Congress of the United States, 1789–1824* (Washington, D. C., 1834–1856), *Register of Debates in Congress 1824–1837* (Washington, D. C., 1825–1837), and *Congressional Globe, 1837–1860* (Washington, D. C., 1837–1860). Although often incomplete, the periodic census reports compiled by the United States government provide important information on the people, economy, and social institutions of Missouri. *The American State Papers: Foreign Relations, Indian Affairs, Military Affairs, Public Lands*, and *Miscellaneous* (Washington, D. C., 1832–1861) also contain some useful documents pertaining to Missouri.

The *Journal of the House of Representatives of the State of Missouri* and the *Journal of the Senate of the State of Missouri*, First through the Twenty-first General Assemblies (St. Charles and Jefferson City, 1821–1860), while not a record of debates comparable to those of Congress, are the official record of the proceedings of the state's legislative body. The laws passed by each General Assembly were regularly published, usually under the title *Laws of the State of Missouri*. Also of value are the *Revised Statutes of the State of Missouri, Revised and Digested by the Thirteenth General Assembly* (St. Louis, 1845), and *The Revised Statutes of the State of Missouri, Revised and Digested by the Eighteenth General Assembly* (Jefferson City, 1856).

For constitutional study, see the *Constitution of the State of Missouri*, 1820, the *Constitution of the State of Missouri*, 1845, the *Journal of the Missouri State* [Constitutional] *Convention*, 1820, and the *Journal of the* [Constitutional] *Convention of the State of Missouri*, 1845.

Essential to the study of the 1820–1860 period is *The Messages and Proclamations of the Governors of the State of Missouri*, vols. 1–3 of 20 vols., edited by Buel Leopard and Floyd C. Shoemaker (Columbia, Missouri, 1922).

PUBLISHED COLLECTIONS, MISCELLANEOUS DOCUMENTS, AND
CONTEMPORARY ACCOUNTS

The State Historical Society of Missouri has published a number of accounts written by observers of the 1820–1860 Missouri scene in the *Missouri Historical Review*. Several of these accounts were of special importance in this study. William Bek translated the highly informative writings of Gottfried Duden as "Gottfried Duden's Report, 1824–27," appearing in the *MHR*, 12 (October, 1917, January, April, and July, 1918), 1–21, 81–89, 163–79, 258–70; and 13 (October, 1918, January and April, 1919), 44–56, 157–81, 251–81. An account less optimistic about the frontier than Duden's is that of "Nicholas Hesse, German Visitor to Missouri, 1835–37," also translated by William G. Bek, *MHR*, 41 (October, 1946, January, April, and July, 1947), 19–44, 164–83, 285–304, 373–90; and 42 (October, 1947, January and April, 1948), 34–49, 140–52, 241–48. Travelers' observations about Missouri society are found in William E. Lass, "Tourists' Impressions of St. Louis, 1766–1859," *MHR*, 52 (July, 1958), 325–38; Vivian K. McLarty, "A Missionary's Wife Looks at Missouri: Letters of Julia Barnard Strong, 1836–1839," *MHR*, 47 (July, 1953), 329–43; Donald

H. Welsh, ed., "Martha J. Woods Visits Missouri in 1857," *MHR*, 55 (January, 1961), 109–23; Ross A. Webb, "Do Right to Me Often," *MHR*, 54 (October, 1959), 18–26; and Eduard Zimmerman, "Travel into Missouri in October, 1838," *MHR*, 9 (October, 1914), 33–43. Durward T. Stokes, ed., "The Wilson Letters, 1835–49," *MHR*, 60 (July, 1966), 495–517, and William D. Hoyt, Jr., "A Clay Countian's Letters of 1834," *MHR*, 45 (July, 1951), 349–53 are two general letter collections from western Missouri. Descriptions of western Missouri society may also be found in W. Darrell Overdyke, ed., "A Southern Family on the Missouri Frontier: Letters from Independence, 1843–1855," *Journal of Southern History*, 17 (May, 1951), 216–37.

For a contemporary's assessment of Missouri towns and town development, see Ralph Gregory, "Count Baudissin on Missouri Towns," *The Bulletin*, 27 (January, 1971), 111–24.

Articles with significant observations of Indian life in Missouri include "Journey to the Land of the Osages, 1835–36," by Louis R. Cortambert, trans. by Mrs. Max W. Myer in *The Bulletin*, 19 (April, 1963), 199–230, and David W. Eaton, ed., "Indian Mode of Life in Missouri and Kansas," *MHR*, 9 (October, 1914), 43–50. Documents relating to George C. Sibley's observations about white settlement in western Missouri and his plans for Indian removals are included in William E. Unrau's "George C. Sibley's Plea for the 'Garden of Missouri'," *The Bulletin*, 27 (October, 1970), 2–13.

Several contemporary publications reveal Missourians' critical attitude toward blacks and their support for slavery. Among these are the Reverend Leander Ker, *Slavery Consistent with Christianity* (Weston, Missouri, 1853); James Adair Lyon, *An Address on the Missionary Aspect of African Colonization* (St. Louis, 1850); Nathan Lewis Rice, *Ten Letters on the Subject of Slavery* (St. Louis, 1855); and Platte County Self-Defensive Association, *Negro Slavery No Evil; or the North and the South* (St. Louis, 1854). The "List of free Negroes licensed by the County Court of St. Louis County, 1847," among the Dexter P. Tiffany Papers, Missouri Historical Society, is an important document showing the occupations of the free blacks. The Missouri Historical Society also holds a rare copy of *The Colored Aristocracy of St. Louis* (St. Louis, 1858) by Cyprian Clamorgan, in which the author provides sketches of wealthy St. Louis blacks. An outstanding memoir for the study of slavery in the state is H. C. Bruce, *The New Man. Twenty-Nine Years a Slave. Twenty-Nine Years a Free Man* (York, Pennsylvania, 1895). A brief note on the free black churches of St. Louis is found in Galusha Anderson, *The Story of a Border City During the Civil War* (Boston, 1908).

The well-known missionary Timothy Flint provided one of the most frequently quoted sources on early Missouri with his *Recollections of the Last Ten Years Passed in Occasional Residences and Journeyings in the Valley of the Mississippi* . . . (Boston, 1826). Although favoring his own role in history, Thomas H. Benton's *Thirty Years View*, 2 vols. (New York, 1859) abounds with information on public affairs. The letters of John B. C. Lucas, opponent of the large Spanish land claimants and enemy of Benton, are available in John B. C. Lucas, Jr., compiler, *Letters of Hon. J. B. C. Lucas from 1815–1836* (St. Louis, 1905), and correspondence of the St. Louis doctor-politician William Carr Lane is available in "Letters of William Carr Lane 1819–1831," *Glimpses of the Past*, 7, Missouri Historical Society (July–September, 1940), 49–114. *Personal Recollections of Many Prominent People Whom I Have Known, and of Events—Especially of Those Relating to the History of St. Louis— During the First Half of the Present Century*, by John F. Darby, a long-time political leader (St. Louis, 1880), is useful but not always fully accurate. William V. N. Bay's *Reminiscences of the Bench and Bar of Missouri* (St. Louis, 1878) contains abundant information about many important pre–Civil War personalities.

Letters of political significance from the artist-politician George Caleb Bingham are in C. B. Rollins, ed., "Letters of George Caleb Bingham to James S. Rollins," *MHR*, 32 (October, 1937, January, April, and July, 1938), 3–34, 164–202, 340–77, 484–522; and 33 (October, 1938, January, April, and July, 1939), 45–78, 203–29, 349–84, 499–526. The Missouri Historical Society has published "Letters of Thomas Caute Reynolds, 1847–1885," *Glimpses of the Past*, 10 (January–June, 1943), 1–54. For a collection of letters and other documents relating to a major figure of the Missouri theatre, see "Sol Smith and Theatre Folk, 1836–1865," *Glimpses of the Past*, 5 (July–September, 1838), 97–136.

For facts on the Santa Fe trade, see William Becknell, "The Journals of Capt. Thomas Becknell From Boone's Lick to Santa Fe, and From Santa Cruz to Green River," *MHR*, 4 (January, 1910), 65–84. Jonas Viles compiled the important "Documents Illustrating the Troubles on the Border, 1858," *MHR*, 1 (April, 1907), 198–215; "Documents Illustrating the Troubles on the Border, 1859," *MHR*, 1 (July, 1907), 293–306; and "Documents Illustrating the Troubles on the Border, 1860," *MHR*, 2 (October, 1907), 61–77.

*Documents Containing the Correspondence, Orders, etc. in Relation to the Disturbances with the Mormans* (Fayette, Missouri, 1841), published by the Missouri State Department, presents the state's side of that controversy. For a Mormon view of their troubles in Missouri, see B. H. Roberts, ed., *History of the Church of Jesus Christ of Latter-Day Saints. Period I. History of Joseph Smith, the Prophet, by Himself*, 6 vols. (Salt Lake City, 1902–1912).

NEWSPAPERS

Of the large number of newspapers published in Missouri for some duration between the years of 1820 and 1860, the following are among the most important: Boonville *Missouri Register*; Columbia *Missouri Statesman*; Franklin, Fayette, and Columbia *Missouri Intelligencer*; Jackson *Independent Patriot*; Jefferson City *Jefferson Examiner, Jefferson Inquirer*, and *Jeffersonian Republican*; St. Charles *Missourian*; and the St. Louis papers: *Intelligencer*; *Missouri Advocate*; *Missouri Argus*; *Missouri Reporter*; *Missouri Republican*; *Morning Gazette*; *St. Louis Beacon*; *St. Louis Enquirer*; *Tri-Weekly Missouri Democrat*. Copies of these and many other newspapers are available in the outstanding collection of The State Historical Society of Missouri in Columbia.

BOOKS AND ARTICLES

BIOGRAPHIES AND BIOGRAPHICAL STUDIES

Historians selecting Missouri personalities as subjects for study have produced a significant body of biographical literature.

William E. Parrish ably portrays the life of Missouri's champion of the South in *David Rice Atchison of Missouri: Border Politician* (Columbia, Missouri, 1961). Edward Bates's role in Missouri political life is covered in Marvin R. Cain, *Lincoln's Attorney General: Edward Bates of Missouri* (Columbia, Missouri, 1965). The brilliantly written *Old Bullion Benton: Senator from the New West* (Boston, 1956) by William N. Chambers is the most complete and authoritative biography of Thomas H. Benton. A second major biography of Missouri's famous senator is Elbert B. Smith's *Magnificent Missourian: The Life of Thomas Hart Benton* (Philadelphia, 1958). Clarence H. McClure concentrated on Benton's fall from power starting with the currency controversy in the early 1840's in *Opposition in Missouri to Thomas Hart Benton* (Warrensburg, Missouri, 1926).

William E. Smith's *The Francis Preston Blair Family in Politics*, 2 vols. (New York, 1933) contains information relative to Frank

Blair and pre-1860 Missouri politics. Norma L. Peterson successfully unravels the shifting career of B. Gratz Brown in *Freedom and Franchise: The Political Career of B. Gratz Brown* (Columbia, Missouri, 1965). *The Life of George R. Smith, Founder of Sedalia, Missouri* (Sedalia, Missouri, 1904) by Samuel B. Harding includes most of the papers of this long-time political leader of central Missouri. The most recent biography of Sterling Price available is Robert E. Shalhope's *Sterling Price: Portrait of a Southerner* (Columbia, Missouri, 1971). Neither James S. Rollins nor Lewis F. Linn has attracted a recent biographer, but material of value will be found in *James Sidney Rollins* (New York, 1891) by William B. Smith and in *The Life and Public Services of Dr. Lewis F. Linn* (New York, 1857) by E. A. Linn and N. Sargent.

For information on Missouri's artist-politician, see Albert Christ-Janer, *George Caleb Bingham of Missouri: The Story of an Artist* (New York, 1940); John Francis McDermott, *George Caleb Bingham: River Portraitist* (Norman, Oklahoma, 1959); and Maurice E. Bloch, *George Caleb Bingham: The Evolution of an Artist* (Berkeley and Los Angeles, 1967).

Several chapters of Merton L. Dillon's *Elijah P. Lovejoy, Abolitionist Editor* (Urbana, Illinois, 1961) pertain to Lovejoy's Missouri years. Some information on Missouri-based operations of the fur trade is contained in Kenneth W. Porter's *John Jacob Astor, Business Man*, 2 vols. (Cambridge, Massachusetts, 1931). For data on a man active in many phases of Missouri life, see Charles T. Jones, Jr., *George Champlin Sibley: The Prairie Puritan (1782-1863)* (Independence, Missouri, 1970).

Several good biographical studies are available in the volumes of the *Missouri Historical Review*. The lack of source material has prohibited the assemblage of a biography of David Barton, but William E. Foley has detailed clearly the basic political philosophy upon which he charted his course of action in "The Political Philosophy of David Barton," *MHR*, 58 (April, 1964), 278-89. A similar study of Benton is Perry McCandless, "The Political Philosophy and Political Personality of Thomas H. Benton," *MHR*, 50 (January, 1956), 145-58. "The Rise of Thomas H. Benton in Missouri Politics," *MHR*, 50 (October, 1955), 16-29, by the same author relates another phase of Benton's career. For good assessments of some of Missouri's governors, see Joseph F. Gordon, "The Political Career of Lilburn W. Boggs," *MHR*, 52 (January, 1958), 111-22; James R. Sharp, "Gov. Daniel Dunklin's Jacksonian Democracy in Missouri, 1832-1836," *MHR*, 56 (April, 1962), 217-29; Fred Fitzgerald, "Daniel Dunklin,"

*MHR*, 21 (April, 1927), 395–403; and Walter B. Stevens, "Alexander McNair," *MHR*, 17 (October, 1922), 3–21.

Frederic A. Culmer traces the career of the Whig leader Abiel Leonard and includes a collection of letters in "Abiel Leonard," *MHR*, 27 (January, April, and July, 1933), 113–31, 217–39, 315–36; and 28 (October, 1933, January, 1934), 17–37, 103–24. A special study on Senator Linn is Michael B. Husband's "Senator Lewis F. Linn and the Oregon Question," *MHR*, 66 (October, 1971), 1–19. Keith L. Bryant's "George Caleb Bingham: The Artist as a Whig Politician," *MHR*, 59 (July, 1965), 448–63, is a recent study of the artist's political activities. The role of a major participant in the troubles on the western border is described by Lester B. Baltimore in "Benjamin F. Stringfellow: The Fight for Slavery on the Missouri Border," *MHR*, 62 (October, 1967), 14–28, and an avid proslavery spokesman is portrayed by David E. Harrell, Jr., in "James Shannon: Preacher, Educator, and Fire Eater," *MHR*, 63 (January, 1969), 135–70. The fluid nature of Missouri politics is revealed in John Mering's "The Political Transition of James S. Rollins," *MHR*, 53 (April, 1959), 217–26.

For an account of an early Missouri editor, see F. F. Stephens, "Nathaniel Patten, Pioneer Editor," *MHR*, 9 (April, 1915), 139–55, and for a later prominent editor and public leader, see North Todd Gentry, "William F. Switzler," *MHR*, 24 (January, 1930), 161–76.

"George Engelmann, Man of Science," *MHR*, 23 (January, April, and July, 1929), 167–206, 427–46, 517–35; and 24 (October, 1929), 66–86, by William G. Bek, contains Englemann's observations on various topics. Two valuable studies of Missouri doctors are Thomas B. Hall, "John Sappington," *MHR*, 24 (January, 1930), 177–99, and Charles F. Mullett, "Doctor John J. Lowry: A Frontier Physician," *MHR*, 38 (January, 1944), 127–37. T. S. Bowdern's "Joseph La Barge, Steamboat Captain," *MHR*, 62 (July, 1968), 444–69, supplies an interesting portrayal of a man who spent years in the river business. A sketch of Alexander W. Doniphan written by Hugh P. Williamson is in the *Journal of the Missouri Bar*, 8 (October, 1952).

Two standard sources of biographical information are the *Dictionary of American Biography*, ed. by Dumas Malone, 44 vols. (New York, 1933) and the *Biographical Directory of the American Congress, 1774–1949* (Washington, 1950). Jerena East Griffen's *First Ladies of Missouri* (Jefferson City, Missouri, 1970) contains interesting information about the wives of Missouri's governors.

POLITICAL ACTIVITY: 1820–1860

Floyd C. Shoemaker's *Missouri's Struggle for Statehood, 1804–1821* (Jefferson City, 1916) remains a standard source on its subject, especially for the state's internal affairs. A more recent volume by Glover Moore, *The Missouri Controversy, 1819—1821* (Lexington, Kentucky, 1953) supplies a detailed and authoritative account of the controversy at the national level. David D. March's "The Admission of Missouri," *MHR*, 65 (July, 1971), 427–49, is an excellent article. In "The Historical Significance of the Missouri Compromise," *Annual Report of the American Historical Association for the Year 1893*, 20: 249–97, James Albert Woodburn focuses on congressional debates over the Missouri question, and Alfred Lightfoot deals with the "great compromiser" in "Henry Clay and the Missouri Question, 1819–1821," *MHR*, 61 (January, 1967), 143–65. Missouri's reactions to congressional action are dramatically presented in Walter B. Stevens, "The Travail of Missouri for Statehood," *MHR*, 15 (October, 1920), 3–35.

The events related to the selection of a site for the state's capital city are discussed in Jonas Viles, "Missouri Capitals and Capitols," *MHR*, 13 (January, 1919), 135–56, and Perry S. Rader, "The Location of the Permanent Seat of Government," *MHR*, 21 (October, 1926), 9–18.

Monas N. Squires provides an authoritative account of the selection of Missouri's first two senators in "A New View of the Election of Barton and Benton to the United States Senate in 1820," *MHR*, 27 (October, 1932), 28–45, and an assessment of state politics is contained in Alan S. Weiner's "John Scott, Thomas Hart Benton, David Barton and the Presidential Election of 1824: A Case Study in Pressure Politics," *MHR*, 60 (July, 1966), 460–94.

Robert E. Shalhope produced two significant articles dealing with the politics of the Jackson period. In "Thomas Hart Benton and Missouri State Politics: A Re-Examination," *The Bulletin*, 25 (April, 1969), 171–91, he demonstrates that Benton was not a political dictator in the state, and he challenges the thesis that state parties and politics centered around the election of a president in "Jacksonian Politics in Missouri: A Comment on the McCormick Thesis," *Civil War History*, 15 (September, 1969), 210–25. A study of six states, including Missouri, "Consensus or Conflict? Political Behavior in the State Legislatures during the Jacksonian Era," *Journal of Ameri-*

*can History*, 63 (December, 1971), 591–621, by Herbert Ershkowitz and William G. Shade supports the thesis that the political parties struggled over more fundamental policy differences than political spoils.

The common man characteristics of Jacksonianism serve as the theme of Hattie M. Anderson's "The Jackson Men in Missouri in 1828," *MHR*, 34 (April, 1940), 301–34, while the art of running for office under the Jackson label by men who were less than pure Jacksonians is revealed in "William Henry Ashley: A Jackson Man with Feet of Clay," *MHR*, 61 (October, 1966), 1–20, by James E. Moss.

The first of Raymond D. Thomas's three-article series, "A Study in Missouri Politics, 1840–1870," *MHR*, 21 (January, 1927), 166–84, offers an overview of the two decades before the Civil War. Thomas H. Benton is a central figure in several special political studies including C. H. McClure, "Early Opposition to Thomas Hart Benton," *MHR*, 10 (April, 1916), 151–96; Perry McCandless, "The Significance of County Making in the Election of Thomas H. Benton," *MHR*, 53 (October, 1958), 34–38; William A. Hansen, "Thomas Hart Benton and the Oregon Question," *MHR*, 63 (July, 1969), 489–97; and P. O. Ray, "The Retirement of Thomas H. Benton From the Senate and its Significance," *MHR*, 2 (October, 1907, January, 1908), 1–14, 97–111.

For a helpful assessment of Missouri's internal problems see Jonas Viles, "Sections and Sectionalism in a Border State," *Mississippi Valley Historical Review*, 21 (June, 1934), 3–22. Dealing with the same problems but with a pro-Union emphasis is George M. Harvey's "Missouri from 1849 to 1861," *MHR*, 2 (October, 1907), 23–40. An expanded and valuable presentation of Missouri's internal struggle is Walter H. Ryle's *Missouri: Union or Secession* (Nashville, 1931). The fluid nature of politics and politicians is made evident in "The Political Fluctuations of B. Gratz Brown: Politics in a Border State, 1850–1870," *MHR*, 51 (October, 1956), 22–30, by Norma L. Peterson. Democratic party politics and the role of David Rice Atchison in the repeal of the Missouri Compromise are considered in the classic study by P. Orman Ray, *The Repeal of the Missouri Compromise: Its Origin and Authorship* (Cleveland, 1909).

For a survey of state tax policy, see Frederick N. Judson, *A Treatise on the Law and Practice of Taxation in Missouri* (Columbia, Missouri, 1900). Specialized works on political party developments include Walter H. Ryle's "Slavery and Party Realignments in Missouri in the State Election of 1856," *MHR*, 39 (April, 1945), 320–32; Reinhard Luthin's "Organizing the Republican Party in the 'Border-Slave' Regions: Edward Bates's Presidential Candidacy in 1860," *MHR*, 38 (January, 1944), 138–61; and John V. Mering's *The Whig Party in Missouri* (Columbia, Missouri, 1967), which is an excellent expanded history of Missouri's minority party.

A brief survey of Missouri's pre-1860 constitutional history may be found in C. H. McClure, "Constitution Making in Missouri," *Proceedings of the Mississippi Valley Historical Association*, 10 (1918–1921), 112–21, and in Perry McCandless, *Constitutional Government in Missouri* (Iowa City, Iowa, 1971). Useful material on early constitutional developments is available in Isidor Loeb and Floyd C. Shoemaker, *Journal of Missouri Constitutional Convention of 1875 . . . with an Historical Introduction on Constitutions and Constitutional Conventions in Missouri* (Jefferson City, 1920). Both F. W. Lehmann's "The Constitution of 1820," *MHR*, 16 (January, 1922), 239–46, and Floyd C. Shoemaker's "The First Constitution of Missouri," *MHR*, 6 (January, 1912), 51–60, offer good assessments of Missouri's first supreme law. The abortive effort to adopt a new constitution in 1845 is discussed by Priscilla Bradford in "The Missouri Constitutional Controversy of 1845," *MHR*, 32 (October, 1937), 33–55. A judicious assessment of the attack upon Lilburn W. Boggs is offered by Monte B. McLaws in "The Attempted Assassination of Missouri's Ex-Governor, Lilburn W. Boggs," *MHR*, 60 (October, 1965), 50–62.

W. Francis English's *The Pioneer Lawyer and Jurist in Missouri* (Columbia, Missouri, 1947) is a study of merit revealing the influential role of lawyers in politics, as well as their broader role as community leaders. Speechmaking was an art and a very real part of politics, and, as Frances Lea McCurdy demonstrates in the lively and revealing study *Stump, Bar and Pulpit: Speechmaking on the Missouri Frontier* (Columbia, Missouri, 1969), the oratory of the day reflected Missourians' democratic values and aspirations.

GENERAL ECONOMIC DEVELOPMENT

James Neal Primm's *Economic Policy in the Development of a Western State, Missouri 1820–1860* (Cambridge, Massachusetts, 1954) shows the government's role in the economy as being a positive one. A number of important topics are treated in Hattie M. Anderson's "Frontier Economic Problems in Missouri, 1815–1828," *MHR*, 34

(October, 1939, January, 1940), 38–70, 182–203. Some information of value relative to business and economics in Missouri is in John L. Bishop, *A History of American Manufacturers from 1608 to 1860* (Philadelphia and London, 1868).

GEOGRAPHY, RESOURCES, AND BOUNDARIES

An excellent brief description of Missouri's land and other natural resources can be found in James E. Collier, *Geographic Areas of Missouri* (Parkville, Missouri, 1959). Information on the Ozarks is available in the same author's *Geography of the Northern Ozark Border Region in Missouri* (Columbia, Missouri, 1953) and Carl O. Sauer's *The Geography of the Ozark Highland of Missouri* (Chicago, 1920). The relation between resources and settlement is discussed by James F. Ellis in *The Influence of Environment on the Settlement of Missouri* (St. Louis, 1929), and a good article on land values and settlement processes is that of Walter A. Schroeder's "Spread of Settlement in Howard County, Missouri, 1810–1859," *MHR*, 63 (October, 1968), 1–37.

For information on Indian territory lines, disputed state boundaries, and the Platte Purchase, see John L. Thomas, "Some Historical Lines of Missouri," *MHR*, 3 (October, 1908, January and July, 1909), 5–33, 210–33, 251–74; Howard I. McKee, "The Platte Purchase," *MHR*, 32 (January, 1938), 129–47; Dorothy Neuhoff, *The Platte Purchase* (St. Louis, 1924); and "A New Sidelight on the Missouri-Iowa Boundary Dispute," *MHR*, 30 (October, 1935), 57–63.

LAND

B. H. Hibbard's *A History of Public Land Policies* (New York, 1924) is useful to the study of land acquisition in Missouri, while Eugene Morrow Violette unravels much about the Spanish grants in "Spanish Land Claims," *Washington University Studies*, 8 (St. Louis, 1921). Donald J. Abramoske's "The Public Lands in Early Missouri Politics," *MHR*, 53 (July, 1959), 295–305, is a good coverage of that subject for the 1820's. Donald Christisen explains men's attitudes toward the prairies in "A Vignette of Missouri's Native Prairie," *MHR*, 61 (January, 1967), 166–86, and Leon Parker Ogilvie traces public policy on swamplands prior to 1860 in "Governmental Efforts at Reclamation in the Southeast Missouri Lowlands," *MHR*, 64 (January, 1970), 150–76.

AGRICULTURE

For a brief survey of pre-1860 agriculture in the state, see F. B. Mumford, "A Century of Missouri Agriculture," *MHR*, 15 (July, 1921), 277–97. George F. Lemmer's important contributions to the history of early Missouri agriculture include "Agitation for Agriculture Improvement in Central Missouri Newspapers Prior to the Civil War," *MHR*, 37 (July, 1943), 371–85; "Missouri Agriculture as Revealed in the Eastern Agriculture Press, 1823–1869," *MHR*, 42 (April, 1948), 226–40; "Farm Machinery in Ante-Bellum Missouri," *MHR*, 40 (July, 1946), 467–80; and "The Early Agricultural Fairs of Missouri," *Agricultural History*, 17 (July, 1943), 145–52.

Important aspects of the production and marketing of livestock in Missouri are elaborated in the following studies: George F. Lemmer, "Early Leaders in Livestock Improvement in Missouri," *MHR*, 37 (October, 1942), 29–39; Virginia Sue Hutcheson, "Cattle Drives in Missouri," *MHR*, 37 (October, 1942), 286–96; Clifford Carpenter, "The Early Cattle Industry in Missouri," *MHR*, 47 (April, 1953), 201–15; John Ashton, *A History of Hogs and Pork Production in Missouri*, Monthly Bulletin of the Missouri State Board of Agriculture, 20 (January, 1923); John Ashton, *History of Shorthorns in Missouri Prior to the Civil War*, Monthly Bulletin of the Missouri State Board of Agriculture, 21 (November, 1923); and Frederic A. Culmer, ed., "Selling Missouri Mules Down South in 1835," *MHR*, 24 (July, 1930), 537–49.

INDIANS AND INDIAN POLICY

Historical writing about the few Indians remaining in Missouri after 1820 is somewhat limited. A brief commentary on the various tribes in the state is included in Joab Spencer's "Missouri's Aboriginal Inhabitants," *MHR*, 3 (July, 1909), 275–92. Aspects of the Indian removals to the west are dealt with in David W. Eaton, "Echoes of Indian Emigration," *MHR*, 8 (January, April, and July, 1914), 93–99, 142–53, 198–205, and in Grant Foreman, *The Last Trek of the Indians* (Chicago, 1946). William W. Graves, *The First Protestant Osage Missions: 1820–1837* (Oswego, Kansas, 1949) is helpful on mission work and reveals something of white attitudes toward the Indians. Three of the last incidents of violence between the Indians and Missourians are objectively recorded by Dorothy J. Caldwell in

"The Big Neck Affair: Tragedy and Farce on the Missouri Frontier," *MHR*, 64 (July, 1970), 391–412; Willis B. Hughes, "The Heatherly Incident of 1836," *The Bulletin*, 13 (January, 1957), 161–80; and Robert A. Glenn, "The Osage War," *MHR*, 14 (January, 1920), 201–10.

*The Osages* (Norman, Oklahoma, 1961) by John Joseph Mathews and *The Sac and Fox Indians* (Norman, Oklahoma, 1958) by William T. Hagen are scholarly accounts of Indian groups with remnants in Missouri after 1820.

## NEGROES AND MISSOURI SOCIETY

The growing interest in black history has resulted in an increasing number of published studies, but the field of black history in Missouri continues to be in need of much additional research. *Slavery in Missouri 1804–1865* (Baltimore, 1914) by Harrison A. Trexler remains the standard work on that subject, but a new study of slavery in Missouri should be undertaken. Arvarh E. Strickland's useful article "Aspects of Slavery in Missouri, 1821," *MHR*, 65 (July, 1971), 505–26, raises important questions about the reasons for such strong support in the state for slavery. An excellent assessment of several facets of slavery for a single county is offered by George E. Lee in "Slavery and Emancipation in Lewis County, Missouri," *MHR*, 65 (April, 1971), 294–317, and Lyle W. Dorsett has highlighted the monetary value of the institution in his county study "Slaveholding in Jackson County, Missouri," *The Bulletin*, 20 (October, 1963), 25–37.

Some special topics are considered in Harrison A. Trexler, "The Value and the Sale of the Missouri Slave," *MHR*, 8 (July, 1914), 69–85, and Lorenzo J. Greene, "Self-Purchase of Negroes in Cole County, Missouri," *Midwest Journal*, 1 (Winter, 1949). Benjamin G. Merkel's published works on the antislavery forces in Missouri include *The Anti-Slavery Controversy in Missouri, 1819–1865* (St. Louis, 1942); "Abolition Aspects of Missouri's Antislavery Controversy, 1819–1865," *MHR*, 44 (April, 1950), 232–53; and "The Underground Railroad and the Missouri Borders, 1840–1860," *MHR*, 37 (April, 1943), 271–85. Benjamin Merkel has contributed a worthwhile article, "The Slavery Issue and the Political Decline of Thomas Hart Benton, 1846–1856," *MHR*, 38 (July, 1944), 388–407.

The legal status of slavery is set forth in Eugene M. Violette, "The Black Codes in Missouri," *Proceedings of the Mississippi Valley*

*Historical Association*, 6 (1912–1913), 287–316, and in Emil Ober-holzer, "The Legal Aspects of Slavery in Missouri," *The Bulletin*, 6 (January and April, 1950), 139–61, 333–51.

A highly significant study by G. Hugh Wamble, "Negroes and Missouri Protestant Churches Before and After the Civil War," *MHR*, 61 (April, 1967), 321–47, covers the relations between whites and blacks in nonsegregated churches and reveals the initiative of the blacks in establishing their independent churches. Russell M. Nolen's "The Labor Movement in St. Louis Prior to the Civil War," *MHR*, 34 (October, 1939), 18–37, contains favorable material on the black workers of St. Louis.

For the most complete account of the Dred Scott case, see Vincent C. Hopkins, *Dred Scott's Case* (New York, 1967). Also of value for the Missouri phase of the case are John Bryan, "The Blow Family and Their Slave Dred Scott," *The Bulletin*, 4 (July, 1948), 223–31; 5 (October, 1948), 19–33, and Harold Schwartz, "The Con-troversial Dred Scott Decision," *MHR*, 54 (April, 1960), 262–72.

One of the most recent books dealing with racism in American history and relating to an episode involving Missourians is James A. Rawley's highly readable *Race and Politics: "Bleeding Kansas" and the Coming of the Civil War* (Philadelphia and New York, 1969).

MISSOURI-KANSAS BORDER TROUBLES

*Bleeding Kansas* (New York, 1954) by Alice Nichols remains one of the best over-all treatments of the Kansas territorial problems, while James A. Rawley highlights the racist theme of the period in *Race and Politics: "Bleeding Kansas" and the Coming of the Civil War* (Philadelphia and New York, 1969). An older article relating Missouri to the Kansas question is "Missouri in the Kansas Struggle," *Proceedings of the Mississippi Valley Historical Association*, 9 (1917–1918), 393–413, by Mary J. Klem. Floyd C. Shoemaker's "Missouri's Proslavery Fight for Kansas, 1854–1855," *MHR*, 48 (April and July, 1954), 221–36, 325–40, and 49 (October, 1954), 41–54, contains im-portant details on that subject, while Hildegarde Rose Herklotz concentrates on violence on the Missouri side of the border in "Jay-hawkers in Missouri, 1858–1863," *MHR*, 17 (April and July, 1923), 266–84, 505–13, and 18 (October, 1923), 64–101. Lloyd Lewis reveals that Missouri got an unfavorable press in national coverage in his "Propaganda and the Kansas-Missouri War," *MHR*, 34 (October, 1939), 3–17. For the treatment of a minister with antislavery views in northwestern Missouri during the Kansas difficulties, see Milton E. Bierbaum, "Frederick Starr, A Missouri Border Abolitionist: The Making of a Martyr," *MHR*, 58 (April, 1964), 309-25.

WESTERN TRADE

Ray Allen Billington's *Westward Expansion: A History of the American Frontier* (New York, 1949) and *The Far Western Frontier* (New York, 1956) contain important background and useful information relating to Missouri's western-directed activities.

Standard over-all treatments of the fur trade include Hiram M. Chittenden, *The American Fur Trade of the Far West*, 3 vols. (New York, 1902) and the more recent work *The Fur Trade*, 2 vols. (Norman, Oklahoma, 1961) by Paul C. Phillips. John E. Sunder deals with the trade in its later years in *The Fur Trade on the Upper Missouri, 1840-1865* (Norman, Oklahoma, 1965). For more special reference to Missouri and the fur trade, see Isaac Lippincott, *A Century and a Half of the Fur Trade at St. Louis* (St. Louis, 1916) and Ada Paris Klein, ed., "The Fur Trade," *MHR*, 43 (July, 1949), 360-80, and 44 (October, 1949, January, 1950), 48-65, 168-78.

After traveling with the traders to Santa Fe, Josiah Gregg wrote his *Commerce of the Prairies*, 2 vols. (New York, 1844), which is considered a classic. A major history of the subject is Robert L. Duffus, *The Santa Fe Trail* (New York, 1930). F. F. Stephens relates the trade specifically to the state in "Missouri and the Santa Fe Trade," *MHR*, 10 (July, 1916), 233-62, and 11 (April-July, 1917), 289-312. A special aspect of the trade is presented in an excellent study by Lewis E. Atherton, "Business Techniques in the Santa Fe Trade," *MHR*, 34 (April, 1940), 335-41, and Ralph P. Bieber demonstrates the importance of the Santa Fe trade after the Mexican War in "Some Aspects of the Santa Fe Trail, 1848-1880," *MHR*, 18 (January, 1924), 158-66.

For interesting information of another western venture see Kate L. Gregg, "Missourians in the Gold Rush," *MHR*, 39 (January, 1945), 137-54. A worthwhile article on the business services offered to western-moving immigrants is Jane Hamill Sommer, "Outfitting for the West, 1849," *The Bulletin*, 24 (July, 1968), 340-47, and Lew Larkin's *Vanguard of Empire: Missouri's Century of Expansion* (St. Louis, 1961) relates to the role of Missouri and Missourians in settling the West.

In *The Urban Frontier* (Cambridge, Massachusetts, 1959) Richard C. Wade assesses the role of cities in the development of the frontier, with St. Louis as one of his selected urban frontiers. A general overview of St. Louis at a later time period can be found in Charles VanRavenswaay, "Years of Turmoil, Years of Growth: St. Louis in the 1850's," *The Bulletin*, 23 (July, 1967), 303–24.

Darrell Garwood, *Crossroads of America: The Story of Kansas City* (New York, 1948) is a general history of that city, while two excellent more specialized books related in part to the pre-1860 years are: A. Theodore Brown, *Frontier Community: Kansas City to 1870* (Columbia, Missouri, 1963) and Charles N. Glaab, *Kansas City and the Railroads: Community Policy in the Growth of a Regional Metropolis* (Madison, Wisconsin, 1962). The latter's "Business Patterns in the Growth of a Midwestern City," *Business History Review*, 33 (Summer, 1959), 156–74, emphasizes the role of real estate promotion in the growth of Kansas City.

A good study for factors contributing to town growth is Stuart F. Voss's "Town Growth in Central Missouri, 1815–1860," *MHR*, 64 (October, 1969, January and April, 1970), 64–80, 197–217, 323–50. Special studies relating to individual towns include Jonas Viles, "Old Franklin: A Frontier Town of the Twenties," *Mississippi Valley Historical Review*, 9 (March, 1923), 269–82; Eugene T. Wells, "The Growth of Independence, Missouri, 1827–50," *The Bulletin*, 16 (October, 1959), 33–46; W. L. Webb, "Independence, Missouri, A Century Old," *MHR*, 22 (October, 1927), 30–50; Lillie Franklin, "Rocheport, Missouri, An Illustration of Economic Adjustment to Environment," *MHR*, 19 (October, 1924), 3–11; Frank S. Popplewell, "St. Joseph, Missouri, As a Center of the Cattle Trade," *MHR*, 32 (July, 1938), 443–57; and Edward M. Shepard, "Early Springfield," *MHR*, 24 (October, 1929), 50–65. A worthwhile article dealing with a major urban problem is A. B. Lampe's "St. Louis Volunteer Fire Department, 1820–1850," *MHR*, 62 (April, 1968), 235–59.

MISSOURI SOCIETY IN GENERAL

Lewis E. Atherton's "Missouri's Society and Economy in 1821," *MHR*, 65 (July, 1971), 450–77, is an excellent recent overview of Missouri's society at the time of statehood; an older but still useful description of early Missouri is found in Jonas Viles, "Missouri in 1820," *MHR*, 15 (October, 1920), 36–52. The cultural attainments in early Missouri are discussed in a study of outstanding merit, "Culture and the Missouri Frontier," *MHR*, 50 (July, 1956), 355–70, by John Francis McDermott; "'Add a Pinch and a Lump' Missouri Women in the 1820's," *MHR*, 65 (July, 1971), 478–504, by Jerena East Giffen is an interesting article on early Missouri women.

Hattie M. Anderson deals with a variety of social and economic developments in a series of articles: "Missouri, A Land of Promise," *MHR*, 30 (April, 1936), 227–53; "The Evolution of a Frontier Society in Missouri, 1815–1828," *MHR*, 32 (April and July, 1938), 298–326, 458–83, and 33 (October, 1938), 23–44; and "Missouri 1804–1828: Peopling a Frontier State," *MHR*, 31 (January, 1937), 150–80. William O. Lynch, "The Influence of Population Movements on Missouri Before 1861," *MHR*, 16 (July, 1922), 506–16, may be consulted on this subject.

Alice H. Finckh summarizes the observations of an important contemporary observer in "Gottfried Duden Views Missouri 1824–27," *MHR*, 43 (July, 1949), 334–43, and 44 (October, 1949), 21–30. General descriptions of selected areas of the state include Helen Devault Williams, "Social Life in St. Louis from 1840 to 1860," *MHR*, 31 (October, 1936), 10–24; Wiley Britton, *Pioneer Life in Southwest Missouri* (Kansas City, 1929); Gerard Schultz, *Early History of the Northern Ozarks* (Jefferson City, Missouri, 1937); Ethel Grant Inman, "Pioneer Days in Northwest Missouri—Harrison County, 1837–1873," *MHR*, 22 (April, 1928), 307–30; and Walter H. Ryle, "A Study of Early Days in Randolph County, 1818–1860," *MHR*, 24 (January, 1930), 214–37.

## TRANSPORTATION AND COMMUNICATIONS

Louis C. Hunter's detailed *Steamboats on the Western Rivers* (Cambridge, Massachusetts, 1949) provides important background for understanding river transportation in Missouri, and H. M. Chittenden's *History of Early Steamboat Navigation on the Missouri River*, 2 vols., Reprint (Minneapolis, 1962) is the traditional work on the subject. An interesting story of a great river is Stanley Vestal's *The Missouri* (New York, 1945). For some special aspects of water transportation see Edgar A. Holt, "Missouri River Transportation in the Expansion of the West," *MHR*, 20 (April, 1926), 361–81; Sam T. Bratton, "Inefficiency of Water Transportation in Missouri— A Geographical Factor in the Development of Railroads," *MHR*, 14

(October, 1919), 82–88; W. J. McDonald, "The Missouri River and Its Victims," *MHR*, 21 (January, April, and July, 1927), 215–42, 455–80, 571–607; and Gerard Schultz, "Steamboat Navigation on the Osage River Before the Civil War," *MHR*, 29 (April, 1935), 175–85.

"The Story of Transportation," a series of articles by Floyd C. Shoemaker in *Missouri Motor News* (1934–1935), chronicles several phases of transportation but is especially helpful on early land roads. A general assessment of one approach to road building is in North Todd Gentry's "Plank Roads in Missouri," *MHR*, 31 (April, 1933), 272–81. For a special study on the subject, see Paul C. Doherty, "The Columbia–Providence Plank Road," *MHR*, 57 (October, 1962), 53–69.

R. B. Oliver's "Missouri's First Railroad," *MHR*, 26 (October, 1931), 12–13 is a popular article about a non-steam-powered railroad. Missouri interest in railroad development is reflected in R. S. Cotterdill's "The National Railroad Convention in St. Louis, 1849," *MHR*, 12 (July, 1918), 203–15. A good survey of the subject is Paul W. Gates, "The Railroads of Missouri, 1850–1870," *MHR*, 26 (January, 1932), 126–41, while two special studies of merit are Homer Clevenger, "The Building of the Hannibal and St. Joseph Railroad," *MHR*, 36 (October, 1941), 32–39, and Robert E. Riegal, "The Missouri Pacific Railroad to 1879," *MHR*, 18 (October, 1923), 3–26. *State Aid to Railways in Missouri* (Chicago, 1896) by John W. Million remains a standard source, and Edwin L. Lopata has detailed the financial participation of local governmental units in *Local Aid to Railroads in Missouri* (New York, 1937). The excitement of promoting a bond issue for railroad construction and the problems of retiring the bonds are described in a significant study by Virginia Rust Frazer, "Dallas County Railroad Bonds," *MHR*, 61 (July, 1967), 444–62.

The Missouri phase of overland mail operations is pictured in Donald Welsh, "The Butterfield Overland Mail, 1858–1861 and Its Centennial Observance in Missouri," *MHR*, 52 (April, 1958), 218–34, and early telegraph developments are traced by John E. Sunder in "St. Louis and the Early Telegraph, 1847–1857," *MHR*, 50 (April, 1956), 248–58, and "The Early Telegraph in Rural Missouri, 1847–1859," *MHR*, 51 (October, 1956), 42–53.

## LABOR

Two studies essential to the study of labor in Missouri are Russell M. Nolen, "The Labor Movement in St. Louis prior to the Civil War," *MHR*, 34 (October, 1939, January, 1940), 18–37, 157–81, and Walter R. Houf, "Organized Labor in Missouri Politics Before the Civil War," *MHR*, 56 (April, 1962), 244–54.

## MANUFACTURING AND MERCHANDISING

A good brief survey of iron production is that of Arthur B. Cozzens, "The Iron Industry of Missouri," *MHR*, 35 (July, 1941), 509–38, and 36 (October, 1941), 48–60. A highly significant study by James D. Norris, *Frontier Iron: The Maramec Iron Works, 1820–1876* (Madison, Wisconsin, 1964), reveals the role of the manufacturer in opening and developing the frontier. Isaac Lippincott's "Industrial Influence of Lead in Missouri," *Journal of Political Economy*, 20 (July, 1912), 695–715, relates especially to St. Louis.

Individual manufactured products are discussed in Miles W. Eaton, "The Development and Later Decline of the Hemp Industry in Missouri," *MHR*, 43 (July, 1948), 344–59; Clarence N. Roberts, "Developments in the Missouri Pottery Industry, 1800–1950," *MHR*, 58 (July, 1964), 464–73; Emily Ann O'Neil Bott's "Joseph Murphy's Contribution to the Development of the West," *MHR*, 47 (October, 1952), 18–28, which deals with wagon making; and Charles Van-Ravenswaay's "The Anglo-American Cabinet-makers of Missouri, 1800–1850," *The Bulletin*, 14 (April, 1958), 231–57.

Lewis E. Atherton, *The Frontier Merchant in Mid-America*, rev. ed. (Columbia, Missouri, 1971) shows the important role of the merchant in community life and development. Two excellent studies of individual Missouri business families are Lewis E. Atherton, "James and Robert Aull—A Frontier Missouri Mercantile Firm," *MHR*, 30 (October, 1935), 3–27, and Harvey A. Kantor, "The Barth Family: A Case Study of Pioneer Immigrant Merchants," *MHR*, 62 (July, 1968), 410–30.

## MINING

The problems of national leasing of mineral lands are explored in Donald J. Abramoske's "The Federal Lead Leasing System in Missouri," *MHR*, 54 (October, 1959), 27–38. Two special articles concerning mining in the state are A. M. Gibon, "Lead Mining in Southwest Missouri to 1865," *MHR*, 53 (April, 1959), 197–205, and Sam T. Bratton, "Coal in Missouri," *MHR*, 22 (January, 1928), 150–56.

## BANKING

John Ray Cable thoroughly assesses the operation and role of the state bank in his still useful *The Bank of the State of Missouri* (New York, 1912). A more recent book on banking in the state is that by Timothy Hubbard and Lewis E. Davids, *Banking in Mid-America: A History of Missouri's Banks* (Washington, 1969). Harry S. Gleick produced a commendable two-article series, "Banking in Early Missouri," *MHR*, 61 (July, 1967), 427–43, and 62 (October, 1967), 30–44. See also Frank F. Stephens, "Banking and Finance in Missouri in the Thirties," *Proceedings of the Mississippi Valley Historical Association*, 10 (July, 1920), 122–34. An interesting item on counterfeiting is by J. W. Vincent, "The Slicker War and Its Consequence," *MHR*, 7 (April, 1913), 138–45.

## LITERATURE

*Missouri Writers: A Literary History of Missouri, 1780–1955* (St. Louis, 1955) by Elijah L. Jacobs and Forrest E. Wolverton is a good general survey of the subject. On a broader scale Ralph Leslie Rusk's *The Literature of the Middle Western Frontier* (New York, 1925) has material related to Missouri. Carle Brooks Spotts produced an excellent study of one phase of Missouri literature in his series "The Development of Fiction on the Missouri Frontier (1830–1860)," *MHR*, 28 (April and July, 1934), 195–205, 275–86, and 29 (October, 1934, January, April, and July, 1935), 17–26, 100–108, 186–94, 279–94. The same author discusses the famous river character in "Mike Fink in Missouri," *MHR*, 28 (October, 1933), 3–8. A good reference source on literary production in Missouri is "Missouri in Fiction: A Review and a Bibliography," *MHR*, 42 (April and July, 1948), 209–55, 310–34, by Joe W. Kraus. Alexander N. DeMenil's "A Century of Missouri Literature," *MHR*, 15 (October, 1920), 74–125, is an older article listing a large number of Missouri authors and their works. See also Minnie M. Brashear, "The Missouri Short Story as It Has Grown Out of the Tall Tale of the Frontier," *MHR*, 43 (April, 1949), 199–219.

## NEWSPAPERS

In *The Pioneer Editor in Missouri, 1808–1860* (Columbia, Missouri, 1965) William H. Lyon ably relates the role of the editor in

Missouri society and also provides a vivid description of all phases of newspaper publication on the frontier. A brief coverage of pre–Civil War newspapers is contained in William V. Byar's "A Century of Journalism in Missouri," *MHR*, 15 (October, 1920), 53–73, while an important study of Missouri papers is Minnie Organ's "History of the County Press of Missouri," *MHR*, 4 (January, April, and July, 1910), 111–13, 149–66, 252–308. For data on St. Louis, see Eleanora A. Bear, "Books, Newspapers, and Libraries in Pioneer St. Louis, 1808–1842," *MHR*, 56 (July, 1962), 347–60.

Each of the following is a good account of an individual newspaper: E. W. Stephens, "The *Missouri Intelligencer and Boon's Lick Advertiser*," *MHR*, 13 (July, 1919), 361–71; Loy Otis Banks, "The *Evening and the Morning Star*," *MHR*, 43 (July, 1949), 319–33; Estal B. Sparlin, "The *Jefferson Inquirer*," *MHR*, 32 (January, 1938), 156–63; and Jim A. Hart, "The *Missouri Democrat, 1852–1860*," *MHR*, 55 (January, 1961), 127–41. A book-length study by the latter author is *A History of the St. Louis Globe-Democrat* (Columbia, Missouri, 1961).

MUSIC, THEATRE, ENTERTAINMENT

For brief surveys of Missouri music, see Ernst C. Krohn, "A Century of Missouri Music," *MHR*, 17 (January, April, and July, 1923), 130–58, 285–320, 440–64, and Susan Arnold McCausland, "A Running Glance Over the Field of Music in Missouri," *MHR*, 8 (July, 1914), 206–10.

Two special studies of value on the theatre are: *Theatrical Entertainment in Rural Missouri Before the Civil War* (Columbia, Missouri, 1958) by Elbert R. Bowen and "Dramatic Criticism in Frontier St. Louis, 1835–1838," *MHR*, 58 (January, 1964), 191–216, by James C. Moss.

Elbert R. Bowen's "Amusements and Entertainments in Early Missouri," *MHR*, 47 (July, 1953), 307–17, and Monas V. Squires's "Merry-Making in Missouri in the Old Days," *MHR*, 28 (January, 1934), 91–102, are both interesting and sound studies of this phase of Missouri life. More specialized treatments within this subject are Wm. G. B. Carson's "Night Life in St. Louis a Century Ago," *The Bulletin*, 1 (April, 1945), 3–10, and 2 (October, 1945), 3–10; Laura Langehenning's "The Steamboat, A Playground for St. Louis in the Fifties," *MHR*, 40 (January, 1946), 205–14; and Dorothy J. Caldwell's "Christmas in Early Missouri," *MHR*, 65 (January, 1971),

125–38. Also see Walter B. Stevens, "Missouri Taverns," *MHR*, 15 (January, 1921), 241–76.

Claude A. Phillips's *A History of Education in Missouri* (Jefferson City, Missouri, 1911) contains some information of value, but it is lacking on interpretation and somewhat dated. For a brief survey that includes the pre–Civil War years, see the same author's "A Century of Education in Missouri," *MHR*, 15 (January, 1921), 298–314. For state school legislation and financing, see Earl A. Collins, *Classification of Chartered Schools in Missouri* (Nashville, 1926) and Howard I. McKee, "The School Law of 1853, Its Origin and Authors," *MHR*, 35 (July, 1941), 539–61.

*The University of Missouri: A Centennial History* (Columbia, Missouri, 1939) by Jonas Viles and the more recent *A History of the University of Missouri* (Columbia, Missouri, 1962) by Frank Fletcher Stephens are both solid histories of that institution. John C. Weaver, a recent president of the university, sketches phases of its history in "Footsteps in the Corridors Behind Us," *MHR*, 62 (April, 1968), 213–34.

John F. Spilman's "History of Sylvan School, Lawrence County, Missouri," *MHR*, 50 (October, 1955), 30–43, is an interesting account of the operation of an elementary school, while John Crighton's "The Columbia Female Academy: A Pioneer in Education for Women," *MHR*, 64 (January, 1970), 177–96, and Dorothy B. Dorsey's "Howard High School, the Outstanding Pioneer Co-Educational High School in Missouri," *MHR*, 31 (April, 1937), 249–66, deal with secondary level education. Lydia Wampler's 1946 manuscript "A Brief History of Johnson County Public Schools" in the Johnson County Heritage Library provides information on educational developments in that county.

Studies relating to individual private colleges include Howard I. McKee, "The Marion College Episode in Northeast Missouri History," *MHR*, 36 (April, 1942), 299–319; Carl S. Meyer, *Log Cabin to Luther Tower: Concordia Seminary During One Hundred Twenty-Five Years* (St. Louis, 1965); Lucinda Deleftwich Templin, "Two Illustrious Pioneers in the Education of Women in Missouri," *MHR*, 21 (July, 1926), 420–27, relating to Major George C. and Mary Sibley, founders of Lindenwood College; William B. Faherty, "St. Louis College: First Community School," *The Bulletin*, 24 (January,

1968), 122–38, Rita G. Adams and others, *St. Louis University: 150 Years* (St. Louis, n.d.), and William E. Parrish, *Westminster College: An Informal History, 1851–1969* (Fulton, Missouri, 1971). The early efforts at teacher training in Missouri are discussed by Monia Cook Morris in "Teacher Training in Missouri Before 1871," *MHR*, 43 (October, 1948), 18–37.

Another important work by John Francis McDermott is "Museums in Early Saint Louis," *The Bulletin*, 4 (April, 1948), 129–39, and Walter B. Hendrickson traces the history of an important organization in "The Western Academy of Natural Science of St. Louis," *The Bulletin*, 16 (January, 1960), 114–29. Valuable information on the Mercantile Library may be found in Brad Luckingham's "A Note on the Significance of the Merchant in the Development of St. Louis Society as Expressed in the Philosophy of the Mercantile Library Association, 1846–1854," *MHR*, 57 (January, 1963), 184–98.

RELIGION

*The Story of Religion in America* (New York, 1950) by William W. Sweet is an excellent survey, and it provides background for understanding religious and church developments within the state. There are a number of published histories of the various denominations. *A History of the Baptist in Missouri* (St. Louis, 1882) by R. S. Duncan is still frequently cited, while Robert S. Douglas's *History of Missouri Baptists* (Kansas City, 1934), with an emphasis upon individual associations, is a somewhat more recent work. E. W. Stephens reviews a part of the church's organizational history in "History of Baptist General Association," *MHR*, 7 (January, 1913), 76–88. Still useful is David R. McAnally's *Methodism in Missouri* (St. Louis, 1881), and Frank C. Tucker's *The Methodist Church in Missouri 1798–1939, A Brief History* (Nashville, 1966) is an excellent denominational history. Hauser Winter discusses the division of the Methodist church in "The Division in Missouri Methodism in 1845," *MHR*, 37 (October, 1942), 1–18.

For the Presbyterian church, see Timothy Hill, *Historical Outlines of the Presbyterian Church in Missouri* (Kansas City, 1871) and the same author's *Presbyterianism in Missouri* (Maryville, Missouri, 1900).

Organizational efforts of the Christian church are surveyed in George L. Peters, *The Disciples of Christ in Missouri, Celebrating One Hundred Years of Co-operative Work* (Kansas City, 1937).

On the Episcopal church, see Charles F. Rehkopf, "The Beginnings of the Episcopal Church in Missouri," *The Bulletin*, 11 (April, 1955), 265–78.

Two articles relating to special phases of Catholic developments in the state are: "Recollections of the First Catholic Mission Work in Central Missouri," *MHR*, 5 (January, 1911), 83–93, by Joseph H. Schmidt and "Kansas City's Pioneer Church," *MHR*, 44 (July, 1950), 364–72, by James J. Schlafly.

Walter O. Forster's *Zion on the Mississippi* (St. Louis, 1953) is an extensive treatment of the Saxon migration to Missouri, while a briefer account of that branch of Lutheranism is P. E. Kretzmann's "The Saxon Immigration to Missouri, 1838–1839," *MHR*, 33 (January, 1939), 157–70. Also see Isidor Bush, "The Jews in St. Louis," *The Bulletin*, 8 (October, 1951), 60–70.

Literature on the Church of Jesus Christ of Latter-day Saints is extensive, but much of it reflects a strong point of view. The generally well-rated *No Man Knows My History: The Life of Joseph Smith the Mormon Prophet* (New York, 1946) by Fawn M. Brodie has important material related to the church in Missouri, as does *The Story of the Church* (Independence, Missouri, 1943) by Inez Smith Davis. Warren A. Jennings has published three interesting and well-researched articles on special Mormon topics: "The Expulsion of the Mormons from Jackson County, Missouri," *MHR*, 64 (October, 1969), 41–63; "The Army of Israel Marches Into Missouri," *MHR*, 62 (January, 1968), 107–35; and "Importuning for Redress," *The Bulletin*, 27 (October, 1970), 15–29. For information on Mormon land disposition, see Rollin Britton, "Mormon Land Titles, A Story of Jackson County Real Estate," *Annals of Kansas City Missouri*, Missouri Valley Historical Society, 1 (1921–1924). The same author has published a series of articles entitled "Early Days on Grand River and the Mormon War," *MHR*, 13 (January, April, and July, 1919), 112–34, 287–309, 388–98, and 14 (October, 1919, January and April-July, 1920), 89–116, 233–45, 459–73.

The following are outstanding articles on special aspects of religion in pre–Civil War Missouri: James Hazlett, "The Troubles of the Circuit Rider," *MHR*, 39 (July, 1945), 421–37; Marie George Windell, "The Camp Meeting in Missouri," *MHR*, 37 (April, 1943), 252–70; G. Hugh Wamble, "Negroes and Missouri Protestant Churches Before and After the Civil War," *MHR*, 61 (April, 1967), 321–47; and Leslie Gamblin Hill, "A Moral Crusade: The Influence of Protestantism on Frontier Society in Missouri," *MHR*, 45 (October, 1950), 16–34.

MEDICINE

A brief survey of medical history with reference to medical leaders is available in H. W. Loeb's "One Hunderd Years of Medicine in Missouri," *MHR*, 14 (October, 1919), 74–81. A phase of medical education and one of its leaders are the topics covered by Marjorie E. Fox Grisham in "Joseph Nash McDowell and the Medical Department of Kemper College, 1840–45," *The Bulletin*, 12 (July, 1956), 358–71. The most rewarding study of medicine and medical practice in Missouri is Roland L. Lanser's "The Pioneer Physician in Missouri, 1820–1850," *MHR*, 44 (October, 1949), 31–47. James T. Barrett, "Cholera in Missouri," *MHR*, 55 (July, 1961), 344–54, and Patrick E. McLear, "The St. Louis Cholera Epidemic of 1849," *MHR*, 63 (January, 1969), 171–81, are both good studies of that feared disease.

Problems and controversies within the medical profession are brought out in two fascinating and informative articles by Cynthia De Haven Pitcock, "Doctors in Controversy: An Ethical Dispute Between Joseph Nash McDowell and William Beaumont," *MHR*, 60 (April, 1966), 336–49, and "The Involvement of William Beaumont, M.D., in a Medical-Legal Controversy: The Darnes-Davis Case, 1840," *MHR*, 59 (October, 1964), 31–45.

SOCIAL REFORM

Fern O. Boan's *A History of Poor Relief Legislation and Administration in Missouri* (Chicago, 1941) provides a general coverage of that subject. George B. Mangold, "Social Reform in Missouri, 1820–1920," *MHR*, 15 (October, 1920), 191–213; Marie George Windell, "The Background of Reform on the Missouri Frontier," *MHR*, 39 (January, 1945), 155–83; and the latter's "Reform in the Roaring Forties and Fifties," *MHR*, 39 (April, 1945), 291–319, all provide information of merit on a broad range of social reform.

Two articles on the efforts to found Utopian communities in Missouri are William Godfrey Bek, "A German Communistic Society in Missouri," *MHR,* 3 (October, 1908, January, 1909), 52–74, 99–125, which deals with the settlement at Bethel and with the work of Dr. William Keil, and H. Roger Grant, "Missouri's Utopian Communities," *MHR*, 66 (October, 1971), 20–48, which covers several such communities.

DEPRESSIONS IN MISSOURI

Dorothy B. Dorsey provides a competent analysis of Missouri's two major pre–Civil War depression periods in "The Panic of 1819 in Missouri," *MHR*, 29 (January, 1935), 79–91, and "The Panic and Depression of 1837–43 in Missouri," *MHR*, 30 (January, 1936), 132–61. The efforts to cope with the impact of the depression of the early 1820's are covered by W. J. Hamilton in "The Relief Movement in Missouri," *MHR*, 22 (October, 1927), 51–92.

## Unpublished Theses and Dissertations

A considerable number of unpublished theses and dissertations were of value in the writing of this history. My own doctoral dissertation, "Thomas H. Benton, His Source of Political Strength in Missouri from 1815 to 1838," Ph.D. diss., University of Missouri—Columbia, 1953, contains more extensive information related to Benton's political career in Missouri. For the development of the Jacksonian organization, see Rudolph Eugene Forderhase, "Jacksonianism in Missouri, from Predilection to Party, 1820–1836," Ph.D. diss., University of Missouri—Columbia, 1968. "The American Party in Missouri, 1854–1860," M.A. thesis, University of Missouri—Columbia, 1949, by Frederick Elmo Brock, and "Frank P. Blair, Jr., and Missouri Politics, 1856–1860," M.A. thesis, University of Missouri—Columbia, 1936, by John Harold Ulbricht are both worthwhile studies. Although his career was more significant after 1860, "The Life and Times of Charles Daniel Drake," Ph.D. diss., University of Missouri—Columbia, 1949, by David D. March contains useful information on Drake's pre-1860 affairs.

Some general themes are brought out in Barry Wayne Ellis's "Development of the Powers and Functions of the State as Exemplified in the Messages of the Governors of Missouri: 1821–1961," M.A. thesis, Central Missouri State College, Warrensburg, 1968, and useful information and assessments were found in each of the following: Ella Johnson, "The Economic Development of the Boonslick Country as Reflected in the Missouri Intelligencer," M.A. thesis, University of Missouri—Columbia, 1931; Cornelios Utz, "Life in Missouri, 1800–1840, As pictured in Travelers' Accounts, Letters and Journals," M.A. thesis, University of Missouri—Columbia, 1933; George Frances Lemmer, "Agriculture Improvement in Missouri:

1830 to the Civil War," M.A. thesis, University of Missouri—Columbia, 1941; Walter R. Houf, "Fifty Years of Missouri Labor, 1820–1870," M.A. thesis, University of Missouri—Columbia, 1958, and especially Halvor Gordon Melon, "The Economic Development of St. Louis, 1803–1846," Ph.D. diss., University of Missouri—Columbia, 1947.

The Dred Scott case is detailed in Walter Ehrlich's "History of the Dred Scott Case Through the Decision of 1857," Ph.D. diss., Washington University, St. Louis, 1950.

Valuable studies for educational developments include: Roscoe Cramer, "State Support of Public Schools in Missouri," Ph.D. diss., University of Missouri—Columbia, 1929; Leo Francis Brown, "Township School Lands and Township School Funds in Missouri," Ph.D. diss., University of Missouri—Columbia, 1935; George S. Reuter, Jr., "The Opinions of Chief School Officers in Missouri as to State School Administration," Ed.D. diss., University of Missouri—Columbia, 1952; Robert Irving Brigham, "The Education of the Negro in Missouri," Ph.D. diss., University of Missouri—Columbia, 1946; William F. Knox, "The Constitutional and Legal Basis of Public Education in Missouri, 1840–1875," Ed.D. diss., University of Missouri—Columbia, 1938.

Warren A. Jennings's "Zion is Fled: The Expulsion of the Mormons from Jackson County," Ph.D. diss., University of Florida, 1962, is the best study on that subject. Walter R. Houf ably assesses the role and influence of the church in Missouri society in "The Protestant Church in the Rural Missouri Community, 1820–1870," Ph.D. diss., University of Missouri—Columbia, 1967. The best study on what early Missourians read is Harold W. Dugger's "Reading Interest and the Book Trade in Frontier Missouri," Ph.D. diss., University of Missouri—Columbia, 1951.

The only study in depth of the Missouri militia system is John G. Westover's "The Evolution of the Missouri Militia, 1804–1919," Ph.D. diss., University of Missouri—Columbia, 1948.

# INDEX

merce and business in, 51, 102–3,
127–28, 129, 130–31, 137, 144, 149,
152, 153, 157, 161; Negroes in, 56,
59, 212–13; labor in, 158–60; cultural activities in, 170, 172, 174, 175,
181, 186, 193, 194, 205, 219–20
*St. Louis Advocate,* 182
St. Louis Agricultural and Mechani-
cal Association, 185
St. Louis Agricultural and Mechani-
cal Society, 47
St. Louis and Iron Mountain Railroad,
147
St. Louis and Missouri Telegraph
Company, 151
*St. Louis Beacon,* 87, 89
*St. Louis Enquirer,* 2, 7, 18, 73, 93,
182
*St. Louis Globe Democrat,* 183
St. Louis Mechanics' and Working-
men's party, 160
St. Louis Mercantile Library Associa-
tion, 172, 185
St. Louis Musical Society Polyhymnia,
186
*St. Louis Observer,* 181
St. Louis Sacred Music Society, 187
*St. Louis Union,* 246
St. Louis University, 198
St. Mary's Seminary, 199
Santa Fe trade, 79, 119, 120, 128–29,
137
Sappington, Dr. John, 216–17
Schoolcraft, Henry Rowe, 163
Schools, 80, 241; public, 190–97; pri-
vate, 194–95; Negro, 196. *See also*
Academies; Education
Scott, Dred, 258–61
Scott, John, 5, 9, 13, 17, 72, 74, 75, 76,
77–78; election to Congress, 15, 72
Scott, William, 260
Scott, Winfield, 262
Seminole Indian War, 118–19
Shaffner, Taliaferro Preston, 150
Shannon, James, 202–3, 272

Shawnee Indians, 55, 57
*Shepherd of the Hills* (St. Louis),
182
Showboats, 176
Sibley, George, 52, 53, 126, 198
Silk culture, 47
Slavery: black, 6–7, 37, 57–66, 270;
controversy over, 2–4, 8, 61–62, 202–
3, 213–15, 233, 243–44, 247, 258, 269,
270–77, 282; legal provisions, 10,
57–58; Indian, 57. *See also* Negroes
Smith, George R., 268, 269–70, 283
Smith, Joseph, 105, 107, 109, 110, 111,
121
Smith, Solomon Franklin, 169, 174
Smith T, John, 90
Social welfare programs, 220–24
Softs, 228, 229, 231, 232, 234, 235–36,
237, 239, 242, 244
Southern Address, 248, 249
Southern Baptist Convention, 215
Southwest Branch of the Pacific Rail-
road, 147, 149
Spanish land claims, 2, 13–14, 17, 18,
70, 84
Special legislation: policy, 241–42
Starr, Frederick, 272
Statehood. *See* Admission of Missouri
into the Union
Steamboats, 136–38
Stewart, Robert M., 276, 285–86, 286–
87; elected governor, 283
Stringfellow, Benjamin, 271–72, 276
Strother, George, 99
Surplus Revenue Act, 95–96
Swinney and Lewis Tobacco Com-
pany, 153–54
Switzler, William F., 179, 182, 203,
269, 284
Swope, Thomas, 133

T

Tallmadge, James, Jr., 3, 6, 7
Tallmadge amendment, 1, 3, 4, 6, 7
Tariff question, 70, 92–93, 98